EAST ASIA

RECOVERY AND BEYOND

THE WORLD BANK
WASHINGTON, D.C.

The findings, interpretations, and conclusions expressed in this paper are entirely those of the authors and should not be attributed in any manner to the World Bank, to its affiliated organizations, or to members of its Board of Executive Directors or the countries they represent. The World Bank does not guarantee the accuracy of the data included in this publication and accepts no responsibility for any consequence of their use. The boundaries, colors, denominations, and other information shown on any map in this volume do not imply on the part of the World Bank Group any judgment on the legal status of any territory or the endorsement or acceptance of such boundaries.

Cover photo: A young beneficiary of a World Bank–supported project in Jakarta in the early 1990s (Curt Carnemark).

ISBN 0-8213-4565-6

Library of Congress Cataloging-in-Publication Data

East Asia: recovery and beyond.
   p. cm.
  Includes bibliographical references.
  ISBN 0-8213-4565-6
  1. East Asia—Economic integration. 2. East Asia—Economic policy. 3. Finance—East Asia. 4. East Asia—Politics and government. I. World Bank.

HC460.5 E2727 2000
388.95—dc21   00-039906

CONTENTS

FOREWORD

When our last regional study—*East Asia: The Road to Recovery*—went to press in September 1998, East Asia was suffering. The recession had just reached its nadir, unemployment was at its highest point in 25 years, and millions had been pushed into poverty. We publish this study under far better circumstances: East Asia's recovery is here, it is solid, and people throughout the region are better off. The recovery is still uneven though—with Indonesia lagging and the Republic of Korea surging—and incomes of the poor have not been fully restored. But countries are now turning from crisis management to long-term issues of development and poverty reduction.

This report examines the region's recovery, assesses its sustainability, and explores the challenges that must be overcome to make it enduring and broadly shared. The conclusion? The pace and duration of the recovery will depend on whether countries can build new institutions to cope with three challenges:

- *Managing globalization.* Countries must both manage potentially volatile capital flows and compete in the global, knowledge-based economy.
- *Revitalizing business.* Systemic collapse severely damaged banks and corporations in Indonesia, Korea, Malaysia, the Philippines, and Thailand—and in China and Vietnam state enterprises are increasingly exposed to international competition.
- *Forging a new social contract and revising the role of government.* Rising public debt and growing popular demand for political accountability have pushed governance squarely onto the development agenda. Moreover, the crisis put more pressure on government to provide social protection and bring the poor into the growth process.

Improving institutions is central to realizing East Asia's potential. Success will require maintaining the momentum of reform that the crisis has unleashed.

Governments and citizens throughout the region should take pride in the speed of the recovery. Under the most difficult circumstances, they have put in place new policies to rekindle growth. The World Bank—in partnership with countries, the International Monetary Fund, the Asian Development Bank, and bilateral donors—is proud to have supported the efforts of East Asians. In the two years after the crisis the Bank doubled its commitments to the region, to more than $9 billion a year. The number of Bank projects more than doubled, social and environmental lending tripled, and the Bank provided a steady stream of technical assistance and policy advice. Even though the exceptional lending levels of the crisis period will soon diminish, the Bank remains committed to continued partnership with the region.

One reason is that our work is not done. Some 278 million East Asians live on less than $1 a day—and 892 million live on less than $2 a day. In many ways the hard part—building new institutions that will raise living standards for the next generation—has just begun.

Jemal-ud-din Kassum
Vice President
East Asia and the Pacific Region
World Bank

ACKNOWLEDGMENTS

This report was a team effort. Richard Newfarmer led the team under the direction of East Asia and the Pacific Region's Chief Economist, Masahiro Kawai, and then-Vice President, Jean-Michel Severino. Chapters 1 and 7 were written by Richard Newfarmer, with substantive contributions from Christina Wood. James Hanson was the principal author of chapter 2, with parts contributed by Li-Gang Liu, Sandeep Mahajan, and Carlos Serrano. Chapter 3 was written by Milan Brahmbhatt, with contributions from Carl Dahlman, Dorsati Madani, William Martin, and Christina Wood. Chapter 4 was written by Sanjay Dhar with contributions from Kathie Krumm and S. Ramachandran. The authors of chapter 5 were Richard Newfarmer and Barbara Nunberg, who benefited from contributions from Naazneen Barma, Li-Gang Liu, and Dana Weist. Chapter 6 was written by Tamar Manualyan-Atinc, with contributions from Norbert Schady. David Bisbee provided valuable research assistance. Gloria Elmore was the team assistant and produced the several iterations of this report.

The report benefited immeasurably from the comments and support of Homi Kharas, Director of East Asia and the Pacific Region's Poverty Reduction and Economic Management Unit, and from the participation of his management team. Several other staff from the World Bank made important contributions: Charles Abelmann, Jill Armstrong, Benu Bidani, Hana Polackova Brixi, Craig Burnside, Steen Byskov, Amanda Carlier, Shaohua Chen, Stijn Claessens, Gaurav Datt, Simeon Djankov, Giovani Ferri, Christine Freund, Swati Ghosh, Alejandro Izquierdo, Bala B.N. Kalimili, Aart Kraay, Will Martin, Jo Ann Paulson, Sergio Schmukler, Su Yong Song, Peter Stephens, Limin Wang, L. Colin Xu, Alexander Yeats, and Chunlin Zhang.

Peer reviewers provided insightful comments and useful guidance: Amar Bhattacharya (World Bank), Nancy Birdsall (Carnegie Endowment for International Peace), Nora Lustig (Inter-American Development Bank), Mari Pangestu (Centre for Strategic and International Studies, Indonesia), John Williamson (Institute for International Economics), and Shahid Yusuf (World Bank). The authors are also grateful to the many Bank colleagues and IMF staff who provided comments.

This report benefited from an Asia-Europe Meeting (ASEM) grant on "Forming Shared Views on Regional Economic Prospects." The grant, among other things, enabled the convening of a workshop to discuss topics shaping East Asia's long-term growth prospects. Paper authors and workshop participants were Mukul Asher (National University of Singapore), Haryo Aswicahyono (Centre for Strategic and International Studies,

Indonesia), Joel Bergsman (Consultant, United States), Romeo Bernardo (Consultant, Philippines), Paola Bongini (Catholic University of Milan, Italy), Anne Booth (School of Oriental and African Studies, University of London), Bijit Bora (United Nations Conference on Trade and Development, Geneva), Yoon Je Cho (Sogang Univresity, Korea), Dieter Ernst (East West Center, Hawaii), Christopher Findlay (University of Adelaide, Australia), Jason Foley (Barents, Washington, D.C.), Junichi Goto (Kobe University, Japan), Donald Hanna (Goldman Sachs, Hong Kong), Hal Hill (Australian National University), Elena Ianchovichina (Kansas State University), Sanjaya Lall (Oxford University), Woropot Manupipatpong (Association of Southeast Asian Nations Secretariat, Jakarta), Warwick McKibbin (Australian National University), Hidenobu Okuda (Hitotsubashi University, Japan), Mari Pangestu (Centre for Strategic and International Studies, Indonesia), Stephen Parker (Asian Development Bank Institute, Tokyo), Graham Scott (Consultant, New Zealand), Andrew Stoeckel (Centre for International Economics, Canberra, Australia), Nguyen Quang Thai (Development Strategy Institute, Hanoi), Shujiru Urata (Waseda University, Japan), Wing Thye Woo (University of California, Davis), Zainal Aznam Yusof (Institute of Strategic and International Studies, Malaysia).

The report also benefited indirectly from a Policy and Human Resources Development (PHRD) grant to facilitate joint research on East Asia. The grant provided resources for, among other things, a Tokyo conference on corporate and bank restructuring, organized jointly by the Asian Development Bank Institute, the Institute of Fiscal and Monetary Policy of Japan's Ministry of Finance, and the World Bank. The conference enabled the region's policymakers, the international financial institutions, and the Japanese government to share information and deepen understanding on corporate and bank restructuring in each country.

The report was edited by Meta de Coquereaumont and Paul Holtz, with Communications Development Incorporated.

EXECUTIVE SUMMARY

East Asia is once again the world's fastest-growing region. This reflects concerted macroeconomic policies that followed a harsh but quick adjustment, progressive implementation of structural policies to contain the systemic meltdown in the financial and corporate sectors and restore confidence, and a turnaround in regional trade, made possible in part by a buoyant international economy.

Attention is now turning to medium-term questions. Is the recovery built on solid foundations? Or will it crumble under the weight of lingering inefficiencies, rising public debt, new competition in the global marketplace, and unfulfilled promises to restructure banks and corporations? Can the recovery be converted into a new era of high growth? Has the crisis fundamentally changed East Asia's development strategy, in its relations with the global economy, in the internal relations of banks and corporations, and in the way people relate to their governments? Or will recovery lead to the resumption of business as usual? These questions are the subject of this report.

In the hardest-hit crisis countries—Indonesia, Republic of Korea, Philippines, Malaysia, Thailand—growth prospects are clouded by corporate debt overhang, rising public debt, and new insecurity among households. Since late 1998, however, new demand has improved enterprise cash flows, shrunk nonperforming loans in banks, and permitted some bank recapitalization. The economic rebound has also eased pressures on public finance.

Prospects for China and Vietnam, by contrast, will hinge on the uncertainties of uncharted reforms. Continued rapid growth will ease the difficult transition from plan to market without triggering a competitive devaluation or social disruption. For example, many workers laid off from state enterprises will be able to find jobs in the fast-growing private economy.

In all countries, economic recovery has created new jobs and permitted poverty reduction to resume. Still, the legacies of the crisis—especially heavy debt and greater insecurity among workers—leave the recovery susceptible to unexpected changes in investor sentiment or world recession.

Maintaining the recovery's pace, broadening its reach, and extending its duration are essential for raising living standards and reducing poverty in the region. Extending the recovery over the next decade will require new sources of productivity growth. Higher productivity depends on policies and institutions—business institutions, government institutions, and social institutions. To achieve their potential, East Asian countries will have to improve institutions and policies in three broad areas: managing globalization (especially financial, trade, and investment integration), revitalizing business, and forging a new social contract and role for government.

Managing globalization

Countries have responded to the crisis not by retreating from globalization but by embracing it and attempting to manage it to their advantage. Rather than backing away from trade liberalization, governments have opened new sectors to foreign direct investment and made capital flows easier—now much better regulated.

Restrictions on capital outflows introduced in the wake of the crisis are the exceptions that prove the point: in both Malaysia and Thailand such controls were quickly scaled back. China, through its World Trade Organization accession offer, has boldly signaled its willingness to deepen its engagement with the global economy. That move will increase market access for imports, subject China to the discipline of global rules, and reinforce ongoing reforms of state enterprises and banks. The region's small countries have not moved as quickly to replace distorted trade regimes and restrictions on foreign direct investment—and so risk being left behind.

Reaping the benefits of increased integration with the global economy requires careful attention to managing the attendant risks. Further attention to reducing restrictions on trade, services, and information flows can generate new productivity gains for the region.

Revitalizing business

In the three years since the crisis hit, laws governing banks and corporations have undergone a sea change. The structure of the financial sector has also been revamped in most of the crisis countries. But progress in resolving systemic banking and corporate distress has not removed the uncertainties hanging over the recovery and future prospects.

Three problems are pressing. Banks remain undercapitalized, which could impinge on renewed lending as the recovery gains force. Corporations are still over-indebted, with loans accruing interest that cannot be paid, inhibiting corporations' creditworthiness and perhaps their ability to expand when unutilized capacity is taken up. And the crisis has increased government ownership of many large banks and corporations at a time when most governments want to reduce their direct role and play a more aggressive regulatory role.

In China and Vietnam problems of corporate governance, corporate debt, and nonperforming loans have had a less dramatic genesis. But if anything, the problems are more acute. They require solutions embedded in reforms of state enterprises and banks, a process under way in earnest since 1993 in China and just beginning in Vietnam. How governments respond to these tasks will shape the pace and sustainability of growth throughout the region.

Forging a new social contract and role for government

Political administrations have changed in many countries, yet institutional innovations in public finance and administration have barely begun. Fiscal pressures—emanating from new debt service burdens and larger changes in society—and globalization are driving governments to become more efficient in managing spending, using human resources, and determining the scope of activities and organization of service delivery.

Governments in the crisis countries have to do more in protecting the poor, the sick, and the elderly from the vagaries of the market. The crisis revealed that by itself growth is no substitute for an effective social policy in support of markets. Analogous problems confront China and Vietnam, where social support mechanisms have not kept pace with the expanding domain of markets and the shrinking protections of state enterprises. East Asia has lagged other developing regions in helping families provide security for the elderly. And to ensure that the poor benefit fully from renewed growth, policies everywhere have to make education more effective.

The international community can help by developing a framework that makes capital flows more manageable and less volatile and by continuing to reduce trade barriers. Regional organizations can spur institutional progress by providing a forum for high-level discussions on Asian solutions to Asian problems and by providing a framework for concerted and collective policy actions in response to problems related to globalization. Ultimately, however, progress will depend on institutional improvements in the countries themselves.

If East Asia succeeds in transforming its business, public, and social institutions and so raises productivity, the region should regain growth rates approaching those of past decades. Converting today's recovery into tomorrow's sustained, broadly shared growth will lift tens of millions out of poverty and raise living standards for all.

CHAPTER 1

RECOVERY GATHERS MOMENTUM

The extraordinary shock of the economic crisis [in Indonesia] devastated all that Mr. Nana had achieved. During the social and political disturbances of 1998, Mr. Nana, owner of eight mini-market shops, could not anticipate the sudden, uncontrolled increase in prices. Information from suppliers came too late. After the riots in May 1998, Mr. Nana, who suspected nothing, did not change his prices when people came shopping in bulk. Retailers and speculators bought out everything from his market. This was the beginning of the failure of his business. In the days after, Mr. Nana could not afford to buy supplies for his shops. He suffered losses ranging from 50% to 80%. Five of his shops were shut down.

—Mukherjee 1999, p. 48.

Three years after hemorrhaging capital outflows caused the collapse of the Thai baht and ushered in the East Asian crisis, economies throughout the region are in resounding recovery. In the five countries hurt most by the crisis—Indonesia, the Republic of Korea, Malaysia, the Philippines, and Thailand—foreign exchange reserves are up, currencies are stable, and interest rates are down. Financial markets are well above their crisis-induced nadirs, and in some cases even above their precrisis highs. Equity markets rose more than 40 percent in 1999 (figure 1.1). The transition economies of China and Vietnam, though with deflating momentum, continue to grow at a pace that buoys the entire region. The high-income economies of Hong Kong (China), Singapore, and Taiwan (China) are performing strongly. And the trade-driven small economies of the Pacific, Indochina, and Mongolia are also benefiting from the rising regional tide. Output is expanding—at varying speeds—in all the major economies (figure 1.2).

Still, challenges remain. The recovery, while no longer fragile, is vulnerable to shifts in market sentiment and external events. And its benefits have not yet restored the incomes

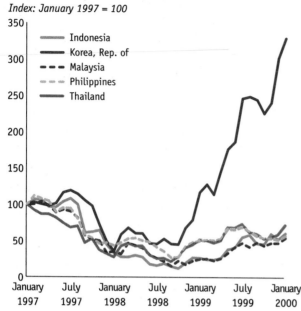

Figure 1.1

The region's stock markets rebounded in 1999

Stock market capitalization in dollars
Index: January 1997 = 100
350
300
250
200
150
100
50
0
Indonesia
Korea, Rep. of
Malaysia
Philippines
Thailand
January 1997
July 1997
January 1998
July 1998
January 1999
July 1999
January 2000

Source: World Bank data.

Figure 1.2

Growth is back on track

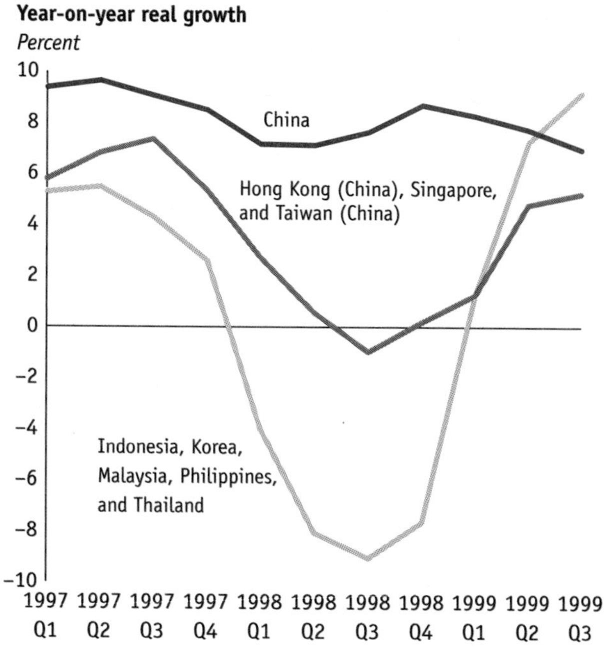

Year-on-year real growth
Percent
10
8
6
4
2
0
-2
-4
-6
-8
-10
China
Hong Kong (China), Singapore, and Taiwan (China)
Indonesia, Korea, Malaysia, Philippines, and Thailand
1997 Q1
1997 Q2
1997 Q3
1997 Q4
1998 Q1
1998 Q2
1998 Q3
1998 Q4
1999 Q1
1999 Q2
1999 Q3

Source: World Bank data.

of the poor. Unemployment, though down, is still unacceptably high in the five crisis countries and China and is rising in Vietnam. The number of poor has increased in the crisis countries, and regional pockets of poverty have spread. The middle class has also suffered. During the downturn many families were forced to cash out their savings in financial markets, and even though markets have bounced back, their wealth has been much reduced.

Throughout the region, the top priorities are maintaining the pace of recovery, broadening its reach, and extending its duration. Achieving those goals turns on the answers to a few fundamental questions:

- Is the recovery built on a solid foundation—or will it crumble under the weight of increased global competition, unfulfilled promises to restructure banks and corporations, multiplying public debt, and lingering inefficiencies exposed by the crisis?
- Even if the recovery lasts beyond 2000, will it launch a new era of high growth? If so, what will be the sources of new growth? How will East Asia fare in a world where knowledge—rather than capital—is increasingly the driving force behind productivity gains?
- Has the crisis changed East Asia's development strategy and institutional underpinnings—its relations with the global economy, the internal dealings between banks and corporations, and the way people relate to their governments? Will this period be seen years from now as a transformation that unleashed profound institutional change, or merely as a brief interlude before the resumption of business as usual?

As if in response to these questions, one investment bank recently proffered this downbeat view:

> The speed of recovery in GDP growth in 1999 through most of Asia has led to policy complacency. Broken banking systems have not been properly fixed. This alone will act as a drag on sustainable growth over the next few years. But it is the continued reliance on export-led growth that is most worrying Asia. Domestic economies have not been reformed and liberalized in an attempt to broaden the longer term sources of growth. (Credit Lyonnais Securities Asia 1999, p. 1)

An early 2000 poll of business executives found that more than 60 percent believed that reform efforts had not slowed. Yet more than half of the respondents from Japan, Korea, and Thailand felt that the reform drive had lost momentum (*Far Eastern Economic Review*, 10 February 2000, p. 34).

Such judgments seem premature. Whether East Asia can transform recovery into a new era of growth depends on government responses to two long-term forces: globalization and domestic demands for increased economic and political participation. This chapter begins with an overview of the recovery, discusses legacies of the crisis that might threaten the recovery, and then turns to the main challenges that are the broad themes of this report.

Dynamics of the recovery

East Asia—including the five crisis countries; the transition economies of China and Vietnam; the newly industrialized economies of Hong Kong (China), Singapore,

and Taiwan (China); and the small economies of the Pacific, Indochina, and Mongolia—grew by 6.5 percent in 1999. After a sharp recession—with growth down 7.8 percent in 1998—growth in the five crisis countries surpassed 5 percent in 1999. Korea is outpacing the other four crisis countries, with growth of more than 10 percent in 1999 (table 1.1). At the other extreme, Indonesia is still faltering with barely positive growth.

Though China and Vietnam continue to outperform most of the rest of the region, their growth—particularly Vietnam's—has decelerated, and structural problems cloud their prospects. The region's smaller economies, bounced around on the waves of the global economy, performed better in 1999 as terms of trade gains, exports, and even tourism provided sources of growth.

The crisis countries: Indonesia, Korea, Malaysia, the Philippines, Thailand

The recession in the five crisis countries began to turn around after mid-1998 for three reasons. Changes in

TABLE 1.1
Real change in East Asia's GDP, 1996–99
(percent)

Economy	Actual			Estimate
	1996	*1997*	*1998*	*1999*
East Asia crisis economies				
Indonesia	8.0	4.5	−13.7	0.2
Korea, Rep. of	6.8	5.0	−5.8	10.7
Malaysia	8.6	7.5	−7.5	5.4
Philippines	5.8	5.2	−0.5	3.2
Thailand	5.5	−1.3	−10.0	4.2
Transition economies				
China	9.6	8.8	7.8	7.1
Vietnam	9.3	8.2	5.8	4.7
Small economies				
Cambodia	7.0	1.0	1.0	4.0
Fiji	3.4	−1.8	−1.3	7.8
Lao PDR	6.8	6.9	4.0	4.0
Mongolia	2.4	4.0	3.5	3.3
Papua New Guinea	3.5	−4.6	2.5	3.8
Solomon Islands	0.6	−0.5	−7.0	−0.5
Newly industrialized economies				
Hong Kong (China)	4.5	5.3	−5.1	2.0
Singapore	7.6	8.4	0.4	5.4
Taiwan (China)	5.7	6.8	4.8	5.5
Industrial economies				
Japan	5.0	1.6	−2.5	0.3
United States	3.7	4.5	4.3	4.1

Source: National accounts and World Bank data.

Figure 1.3

The five crisis countries saw a harsh adjustment—and a rapid recovery

A contraction in imports produced a huge trade surplus...
Billions of dollars

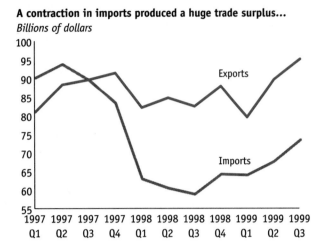

...that led to rising reserves...
Billions of dollars

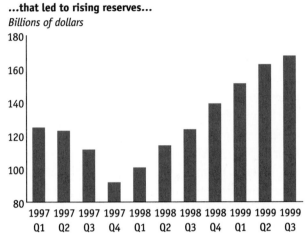

...increasing confidence in currencies...
Currency/dollar

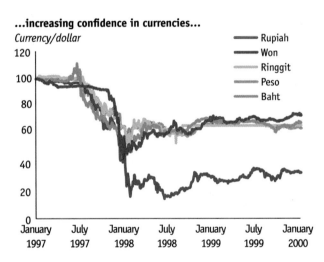

...allowing looser monetary policy...
Nominal interest rates (percent)

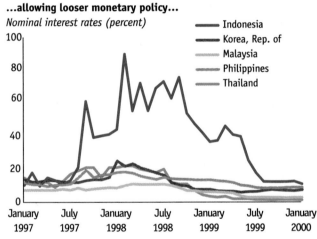

...which, togther with fiscal expansion...
Budget balances (percentage of GDP)

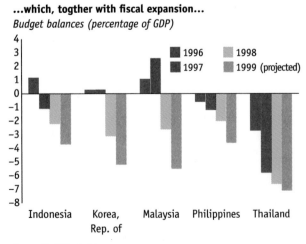

...has led to signs of recovery
Quarter-on-quarter growth (percent)

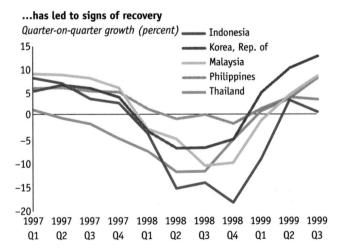

Source: World Bank data.

What did the crisis cost?

How much output did East Asia lose because of the crisis? Decomposing real annual GDP during 1960–96 into its cyclical and growth components—done using the Hodrick and Prescott (1997) method—shows the long-term trend in output growth. Comparing this trend with the actual path of output shows the cost of the crisis in lost output. Because past growth trends might not have been sustainable, the post-1997 trend was adapted to market expectations of growth on the eve of the crisis; for 1998–2000 the trend projection is based on consensus forecasts and their extrapolation into 2001.

Indonesia, Korea, Malaysia, and Thailand suffered big output losses as a result of the crisis. Though recovering, in 1999 they were still far from their precrisis trends. Indonesia's output was the furthest below its growth trend—16.6 percent. Malaysia's gap showed the fastest and strongest recovery: in 1999 its output gap was 7.2 percent of its precrisis trend. The equivalent figure for Korea was 12.9 percent and for Thailand, 14.5 percent. China and the Philippines, by contrast, were above their long-term trends—even during the crisis years.

East Asia's crisis countries experienced considerable losses

Actual and trend GDP

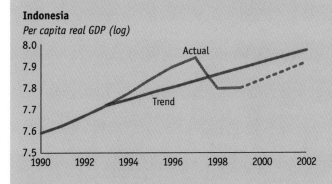

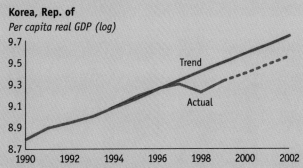

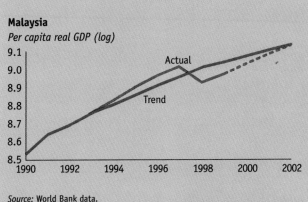

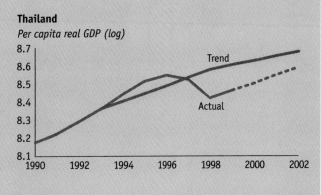

Source: World Bank data.

macroeconomic policy, as exchange rates stabilized, allowed interest rates to fall and consumption to recover. Assertive structural adjustments helped restore credit flows and boosted consumer and investor confidence. And the regional recovery, supported by strong growth in the United States and Europe, bolstered external demand.

The crisis caused harsh but brief changes in macroeconomic indicators. Capital flight and the collapse in currencies deflated domestic demand, contracted imports, and propelled trade balances from large deficits into massive surplus (figure 1.3). Between 1996 and 1998 the five crisis countries' current accounts swung almost $125 billion from deficit to surplus (see table 2.3 in chapter 2). This shift allowed for the accumulation of reserves—but at the huge sacrifice of lost output (box 1.1), lower investment, and forgone consumption.

Contractions in consumption have been reversed in the crisis countries

Contribution to growth by expenditure

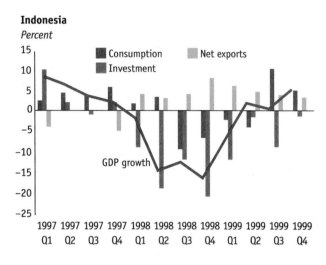

Indonesia

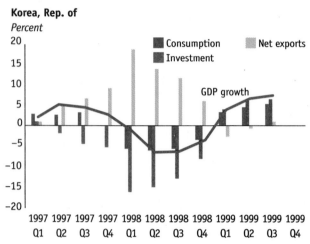

Korea, Rep. of

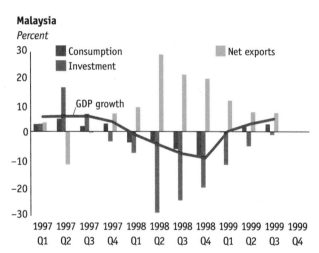

Malaysia

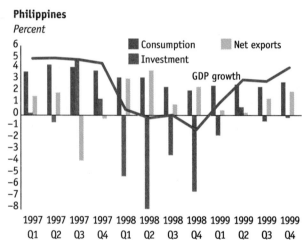

Philippines

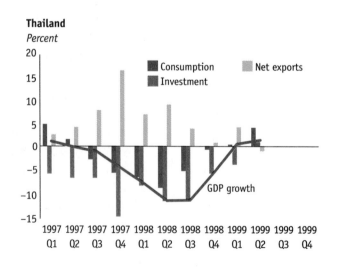

Thailand

Source: World Bank data.

Among the main components of demand, the turn-around in consumption has underpinned the recovery. Private consumption contracted in 1998, most sharply in Thailand and to a lesser extent in Korea and Malaysia (figure 1.4). The wealth lost from the decline in capital markets and property values undoubtedly diminished middle- and upper-class consumption in these countries. But after mid-1998 lower interest rates and a fiscal stimulus in Korea, Malaysia, and Thailand began to ignite a recovery—and by early 1999 consumption rose, at first through government spending and then through private consumption. Neither Indonesia nor the Philippines mounted a serious fiscal stimulus. Indonesia lacked the funds to ramp up government spending, and the Philippines, already heavily indebted, lacked borrowing capacity and had less need because its recession was not as deep. Investment absorbed the deepest cuts of any GDP component and has been the slowest to bounce back. By mid-1999 investment had contributed to growth only in Korea.

Though exports supported East Asian economies during the darkest days of 1998, rising net exports did not play the dynamic role that the region's enormous currency depreciations would have predicted. Why? Because unit prices of the region's main exports plummeted while import prices remained high, causing a huge terms of trade shock.[1] By the end of 1998 the terms of trade shock began to reverse—driving the V-shaped recovery. Electronics suddenly boomed, spurred by Y2K fears, Internet fever, and consumers in OECD countries eager to take advantage of low prices (figure 1.5). At the same time, oil prices recovered. Export revenues finally began to firm up and supported the recovery in 1999.

The restoration of investor confidence contributed to positive developments in the balance of payments. Although hefty current account surpluses carried into 1999, rising exports accommodated the growing import demand associated with the recovery. Net capital outflows began to attenuate sharply. After reaching $70 billion in 1996, private inflows plummeted to –$60 billion in 1998 and then eased to –$23 billion in 1999. Even though private banks and other creditors continued to reduce their exposure in 1999, portfolio investment rebounded in the second half of 1998—and rose to $8.5 billion in 1999 (see table 2.3 in chapter 2). Rising portfolio inflows, coupled with the willingness of savers to invest in financial markets, underpinned the

Figure 1.5

East Asia's industrial production has bounced back—as have semiconductor sales

Three month moving averages

Source: JP Morgan.

recovery of equities. By the end of 1999 stock market capitalization was more than 50 percent higher (in U.S. dollar terms) than in September 1998 for Hong Kong (China), Indonesia, Korea, Malaysia, the Philippines, Taiwan (China), and Thailand (see figure 1.1). And foreign direct investment reached new heights.

The transition economies: China and Vietnam

By early 1998 it was obvious that China was facing anemic internal demand. Deflationary pressure pushed growth down to 7.8 percent in 1998 and 7.1 percent in 1999. Four forces were responsible.

First, the government's five-year campaign to modernize the monetary authority finally reined in "franchise central banking" in the huge branch network of the People's Bank, restraining credit growth. Provincial and municipal authorities lost the power to create credit for favored activities and enterprises, prompting reform of state-owned enterprises. The subsequent reform of state-owned commercial banks laid down strict guidelines for lending, made the banks responsible for their financial performance, and even threatened to hold managers personally accountable for bad loans. These new incentives, coupled with the absence of managerial capacity to accurately evaluate credit risk, have made bank managers extraordinarily cautious about extending loans. Because it is difficult for state banks to lend to dynamic nonstate enterprises, credit growth became stifled.

Second, state enterprise reform and government downsizing increased household insecurity, as evidenced by weakening urban consumption. Third, large declines in farm procurement prices, mirroring international commodity prices, and declining labor absorption in rural industries weakened rural income growth and rural consumption. Finally, export growth, robust in 1997, sagged in 1998 under the weight of Japanese and Korean contraction and the loss of price competitiveness with competing products originating in East Asia.

The Chinese government responded with several new measures. Monetary policy was eased further in June 1999, with interest rates cut by 0.75 percentage points. To stimulate foreign sales, the government increased value added tax rebates on exports by 2.95 percentage points in July—the latest in a series of increases dating to 1998, though the total rebate is still below the imputed share of domestic value added taxes paid on production. In August the government adopted

a supplementary 60 billion yuan fiscal package that augmented the fiscal stimulus of 1998. The government also raised pay for civil servants and increased lending to small banks. In 1999 consumption stabilized, the government stimulus began to have an effect, and net exports and investment were strong, so all components of GDP contributed to GDP growth (figure 1.6).

These results dampened market speculation that the yuan would soon be devalued. The governor of the People's Bank recently ruled out changes for the yuan in 2000. This, together with better export performance and a rising yen, eased private fears and may have improved capital account performance in 1999. Deutsche Bank recently calculated that the probability of a devaluation greater than 10 percent over the next six months had fallen from 22 percent in August 1999 to 14 percent in late 1999 (Deutsche Bank 1999).

Vietnam experienced steady but slower growth in 1999. After humming along at 8.6 percent a year in 1992–97, growth slipped to 4 percent in 1998 and 1999, dragged down by internal factors and decreased demands for exports. Lagging productivity growth in the state-dominated industrial sector and a highly regulated service sector were major contributing factors. A continued slide in both sectors in 1999 was offset only by an abundant agricultural harvest. Since nearly 60

Figure 1.6

All the components of GDP contributed to China's growth in 1999

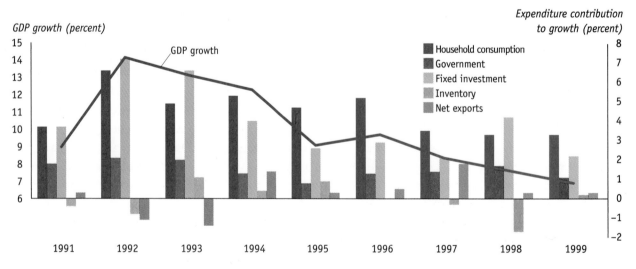

Source: World Bank data.

percent of Vietnam's exports go to Asia, the regional recovery was crucial for the country's growth.

Still, without deeper structural reforms, Vietnam may not fully share in the region's recovery. Investment from every source continues to slide: the government (because of low revenue mobilization), state enterprises (because of low retained earnings and lingering inefficiencies), the nonstate sector, and foreign direct investment (because of excessive regulation). Foreign direct investment may begin to pick up, but deregulation has made Vietnam's competitors more attractive to foreign investors. The reforms being considered by the government could, however, sharply accelerate Vietnam's growth.

The small economies: the Pacific, Indochina, Mongolia

The region's recovery has contributed to a bounce for the small economies of the Pacific, Indochina, and Mongolia. Unlike the main crisis countries, the 1997–98 declines in the small economies stemmed primarily from trade effects rather than capital outflows. The Solomon Islands suffered a steep recession as demand for tourism and logs from its high-income neighbors—notably Japan—dropped sharply. Papua New Guinea's recovery from the El Niño–induced drought of 1997 was tempered by adverse terms of trade shifts for its main exports (gold, copper, oil) and by civil strife.

In Mongolia reforms aimed at strengthening the environment for private growth stalled in the face of adverse terms of trade for its main exports (gold and copper) in 1998–99. Budget revenues and international reserves fell, and the loan portfolios of major commercial banks deteriorated. Poor domestic policies in Cambodia and Lao PDR in the years before the crisis translated into worsening fiscal performance, loosening monetary policy, rising inflation, and weakening currencies (which were exacerbated by crisis-induced currency depreciations). Subsequent improvements in both countries stemmed from better terms of trade, stronger demand for exports, and a return to domestic reforms. Cambodia, Lao PDR, Mongolia, and Papua New Guinea recorded growth of 3–4 percent in 1999. Fiji, buoyed by tourism and a rebound in sugar production, grew nearly 8 percent.

Legacies of crisis—and the new vulnerability

The crisis has left two legacies: heavy debt and greater household insecurity. It has also left the region more vulnerable to external shocks.

Heavy debt

The increase in debt has created challenges across the region. High corporate debt eats into earnings. High nonperforming loans force wide spreads on bank loans and limit loanable funds. And in some countries the public sector owes three times as much in debt service as before the crisis.

The five crisis countries have yet to complete the painful process of writing down their national balance sheets, restructuring debts and absorbing the associated capital losses, and undertaking the operational and ownership restructuring that can unlock future productivity gains. Banks are saddled with nonperforming loans, which at the end of 1999 hovered around 35 percent in Indonesia, 20 percent in Korea, 10 percent in Malaysia, and 40 percent in Thailand. Official estimates in China put nonperforming loans at 25 percent (though private estimates range much higher). The arduous process of resolving the nonperforming loans may push public debt beyond current levels. Government debt, driven by financial bailouts and deficit spending to jumpstart demand, has already risen to 35–50 percent of GDP in Korea, Malaysia, and Thailand—and to 90–100 percent of GDP in Indonesia and the Philippines. China has also seen public debt rise, to 30 percent of GDP.

The recovery, however, has mitigated the depressing force of the debt overhang. New demand has increased the cash flow of corporations, allowing them to begin to repay some debt, reschedule some, and seek equity infusions that lower leverage ratios. Indeed, cash flows have proven surprisingly resilient among leading corporations (chapter 4). The strong recovery and rising exports in 1999 made companies more creditworthy—because the value of their assets rose—and strengthened bank portfolios.

Because financing requirements during this first stage of recovery are limited to securing working capital and rebuilding inventories, and because underused capacity allows firms to meet demand, increases in bank lending will be modest. For example, capacity utilization rates in Thailand, while up, ended 1999 at 62 percent. Even in Korea only 81 percent of capacity was being used at the end of 1999. It remains to be seen what will happen as firms require new capacity to satisfy demand.

The recovery has also relieved the debt-driven pressures on public finance. Even so, the five crisis countries will have to reduce their fiscal deficits by 1–3 percent of GDP (relative to 1999), accommodate a larger share of interest payments in total spending, and create new policy headroom through eventual debt reduction (chapter 5). Here too continued growth is essential. Any needed fiscal consolidation will be 0.6–1.8 percent of GDP less for the crisis countries if their growth rates are 2 percentage points higher than—rather than the same as—the real interest rate (chapter 5).

In China and Vietnam the debt overhang is less likely to constrain growth than will the need to create new institutions to support market incentives. Nearly 40 percent of China's state enterprises are unprofitable, and unpaid debt obligations are high even by the standards of the crisis countries. The government has introduced a program to remove nonperforming loans from the books of banks (for resolution in asset management companies) and to recapitalize banks. With continued rapid growth, the government will be able to encourage banks to lend to dynamic enterprises (rather than simply to roll over bad loans from lethargic state enterprises), to remove nonperforming loans from their books, and to work the financial system out from under the dead weight of nonperforming loans.

Vietnam, far behind China on reform, may see its window of opportunity for adopting a similar strategy squeeze shut. Growth is being stifled under the weight of increasing inefficiency in state enterprises, without relief from economic expansion in the shackled nonstate sector—making reforms much more politically difficult.

Greater household insecurity

The increase in insecurity is especially pronounced among low-income and urban households. In the five crisis countries and in China the number of people living below the international poverty line of $1 a day (in 1993 purchasing power parity terms) jumped about 13 million between 1996 and 1998, pushing East Asia's total number of poor people to 278 million (table 1.2). Of these, 213 million are Chinese. Because another 150 million people rose above the poverty line only in the decade prior to the crisis—60 million East Asians and 90 million Chinese—the region also contains a huge group of near-poor. The recession made their lot more precarious as demand for labor slackened and unemployment rose, especially in urban areas. In the crisis countries many of these workers are young and had never experienced a serious recession. In China (and Vietnam) unemployment has affected older workers—a painful by-product of state enterprise reform and government downsizing. In both groups of countries the newly unemployed face rising insecurity over jobs and incomes.

TABLE 1.2
Poverty in East Asia, 1987, 1996, and 1998
(millions of people)

Poverty line/area	1987	1996	1998	Crisis-induced increase Millions	Percent
Less than $1 a day					
East Asia	417.5	265.1	278.3	13.2	5.0
East Asia excl. China	114.1	55.1	65.1	10.0	18.1
China	303.4	210.0	213.2	3.2	1.5
Less than $2 a day					
East Asia	1,025.3	863.9	892.2	28.3	3.3
East Asia excl. China	299.9	236.3	260.1	23.8	10.1
China	752.4	627.6	632.1	4.5	0.7

Note: The international poverty line is fixed at the equivalent of $1 a day in 1993 purchasing power parity (PPP) dollars. Estimates for China are based on the income distribution, adjusted to yield the consumption distribution using average per capita consumption rates from household surveys. National poverty lines are different; see table 6.1.
Source: World Bank staff estimates.

Economic expansion, by creating new jobs, has offered hope to workers and eased insecurity. Unemployment has fallen in the five crisis countries and stabilized in China. Continued expansion is crucial for restoring lost income to the poor. The most effective poverty reduction tool is an expanding economy that creates jobs and demand for the resource the poor most control—their labor.

If growth stays at 5 percent a year through 2008 and is equally shared, the number of poor people in East Asia (including China) will fall from 278 million to 84 million. But slower growth of 3 percent a year and a deteriorating income distribution (with a 10 percentage point increase in inequality) would leave 229 million in poverty in 2008 (see chapter 7). In addition, urban groups, ever larger and more educated, are likely to demand better services to help them deal with market fluctuations—and more voice in policymaking to ensure that their interests are represented. Economic growth is essential for these groups, which are likely to be less willing to peacefully accept additional wage cuts from new shocks.

The new vulnerability

East Asia is vulnerable to external shocks in ways fundamentally different from the days before the crisis. For all its damage, the huge outflow of hot money that caused the crisis also purged the region of one of its greatest sources of vulnerability. Short-term private foreign debt has shrunk to low levels, and international reserves have surpassed precrisis levels. As a result ratios of short-term debt to reserves are generally far lower (figure 1.7). Similarly, currency depreciations have reduced the value of money held in foreign currencies that might seek a sudden exit. Both factors have helped restore investor confidence by reducing the region's vulnerability to sudden shifts in capital.

But recovery remains dependent on the virtuous cycle that growth has unleashed—and a global recession could reverse this cycle. Companies that can now pay their debt and begin to invest could suddenly go under. Governments that depend on healthy revenues to service debt might suddenly have to cut back on

Figure 1.7

Short-term debt is far lower than before the crisis

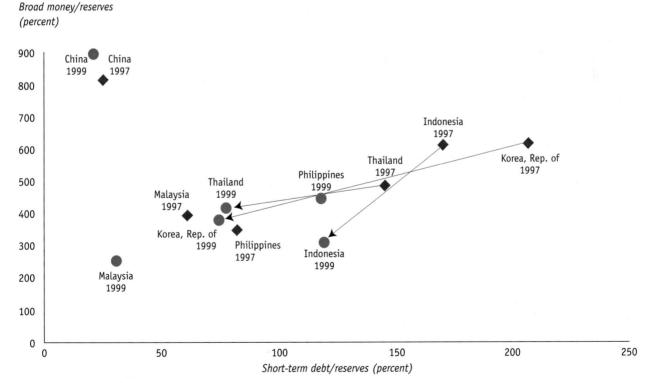

Broad money/reserves (percent)

Short-term debt/reserves (percent)

Note: Data are for June 1997 and June 1999.
Source: World Bank data.

social or other important spending. Investors have emerged from the crisis much more fleet-footed, ready to exit at the slightest provocation. And the poor and near-poor, having seen their incomes fall already, may be less patient with governments that ask them to sacrifice more. For these reasons, propelling today's recovery well into the future is not only desirable—it is essential.

From recovery to a new era of high growth?

Can today's recovery develop into a sustained and broadly shared economic expansion—an expansion measured in years rather than quarters? The answer depends on how East Asia responds to two forces. On the one hand, trade, investment, and finance, together with unprecedented advances in communications and transport, are closely integrating markets around the world—a process known as globalization. On the other, three decades of rapid growth have generated vast improvements in education and increases in wealth, spawning new demands from the middle and lower classes for increased participation in economic and political decisionmaking as well as in the fruits of economic growth.

In many respects the recent crisis can be seen as a failure of East Asian countries to cope with these two forces. True, the explosion of the crisis can be laid squarely on the financial panic of international and domestic investors suddenly concerned about the fate of their portfolios. But the buildup of structural vulnerabilities—sharp rises in short-term debt that far exceeded international reserves, a financial sector that had poorly intermediated international inflows and found itself saddled with huge mismatches between assets and liabilities, and corporations massively over-leveraged and exposed to changes in interest and exchange rates—provided the dynamite for the explosion. The collapse of the Thai baht sparked a regional crisis that reflected the failure of the affected countries to manage globalization (chapter 2).

Too sharp a focus on managing financial integration might, however, overlook another important change: the transformation of the global economy itself. The global economy is rapidly changing from one based on trade in agricultural and industrial products to one in which knowledge-based activities are the most dynamic (World Bank 1999b). The increasing importance of technology in production and in products, the rise of services, and the geometric expansion of information as a source of productivity gains is transforming the world in which East Asia competes. Even if East Asian countries learn to manage global financial flows, they may have to transform their development strategy to ensure continued high growth.

The second set of longer-term trends—brought about by rising incomes, urbanization, and improvements in education—intersected with globalization during the crisis, leading groups that were newly empowered economically to seek greater political participation and accountability from government institutions. One precursor of this change was the rapid growth of newspapers, radio, and television throughout the region. The integration of global media markets reinforced these trends. Among other things, these media have exposed with increasing boldness the corruption of civil servants and politicians.

Another factor has been the explosive growth of the Internet, which has provided urban middle classes all over the region with new sources of information—and new outlets for expression. A third manifestation has been the emergence of nongovernmental organizations and social groups, many with political objectives different from government's. Finally, citizens outside national capitals have been demanding bigger roles in resource allocation and governance, leading to pressures for decentralization.

The crisis exposed the interaction between these two forces. Korea and Thailand have arguably avoided the social crisis that has plagued Indonesia because of an institutional capacity for political change. In the 30 years before the crisis Indonesia made enormous advances, lifting 30 percent of its people out of poverty. But it failed to incorporate new groups into the process of governance and increasingly assigned key economic activities to a family elite—until the legitimacy of the Soeharto regime came to rest solely on its ability to provide annual pay increases to everyone. The Philippines has provided for greater participation but has still suffered reverberations from the crisis in neighboring countries.

Whether East Asia can regain and sustain the high growth of the past depends on how countries respond to globalization and new demands for participation. These forces generate three future policy challenges: managing globalization, revitalizing business, and forging a new social contract.

Managing globalization

After receiving large capital flows for four years or more, the four most affected crisis countries—Indonesia, Korea, Malaysia, and Thailand—suffered heavy losses following the sudden shift in investor sentiment. The penalties for policy missteps were excessive, fed as much by investor reactions to each other's behavior as by the underlying fundamentals. The region is emerging from the crisis with investors—domestic as well as foreign—that are more skittish, ready to flee with an alacrity born of recent experience.

The challenge of managing globalization is to capture its benefits without suffering the high costs of sudden capital reversals or trade shocks. This requires that East Asia put in place macroeconomic and structural policies for capital flows that encourage stability. It also means formulating options for the transition economies—China and Vietnam—that minimize risks that their vulnerable financial systems will be exposed to the same forces that have wreaked havoc on the crisis countries. China is partway down the path of reform, and its trade and selective financial openness have already spawned an inevitable trend toward financial integration. Developing a coherent program to manage this process—and avoid disruption—involves difficult issues of pace and sequencing (chapter 2).

Export growth, a mainstay of growth during the miracle years, faltered in 1996–97 for most East Asian countries. Some of this slippage may have been due to short-run factors, but the year-in, year-out high growth that powered the region's prosperity can no longer be taken for granted. High tariffs on certain products and varying limitations on foreign direct investment lasted well into the 1990s. But other regions have markedly improved their trade competitiveness—and even surpassed East Asia in their external policies. Even within the region, China has embarked on trade integration following the path of its neighbors, and so constitutes a new force in world markets that could erode the market share of other

East Asian countries. In addition, the global marketplace is rapidly shifting toward trade in high-technology products and knowledge-based industries, so the policy response must go beyond trade and investment (chapter 3).

Revitalizing business

The crisis left in its wake insolvent banks and corporations. As noted, countries have not completed the painful process of writing down national balance sheets, restructuring debts and absorbing the associated capital losses, and undertaking the operational and ownership restructuring that can unlock future productivity gains.

Without a healthy financial system, the recovery will be subject to sudden portfolio shifts by foreign investors suddenly wary of corporations' capacity to service debt—as shown by the July 1999 financial turmoil around Korea's Daewoo. Without corporate debt workouts and operational restructuring, potentially viable corporations will not be considered creditworthy. More important, new loans will not be put to the most productive uses, with adverse long-term implications for growth.

Recovering from systemic distress in the financial sector involves:

- Restoring investor confidence by intervening in nonviable financial institutions to protect depositors.
- Developing a strategy for rehabilitation and recapitalization.
- Strengthening medium-term supervision and examination.
- Improving regulations to ensure adequate financial governance.
- Resolving and restructuring impaired assets.

Restructuring corporations means not only restructuring their debt but also hiving off or closing down inefficient operations. For both banks and corporations, restructuring means that owners unable to pay their debts forfeit their capital and corporate control. An analogous process is occurring in the state sector in China and Vietnam, where enterprises and banks are undergoing reforms to cut losses and clean up balance sheets.

The pace and approach to resolving systemic insolvency will influence the speed and sustainability of future growth. There are dangers on all sides. Going too slow will increase the costs to taxpayers, impose costs on intermediation, and drag down investment. Going too fast risks incurring unnecessary costs for government and wasting potentially viable capacity and managerial talent. Similarly, if the resolution bails out owners of banks and corporations in an attempt to speed recovery, it risks sending a signal that the government will cover losses from bad investment decisions—a sure incentive for such behavior to be repeated.

No less important is whether bank and corporate governance changes. If banks are relieved of the responsibility for monitoring their loans and large families or economic groups are allowed to capture deposits from related banks or resources from minority shareholders, future economic growth will be in jeopardy. Considerable banking and corporate assets have been devolved to the state, and the way these assets are privatized may shape the distribution of assets for generations to come—as well as the course of economic performance (chapter 4).

Forging a new social contract

Countries throughout East Asia are experiencing profound changes in governance. Pressures emanate from several sources. Because government debt has doubled or even tripled, interest payments account for a larger share of public spending. This has put new pressure on noninterest spending—a pressure that will only intensify as fiscal policy shifts away from stimulus to deficit reduction. Governments everywhere are looking for ways to make their spending go further. On the one hand, many people have felt the sting of unemployment and want stronger social safety nets to protect against volatile, globalized markets. On the other, remaining competitive in a global market requires efficient provision of infrastructure and education. Finally, citizens, aided by advances in press freedom, have grown less tolerant of official corruption. All these pressures place demands on governments to revamp their roles, recast their public institutions to deliver more efficient and effective services, and increase their accountability (chapter 5).

Globalization has also placed new pressures on government to ensure that the poor are insulated from downturns during bad times and benefit from growth during good times. The crisis has revealed gaps in social safety nets. With the simultaneous growth in urban labor markets and the gradual aging of East Asian societies, there will likely be new demands on social safety nets and pension systems. No less worrisome, during the miracle years the income of the poor failed to grow as rapidly as that of the better-off in several East Asian countries. With growth increasingly dependent on skills and knowledge rather than on labor or labor augmented by capital, the risk should not be dismissed that the poor could be left out of the growth process. Demand could rise faster for skilled labor than for unskilled labor, and wage gaps could widen. This risk underscores the important role of government, and the effects its revenue and spending policies have on incorporating low-income groups into the growth process—or leaving them by the wayside (chapter 6).

Answers to questions about the duration of East Asia's recovery and about whether the region can propel itself into a new era of high growth hinge critically on how it manages globalization, whether it revitalizes a badly damaged business sector, and whether it succeeds in forging a new social contract. Chapter 7 examines the region's long-term potential and summarizes the report's many suggestions for institutional improvements that will affect growth and poverty reduction.

Note

1. With nominal depreciations of 40 percent or more, exports were expected to surge 20–25 percent. That did not happen because, although export volumes rose, prices declined precipitously. Four forces explain the region's massive terms of trade shock. First, East Asian economies are highly integrated, so recession in one country soon spilled into neighboring economies, unleashing a collective contraction. Second, the regional contraction, including the Japanese recession, depressed commodity prices, including for rice, rubber, and oil. Third, excess capacity in the electronics industry, notably semiconductors, drove prices through the floor—and these exports accounted for a large share of manufactured exports from Korea and Malaysia. Finally, the sudden surge of exports from within the region in competing product lines cut prices for all. The terms of trade shock added to the shock of capital flow reversals and dug the hole of recession deeper than anyone expected.

References

Credit Lyonnais Securities Asia. 1999. "Eye on the Asian Economies." Global Emerging Market

Deutsche Bank. 1999. *Emerging Markets Weekly*, September 17.

Hodrick, Robert J., and Edward C. Prescott. 1997. "Post War U.S. Business Cycles: An Empirical Investigation." *Journal of Money, Credit and Banking* (U.S.) 29 (February): 1–16.

Montes, Manuel F. 1998. "The Currency Crisis in Southeast Asia." Institute of Southeast Asian Studies, Singapore.

Mukherjee, Nilanjana. 1999. "Indonesia: Consultations with the Poor." Paper prepared for World Bank Global Synthesis Workshop, 22–23 September, Washington, D.C.

World Bank. 1999a. *East Asia: The Road to Recovery.* Washington, D.C.

———. 1999b. *World Development Report 1998/99: Knowledge for Development.* New York: Oxford University Press.

———. 2000. *Global Economic Prospects and the Developing Countries.* Washington, D.C.

CHAPTER 2

MANAGING FINANCIAL INTEGRATION

It's the end of March and Alfred Ho, a director at Invesco Hong Kong, is in an expansive mood. "The systemic danger of Asia is less," he proclaims. "Now is the time to look at the dogs and take a risk. Companies will either restructure and deleverage or go under." Last year, Ho wasn't sure what to tell his clients. "This year I can tell them 'I won't lose your money,'" he says. At a time when many Asian markets are down 80% from their peaks, fund managers have concluded that the greatest risk to investors lies in not investing. There hasn't been a return to the good old days of five years ago. But it is time for some careful homework and a search for genuine turnaround plays and companies that are serious about restructuring. "You have to ask, 'Will they repay their debt? Will they focus more? Will they improve their return on assets?'" says Ho.

—Far Eastern Economic Review, 22 April 1999, p. 32

The East Asian crisis grew out of inadequate management of the risks associated with integration with global financial markets.[1] Overleveraged and poorly regulated financial institutions and firms borrowed offshore to finance investments that became progressively less productive. As the region's boom slowed, growing weaknesses in financial institutions and firms interacted with economic policies to encourage excessive offshore borrowing—particularly short-term borrowing. Rather than slowing or offsetting inflows, policies sometimes encouraged more short-term flows by further opening the capital account and facilitating the expansion of poorly regulated financial institutions, including nonbanks and offshore domestic banks.

Such policies helped maintain growth, but they also increased risks. Because of East Asia's good performance and with lower-return lending opportunities at home, external lenders were eager to lend. In retrospect, they lent beyond levels that prudence would have dictated, perhaps because of expectations that exit would be easy or that governments would take over loans—expectations that were largely fulfilled. As risks mounted in the mid-1990s, lending became increasingly short-term, and capital outflows rose, suggesting that asset holders in these countries were becoming increasingly nervous. After Thailand's crisis hit, investors' concerns about country risks increased sharply, leading to massive outflows from countries they considered similar to Thailand.

The crisis countries' recent experience with financial integration can be assessed in three phases. After a decade in which partial capital account openings produced large private long-term flows, the 1990s began with a new phase of financial integration. Booming global private flows, attracted by East Asia's strong performance, interacted with underlying financial weaknesses (and in some cases macroeconomic weaknesses) to increase vulnerabilities. The second phase began when risks became realities and the crisis hit. Macroeconomic policy struggled to cope with massive private capital outflows, enormous official capital flows mitigated the adverse financial and real effects, and monetary policy was caught between the objectives of limiting exchange rate impacts on heavily indebted firms and of supplying liquidity to the financial system. In the third phase, as outflows slowed and stability was restored, policy turned toward setting up new frameworks to manage financial integration. China, integrating with global financial markets under a very different framework, requires separate consideration.

The first phase: emerging vulnerabilities

Despite remarkable growth, East Asia was already exhibiting a few vulnerabilities before the crisis. Among the most important were rapidly rising inflows, increasingly less productive investment, and policy choices that sustained growth but increased vulnerability.

Rapidly rising inflows

Even in 1990 the four countries hit hardest by the crisis—Indonesia, the Republic of Korea, Malaysia, and Thailand—were relatively well integrated with global financial markets. Reflecting their integration and strong performance, they had high ratios of private long-term nonguaranteed debt and private short-term debt to GDP, higher even than large Latin American countries (figure

Figure 2.1

East Asia had high private debt even before the crisis

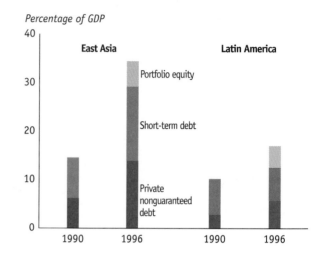

Percentage of GDP

Note: East Asia data are an average for Indonesia, Republic of Korea, Malaysia, and Thailand. Latin America data are an average for Argentina, Brazil, Colombia, Mexico, and Peru.
Source: World Bank data.

2.1).[2] Other large East Asian countries—China, the Philippines, Vietnam—had much less private debt.

After 1990 the region entered a new phase of financial integration with the global economy. The four crisis countries took on even more private debt, and at a faster pace than other developing countries, especially after 1993 (see figure 2.1).[3] Policy changes indirectly favored foreign borrowing (boxes 2.1, 2.2, and 2.3). The countries' ratio of private nonguaranteed and short-term debt to GDP rose by almost 3 percentage points a year. Short-term debt grew especially fast, with Thailand and (after 1994) Korea seeing the largest relative increases.[4]

In addition, the four countries received enormous portfolio and foreign direct investments. Annual portfolio inflows averaged more than 1 percent of GDP, 50 percent more than in large Latin American countries. Significant foreign direct investment (above the average for large developing countries) went to Malaysia, Indonesia, and Thailand. The inflows were responding to these countries' continued good performance and increasingly open capital accounts. Thus the countries benefited from, and accounted for about one-quarter of, the explosion in global private financial flows in the 1990s.

In the early 1990s the inflows financed a sharp rise in domestic investment and international reserves (figure

Thailand's financial integration, financial policies, and the crisis

After 1990 Thailand had the highest growth rate of the four crisis countries but also ran the largest current account deficit—averaging 7 percent of GDP in 1990–96 and 8 percent in 1995–96. External debt, particularly short-term debt, increased quickly. Investment rose but growth actually fell relative to the late 1980s.

Thailand's capital account was already relatively open in the mid-1980s. Liberalization of current account transactions was completed in 1990, and by 1996 most capital account restrictions had been removed (Alba, Hernandez, and Klingebiel 1999). The exchange rate was fixed, reducing the apparent risk for borrowers in foreign currency. Although the real exchange rate appreciated less than 10 percent in the 1990s (according to the IMF), a large shift occurred between the prices of tradables and nontradables (Warr 1998). The question remains whether a more flexible exchange rate, which would have allowed a nominal appreciation, would have deterred some inflows and accomplished that shift in a way that could have been reversed later at lower cost.

The domestic banking system's interest rates and directed credit allocations had been liberalized in the early 1990s. Although there was no formal deposit insurance, in the crisis of 1983 depositors' losses were limited, even in nonbank financial institutions (Johnson 1991).

In 1993 capital account openness increased sharply and changed in form with the opening of the Bangkok International Banking Facility. The facility was created with the hope of creating an international financial center and to attract capital to sustain Thailand's boom. The facility's rules encouraged short-term, foreign currency financing for domestic firms. Participating banks enjoyed tax and regulatory advantages. Domestic banks shifted some operations offshore, which may have increased their foreign currency liabilities to depositors (Kawai and Iwatsubo 1998).

Thailand's high growth in the 1990s partly reflected a massive building boom, with much of the financing coming from offshore, through weak, unregulated finance companies. Because they could not take deposits, the finance companies depended on volatile commercial paper for funding. Their rapid expansion partly reflected the hope that the largest ones would receive new bank licenses. The banking system was also poorly regulated (in terms of loan loss provisioning and income recognition), had weak assets (with 7 percent nonperforming assets before the crisis), and was exposed, directly and indirectly, to property lending.

Fiscal policy probably added to, rather than offset, the impact of the inflows. The fiscal surplus fell from 3.2 percent of GDP in 1990 to 0.9 percent in 1996 (IMF, *International Financial Statistics*; data include privatization revenue). The Bank of Thailand's attempt to contain the boom with high interest rates only attracted more inflows under the open capital account, fixed exchange rate regime.

When the economic slowdown began in 1996, the government provided massive support for finance companies (and investors in the stock market) rather than forcing them to resolve their affairs on their own (as India did in 1998). Between December 1996 and June 1997 the Bank of Thailand's loans to nonbanks would have increased base money by 66 percent had reserves not fallen. Not surprisingly, holders of baht—already nervous because of the falling stock market and deteriorating fiscal balance—feared that these policies would rupture the fixed exchange regime and so fled the currency. The government was forced to float the baht in July 1997, when its reserves (net of forward contracts) were nearly exhausted (Lane and others 1999). Large external debt and sharply higher interest rates led to widespread bankruptcies.

2.2). Higher net inflows to Korea, Malaysia, and Thailand financed most of their sharp rise in investment; the rest was financed by domestic saving.[5] Indonesia's investment increased less (3 percent of GDP) and was largely financed by domestic saving.

In 1994–96 the four countries allowed themselves to become even more vulnerable, and there were signs that investors were becoming concerned about the sustainability of the boom. Countries increasingly used inflows to finance investment—investment remained roughly constant as a share of GDP (except in Malaysia), while the current account widened by 1 percent or more of GDP. Moreover, short-term debt and unaccounted-for capital outflows increased sharply.[6] Finally, growth in

international reserves slowed (see figure 2.2). Lower reserves relative to rapidly growing short-term debt and domestic deposits meant a smaller cushion against shifts by short-term lenders and domestic depositors through the open capital account. This vulnerability was in addition to the potential of reversals in portfolio flows and any problems in rolling over long-term debt that would come with any loss of confidence. (Debt service obligations on long-term debt averaged 8.2 percent of GDP in Indonesia and 7.7 percent in Malaysia.)

Avoiding the loss of confidence that would reverse capital flows and cause a crisis depended on using the inflows productively (so that the resulting assets could service the resulting debt) and maintaining sound

Figure 2.2

Net inflows financed a sharp rise in domestic investment and international reserves

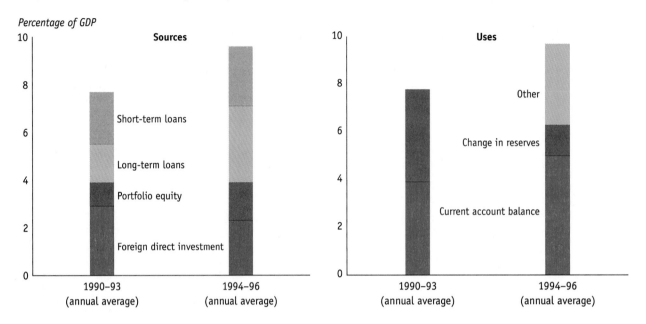

Note: Data are an average for Indonesia, Republic of Korea, Malaysia, and Thailand.
Source: World Bank, *Global Development Finance database;* IMF, *International Financial Statistics.*

macroeconomic policies (with consistency between monetary and exchange rate policies even if external or internal conditions changed). But during the 1990s, and especially after 1993, the crisis countries increasingly did not meet these conditions—raising the risk of a sudden shift in funds.

Less productive investment

East Asian investment became less productive in the 1990s. At the macroeconomic level increased investment did not lead proportionally to increased growth. In Korea and Thailand growth rates actually declined. At the microeconomic level, profit rates were low and falling (Claessens, Djankov, and Lang 1998). With debt and interest rates rising, earnings fell (Alba and others 1999). Part of the slowdown in productivity and profits probably reflected a shift into property lending (Goldstein 1998). Declines in stock markets and residential property prices began in 1996 (Berg 1999). In Korea low profits fell even further, partly reflecting external shocks, and in 1996 and early 1997 six *chaebols* (corporate conglomerates) went bankrupt. In all

countries weak, overleveraged, and poorly regulated financial institutions (particularly nonbanks and offshore local banks) and their clients were highly vulnerable to the declines in stock and property prices.

Why did flows to East Asia lead to less productive investment? One reason is that they passed through weak financial institutions with poor evaluation capacity, low capital, and weak regulation and supervision—particularly state banks in Indonesia and nonbanks in Korea and Thailand (chapter 4; Alba and others 1999; Claessens and Glaessner 1997; Alba, Claessens, and Djankov 1998; Claessens, Djankov, and Lang 1998; Gray 1999). But this is not the complete answer. Much of Indonesia's external borrowing did not pass through the domestic financial system but went directly from international banks to nonfinancial firms.

For every offshore borrower there was an offshore lender. The natural question is, why was private lending so massive to financial institutions and corporations that were generally known to be weak? One possible explanation is the good performance of the countries and the borrowers, combined with a search for higher profits than could be obtained at home. Japanese banks, for

BOX 2.2

Indonesia's capital account openness, policies in the 1990s, and the crisis

In many ways Indonesia seemed like a strong economy in early 1997. Yet it suffered the most from the crisis when its financial and governance weaknesses interacted with policy errors and high external debt. Indonesia had opened its capital account long before the crisis, in 1970, with the aim of reducing the corruption that had plagued its capital controls. The exchange rate regime was shifted in 1994, from a crawling peg to a band around a crawling peg, but the width of the band was kept relatively small. Although the capital account was open, in the 1990s dollar deposit rates were about 1 percentage point higher than in Singapore and local currency rates, adjusted for depreciation, were far higher than offshore rates (World Bank 1995b), suggesting large risk premiums. Nonetheless, external loans were offered and Indonesian corporations borrowed directly offshore, in massive amounts. Thus much of Indonesia's global financial integration and corporate financing did not take place through its banks but directly with international banks. Corporations took no hedges, a risky strategy that paid them large dividends for a time but contributed heavily to the severity of the crisis.

Banks dominated Indonesia's domestic financial sector. The ratio of broad money to GDP increased only slightly faster than GDP during the 1990s—suggesting that domestically based credit expansion was not excessive. But the private capital market was small (World Bank 1995a), and there was no government debt market because of a 1967 regulation prohibiting government onshore borrowing. Interest rate ceilings were lifted in 1984. In 1988, to stimulate competition, foreign and new private banks were allowed nearly free entry, and capital and reserve requirements were minimized (Hanna 1994). To curb the credit expansion that followed, monetary policy was tightened sharply—but this only stimulated capital inflows under the open capital account and generated a large quasi-fiscal deficit that was largely unwound in 1993 (World Bank 1994).

Bank regulation and supervision were tightened in the early 1990s, but inaction against those not in compliance allowed many weak banks to stay in business. Nonperforming assets averaged 9 percent. State banks, which accounted for 40 percent of deposits, probably had less than 3 percent capital, taking into account underprovisioning. And 27 percent of banks exceeded exposure limits (World Bank 1995b). No formal deposit insurance existed. In the first major private bank crisis in the 1990s large depositors lost substantial interest; in the second there was no loss to depositors because a takeover was arranged. Many foreign banks were licensed, but they typically booked loans offshore, probably because of the weak legal framework for collection and the capital required to book onshore.

Fiscal policy was tightened in the 1990s, initially to offset high oil prices, then with a 2.6 percent of GDP deficit reduction

between 1992 and 1996 to offset overheating. Public external debt was prepaid using privatization revenues and the 1995 budget surplus. But monetary policy was considered the primary stabilization instrument, especially in 1995–96, and low reserve requirements were raised in February 1996 and April 1997. This monetary tightening, like the previous one, was offset by inflows under the open capital account and relatively fixed exchange rate, and had little impact on interest rates or credit volumes (World Bank 1996c). And as noted, corporations were also borrowing directly offshore.

At the start of 1997 Indonesia had the lowest current account deficit of the crisis countries, a smaller investment boom, and a massive increase in foreign direct investment. But its high external debt, especially short-term debt, and its open capital account left the economy vulnerable to shifts in confidence. Moreover, the country suffered from longstanding, well-known weaknesses in finance and governance (World Bank 1993, 1995b, 1996c, 1997c). Capital outflows had risen in 1994–96. The likelihood of a new cabinet after the election and a deteriorating macroeconomy heightened concerns in 1997. The float of the Thai baht increased them sharply.

Indonesia responded to Thailand's float by widening its exchange rate band in July and then announcing a float of the exchange rate in August, with little use of reserves to defend the currency during the interval. Interest rates were raised but soon lowered because of political pressure (Ohno, Shirono, and Sisli 1999). By the end of September central bank credit was up 11 percent relative to the end of June. To help defend the exchange rate, limits were placed on banks' foreign exchange positions at the end of August. By the end of October the crisis had left Indonesia's exchange rate depreciated, though not much more than Malaysia's and Thailand's.

In November Indonesia received a large package of multilateral support. In addition to macroeconomic conditions, the economic program called for deregulation and the closure of 16 weak banks. A run developed on these banks, then spread to others, despite the announcement of deposit insurance for small depositors that was soon followed by general coverage. The central bank offered large credits to support the banking system and in response to pressure to keep down interest rates. By the end of December credit to banks had more than tripled—an increase that would have doubled the money base had international reserves not declined. Concerns about Soeharto's health and the announcement of a budget for 1998–99 that appeared to bear little resemblance to IMF targets increased capital flight. By December 1997 the rupiah had fallen to about half its value at the end of 1996, and political concerns were compounding economic problems.

Korea's capital account liberalization, financial integration, and the crisis

Korea's capital account liberalization began in earnest in the early 1990s. But for three reasons these efforts encouraged a buildup of short-term external debt intermediated mainly through the financial sector. First, short-term borrowing for both banks and corporations was liberalized while longer-term borrowing, including access to supplier credits and foreign bond markets, remained restricted. Second, debt flows were encouraged relative to equity inflows. Although foreign equity flows into the stock market were liberalized in January 1992, they remained subject to restrictions—including a 10 percent ceiling on foreign holding of any stock (raised to 12 percent in December 1994 and 15 percent in July 1995). Third, financial institutions' borrowing was liberalized, but corporations' borrowing required government approval, and its uses were restricted.

Korea also resumed domestic financial liberalization in the early 1990s. In 1991 a four-stage plan for deregulating interest rates was announced. Financial institutions were given greater freedom in asset-liability management, including liberalization (in 1993) of foreign currency–denominated lending. In 1994–96 more financial institutions were allowed to offer foreign currency loans through the transformation of 24 finance companies into merchant banking corporations (which could operate in foreign exchange markets) and the opening of 28 new offshore branches by banks.

In addition, the macroeconomic policies used to deal with inflows at least partly encouraged the accumulation of short-term external liabilities. To relieve inflationary pressures, the authorities both sterilized a sizable portion of foreign inflows and allowed some exchange rate appreciation. A significant differential between domestic and foreign interest rates was sustained, leading to strong demand for cheaper foreign funds. For all these reasons, external debt grew sharply—particularly short-term borrowing, which had been liberalized more.

Korean financial institutions were inadequately prepared to manage these large inflows. There was limited experience with credit analysis, risk management, and due diligence—a legacy of the past development strategy, which, despite its successes, had resulted in a passive financial system. As a result financial institutions became vulnerable to increasing currency and maturity mismatches. Lending was channeled to manufacturing and export-oriented sectors. But corporations' rates of return were low and fell in the 1990s, while their investment and borrowing did not. External financial flows eased corporations' budget constraints and added to their high leveraging. Thus the approach to financial integration appears to have exacerbated underlying structural weaknesses.

Until 1995 Korea's strong performance masked these weaknesses. When the economy slowed in 1996, the underlying fragility gave way to corporate distress. Corporate after-tax profits declined from 4 percent of GDP in 1989–95 to less than 2 percent in 1996. Moreover, net corporate borrowing rose considerably—from 4 percent of GDP in 1989–95 to almost 18 percent in 1996. The first evidence of distress surfaced in late 1996 and early 1997. In January 1997 Hanbo, the fourteenth largest chaebol, declared bankruptcy with debts estimated at $6 billion. This was followed by a string of other business failures.

By mid-1997 it was clear that corporate difficulties would have significant repercussions on the financial sector. The Thai devaluation in July raised investor concerns, and growing difficulties in the financial sector heightened nervousness. The decision to bail out the near-bankrupt Kia in October, and the stock market crash in Hong Kong (China), appear to have triggered more intense pressure on the won. Foreign banks refused to roll over loans—adding to pressures on the exchange rate.

Throughout the period, foreign investor uncertainty was fueled by the lack of timely, reliable information on nonperforming loans, foreign exchange reserves, and foreign debt. The government's initial response in August 1997 was to guarantee the deposits and foreign liabilities of financial institutions. But this move may have called into question the Bank of Korea's ability to act as the lender of last resort, and so failed to reassure investors. Attempts to maintain the exchange rate by intervening in the foreign exchange market led to a $10 billion loss in reserves between the end of August and the end of November. Attempts to maintain the exchange rate policy were abandoned on 17 November. A few days later, Korea sought emergency support from the international community to avoid defaulting on external debt.

---

example, may have increased offshore exposure to offset falling domestic returns and to support Japanese corporate investment—much as U.S. and European banks did in Latin America in the 1980s. Another hypothesis relates to financial bubbles and herd behavior.

A third hypothesis relates to the idea that flows were encouraged by expectations of an ability to exit (while government supported the exchange rate) or of government takeovers of private debt if things went wrong. No formal guarantees existed.[7] However, Thailand defended its pegged exchange rate in the first half of 1997—and all countries used reserves and official borrowing to limit exchange rate depreciation after their pegs were abandoned (see below). Once the crisis hit, the Korean government effectively took over private external debt and Indonesia, Korea, and Thailand guaranteed bank and nonbank deposits. Thus if there had been expectations of bailouts, they were largely fulfilled because external lenders and asset holders, domestic and foreign, were able to exit and government guarantees were offered (except in the case of Indonesian corporate debt).

Policymaking problems

During the 1990s various pressures led to increasingly inconsistent macroeconomic policies—defined as the mix of monetary, exchange rate, fiscal, and external debt management policies. The crisis countries had long pursued conservative macroeconomic policies (World Bank 1993). When capital inflows picked up in the early 1990s, the countries faced new challenges and tougher decisions, often outside the realm of traditional macroeconomic policy. The choices made often kept growth going in the short run but provided limited cushions against increasing vulnerability.

The crisis countries (especially Indonesia and Thailand) tried to use monetary policy to sterilize inflows. But attempts to tighten credit encouraged additional inflows under relatively fixed exchange rates. This exchange rate policy (as opposed to a one-time appreciation) was guided by a desire to sustain the export drive on which these countries' growth had been built and to provide predictability for cross-border traders, investors, and borrowers. But the policy not only contributed to inflows, it also encouraged unhedged positions.

Nor did fiscal policy offset the expansionary impacts of capital inflows. In Korea and Thailand little fiscal tightening occurred. In Indonesia and Malaysia tightening was fairly large by international standards between 1989 and 1995 (3.2 and 4.2 percent of GDP). But even in those two countries the increase in fiscal surpluses was much less than the massive increase in annual inflows. In 1996 the fiscal surplus deteriorated in all four countries, especially Malaysia and Thailand. In the first half of 1997 Thailand also began providing massive support to its banks and nonbanks (see box 2.1).

Inadequate management of financial integration in the context of weak domestic financial institutions and corporations was perhaps the greatest policy weakness in East Asia. This area lies outside traditional macroeconomic policy but has been a major issue since the Latin American debt crisis of the 1980s, particularly in Chile.[8] In East Asia the problems related to moral hazard—the lack of concern for prudent, productive lending that develops when financial institutions and firms have little stake in financial outcomes and depositors and lenders expect to be protected by governments. Links between financial institutions and corporations increase moral hazard.

These problems were magnified by East Asia's financial integration with world markets. Thus, as the Asian boom began to slow, financial institutions and corporations with increasingly less to lose did their best to borrow and sustain their activities in hopes that returns would improve. External lenders allowed borrowers to escape the limited size of the domestic credit market; they were willing to lend increasingly short-term funds with the idea that they could get out and the governments would probably take over the loans if they went bad.

Governments did not intervene in weak institutions until they had openly experienced a crisis. Indeed, the Korean and Thai governments allowed poorly regulated institutions to expand rapidly through offshore borrowing. Korea and Thailand also eased regulations on inflows, particularly short-term debt. These polices encouraged additional inflows and temporarily sustained growth—but also increased vulnerability.

In sum, East Asia's crisis countries were unprepared to manage the sharp increase in financial integration during the mid-1990s. Increasingly large financial inflows, attracted by the region's past success, swamped the capacity of financial institutions to make productive loans. Macroeconomic policy did not offset the boom and was lulled into a false sense of security by the private nature of flows. When growth slowed and adjustments became desirable, as in Korea and Thailand in 1995–96, policymakers opted to try to keep the boom going with more external borrowing, rather than by making adjustments that would have further slowed growth in the short run. Foreign inflows increased, particularly short-term flows, responding to further financial opening and perhaps to the expectation of government guarantees if something went wrong.

When Thailand's monetary and fiscal policies appeared inconsistent with the exchange rate regime in the first half of 1997, strong speculation developed against the baht. Thailand was forced to announce a float of the baht when it exhausted its reserves in defense of the peg.[9] Elsewhere there were no obvious signs of problems before the baht was floated,[10] despite the problems discussed above. Nonetheless, the baht's collapse led the herd of investors to quickly flee other countries in the region.[11] Pressure developed on exchange rates and interest rates, triggering corporate and financial bankruptcies. Investment collapsed. Making matters worse, negative shocks, in many cases unrelated, hit exports and agriculture.

The second phase: responding to the crisis

The crisis plunged East Asia's financial integration into a new and difficult phase, closely tied to macroeconomic policy responses and characterized by three elements:

- A massive withdrawal of private capital (including deposits) as investors, domestic and foreign, fled from assets denominated in domestic currency or located in domestic financial markets.
- A partly compensatory movement of official capital inflows to offset private outflows and a guarantee (or takeover) of private debt by governments.
- A monetary policy caught in a dilemma: either fulfill lender of last resort functions (in hopes of maintaining confidence) and expand domestic credit (to try to lower interest rates), at the risk of fueling the portfolio shift and exchange rate depreciation, or limit domestic credit creation (to stabilize the exchange rate and offshore borrowing costs), at the risk of causing a systemic banking crisis. Countries switched between these options (Ohno, Shirono, and Sisli 1999).

Private outflows—and official inflows

After the baht collapsed, domestic and foreign asset holders scrambled for the exit—causing a spectacular wave of capital outflows. Commercial banks led the exodus, reducing their exposure by nearly $100 billion in 18 months (table 2.1).

The crisis countries tried to support their weak financial systems with large central bank loans and, from time to time, tried to lower interest rates. Deposits were guaranteed and private debts were effectively taken over by governments in an attempt to boost confidence. Nonetheless, a lack of demand for local assets meant that most of the increases in central bank credit leaked out into the foreign exchange market, contributing to depreciation pressures and reserve losses. Capital controls were used by Thailand briefly in mid-1997 and by Malaysia after September 1998. Fiscal deficits increased as GDP fell—and the quasi-fiscal deficits associated with support for financial systems were large—but fiscal loosening was insufficient to offset the huge drop in demand.

Large official support packages in Indonesia, Korea, and Thailand tried to restore confidence and provide resources to stem the depreciation and meet the reduction in private demand for assets (table 2.2). The support was larger than in the Latin American debt crisis of the 1980s and similar to that in the Mexican peso crisis of 1994–95. As is usually the case, the funding was not disbursed all at once, but over time in response to changing conditions and various cross-linkages (Lane and others 1999).[12] Malaysia, with relatively less external debt, did not enter an IMF-supported program and received much less official support, largely meeting the exchange rate pressure with a mix of reserve sales and depreciation.

As noted, governments offered guarantees in an attempt to preserve confidence in financial systems. Before their IMF programs, Korea and Thailand effectively guaranteed deposits in banks and nonbanks. Indonesia offered guarantees after closing 16 banks, first to small depositors and then to all depositors.

Attempts were also made to limit outflows by external creditors. Thailand received assurances at the start of its IMF program that foreign (mostly Japanese) banks resident in Thailand would continue their lines of credit, but rollovers to Thai banks declined. Korea lost short-term credits even after its standby agreement with the IMF was announced. With its reserves largely depleted, Korea reached an agreement with it creditors in January 1998 that calmed markets. The agreement

---

TABLE 2.1

Changes in commercial bank exposure to East Asia, 1997–98

(billions of U.S. dollars)

Recipient	1997 first half	1997 second half	1998 first half	1998 second half
Indonesia, Rep. of Korea, Malaysia, and Thailand	18.4	−20.3	−46.9	−21.2
Other	15.4	12.5	−10.7	−6.8

Source: IMF 1999b.

included a voluntary, cooperative understanding to maintain interbank lines of credit until March 1998. Under a debt restructuring agreement signed at the end of March, $21.8 billion of private banks' short-term debt was exchanged for one- to three-year government-guaranteed debt.

Restructuring of Indonesia's debt did not begin until February 1998, hampered by large private corporate debt, numerous creditors, and difficulties in getting a good assessment of debts. In June 1998, interbank debt was restructured and guaranteed by Bank Indonesia, and banks agreed to try to maintain trade credit at the April 1998 level for one year. Indonesia also set up exchange rate guarantees for corporate debt restructuring. By October 1998, however, this program had attracted only $2.9 billion.

Capital controls were tightened in Thailand in mid-1997 and in Malaysia in September 1998 (see below). Large capital outflows from domestic depositors (IMF 1998) and large reductions in bank exposures (see table 2.1) suggest that all these efforts to limit outflows by external creditors were ineffective. Finally, there were also substantial outflows from capital markets.

The massive outflows, the reserves and official borrowing used to meet them, and the sharp improvement in current accounts are shown for Indonesia, Korea, and Thailand in figure 2.3. In Korea private outflows totaled $38 billion—equivalent to 20 percent of GDP—in the fourth quarter of 1997 and first quarter of 1998, the two quarters of greatest outflows.[13] Official inflows covered 46 percent of these outflows (and the gain in reserves in the first quarter of 1998); reserve losses in the fourth quarter and current account surpluses covered the rest.

In Thailand private outflows totaled $15 billion in the third and fourth quarters of 1997, equivalent to 23 percent of GDP, and official flows covered 61 percent. In 1998 Thailand lost an additional $18 billion. In Indonesia the fourth quarter of 1997 and first quarter of 1998 saw private outflows of $16 billion, equivalent to 26 percent of GDP. Official flows covered 18 percent of the outflows; reserve losses and current account surpluses covered the rest. The lower coverage of Indonesian outflows reflects limited official disbursements associated with difficulties in meeting the conditions of the IMF program.

In the third quarter of 1998 private capital outflows increased again in all three countries. This interruption probably reflected the turbulence in international markets related to Russia's August default and the collapse of the Long Term Capital Management hedge fund. But the increase in outflows was not large (except in Indonesia, where political uncertainties may have played a role). In the fourth quarter of 1998 outflows slowed again and growth began to recover (except in Indonesia, where the increase in growth was delayed until 1999).

Monetary policy and lender of last resort: the dilemma of integrated economies

East Asia's globally integrated corporations and financial institutions were hit hard by currency depreciations and nonrenewals of external loans. In theory the outflows and the pressures on exchange rates could have been limited by tighter money policy (box 2.4). But tight money would have limited the ability of central banks to act as lenders of last resort in response to withdrawals of funds by foreign lenders and domestic depositors. Tight money also would have hurt indebted domestic corporations and financial institutions—particularly if it lasted for a long time. Thus policymakers faced a tradeoff between allowing depreciation and tightening money, with their different allocational and distributional effects on depositors and different groups of debtors.

TABLE 2.2
Packages of official support for crisis countries
(billions of U.S. dollars)

	Indonesia	Korea, Rep. of	Thailand	Mexico
Total	38.1[a]	58.2	17.2	50.0
(As percentage of 1997 GDP)	18.0	13.0	12.0	12.0
IMF	10.1	21.1	4.0	
World Bank	4.5	10.0	1.5	
Asian Development Bank	3.5	4.0	1.2	
Other (largely Japan)	20.0[b]	23.1[b]	10.5[c]	
Date of IMF approval	11/5/97	12/4/97	8/20/97	

a. Augmented by $42 billion (including debt rescheduling and new funds) in June 1998.
b. Second line of defense. Indonesia includes $5 billion of its own reserves.
c. Japanese funding disbursed in parallel with IMF loans.
Source: Lane and others 1999; World Bank data.

Figure 2.3

Inflows, outflows, and growth during the crisis

Indonesia

Percentage of GDP

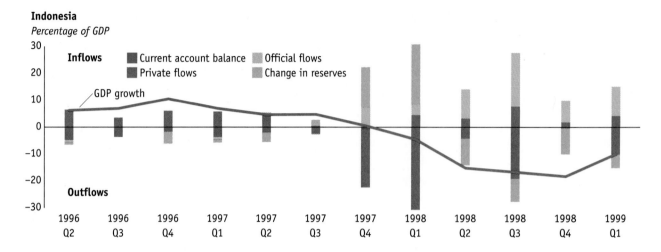

Korea, Rep. of

Percentage of GDP

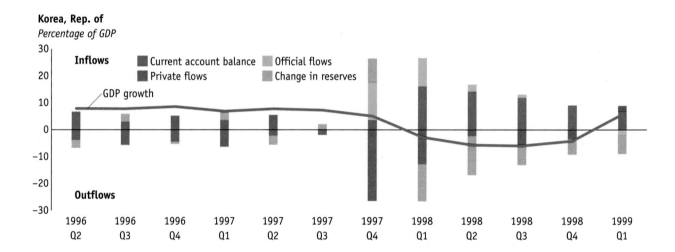

Thailand

Percentage of GDP

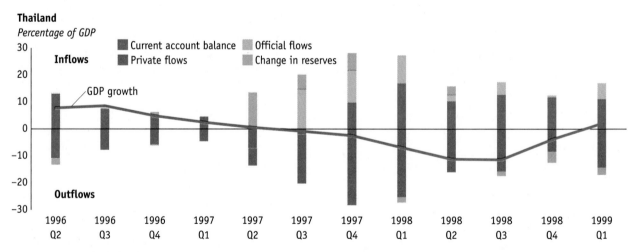

Source: IMF, *International Financial Statistics.*

In practice, the crisis countries vacillated in their approaches to monetary and exchange rate policy. At times they substantially increased central bank credit, acting as lenders of last resort, paying off depositors, and occasionally trying to lower interest rates while selling their own and borrowed international reserves to limit the impact of outflows on the exchange rate. During these periods countries were trying to support weak financial institutions and to replace lost foreign credits and deposit outflows with central bank credit. While no longer supporting their original exchange rates, countries' large sales of reserves limited the depreciation. Hence, despite the large depreciations, countries were far from floating their exchange rates freely.[14]

At other times, countries tightened central bank credit to limit depreciation and outflows and to rebuild reserves.

Increases in central bank credit dominated the early days of the crisis and tightening later, but sometimes the policies alternated within a short period (see box 2.2; Tanner 1999; Ohno, Shirono, and Sisli 1999; and Lane and others 1999). As discussed below, the issue here goes beyond the policy stance to, more fundamentally, policymakers' ability to affect monetary and credit conditions in fairly open economies when they are also selling large amounts of reserves to limit exchange rate movements and a large part of credit is denominated in foreign currency.

BOX 2.4

Counterfactuals: Alternative policy packages?

It is obviously a lot easier to offer policy recommendations with the benefit of hindsight. Certainly, the crisis would have cost less if countries had taken preventive steps beforehand—tightening fiscal policy, dealing with weak financial institutions quickly, abstaining from additional capital account liberalization to keep an unsustainable boom going. But these policies were politically difficult, especially with political transitions and elections in Indonesia, Korea, and Thailand (Berg 1999). Moreover, governments everywhere find it tough to take action on the basis of projections, especially when things are going well.

Once the crisis began, the stress on policymaking increased dramatically. One alternative response might have been looser fiscal policy and tighter monetary policy, in the sense of less domestic credit creation and more concern for reserve losses. But looser fiscal policy would have required even more official financing upfront. And without official support, looser fiscal policy might have reduced investor confidence, as occurred in Indonesia in January 1998. Finally, achieving looser fiscal policy quickly would not have been easy: new spending or tax cuts might have raised investor concerns. Increases in new infrastructure spending (other than speeding up existing contracts) would have taken time. And implementing new social spending and safety nets would have required major institutional improvements. Tighter monetary policy—avoiding attempts to hold down interest rates and making stronger efforts to avoid reserve losses—might have brought a quicker end to the exchange rate fall, but much of the domestic credit creation was to provide liquidity support for weak financial institutions. Once their IMF-supported programs were in place, Korea and Thailand followed the tightness agreed to fairly closely.

Other alternatives to combat the crisis might have involved greater concern for dealing with domestic financial institutions and offshore creditors. As long as deposits were not insured, governments might have required weak intermediaries to suspend payments and clear liabilities as loans were repaid—as India did with its uninsured nonbank financial institutions in 1998. Goldstein (1998) argues that all weak intermediaries should have been closed. Depositors and creditors might have been given the option of receiving a government bond equal to a fraction of their claims (say, for five years' tenure). That approach might have generated runs on other institutions, but in reality all institutions were hit hard—despite guarantees and liquidity support.

In constructing the official packages, more attention might have been paid to dealing with external creditors along the lines of the G-10 recommendations after Mexico's 1994–95 crisis (G-10 1996). Revised payment schedules might have created some risk of a systemic international crisis, but Stulz (1999) argues that the risk was small. In fact, countries were largely left to sort out their external debt. Implementing such a policy would have created enormous technical and political problems for official lenders and countries, given the hopes that government guarantees would stem the outflows. And while such actions might have stemmed the outflows, they would also have shifted deposits to public banks—where it would have been harder to reduce obligations, as in Indonesia, and probably would have limited the flow of new money after the crisis subsided.

Finally, countries might have closed their capital accounts at the first sign of crisis. The rationale would have been to allow looser domestic money to reduce onshore interest rates relative to offshore rates without creating depreciation pressures. In other words, countries could have tried to create another policy instrument to manage the capital account of the balance of payments and correspondingly reduce spillovers from other policy instruments. This option is discussed in the next section.

Figure 2.4

Domestic credit increases were largely offset by reserve losses

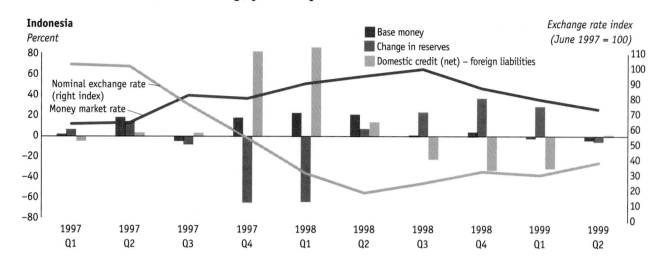

Indonesia
Percent

Base money
Change in reserves
Domestic credit (net) – foreign liabilities

Exchange rate index
(June 1997 = 100)

Nominal exchange rate (right index)
Money market rate

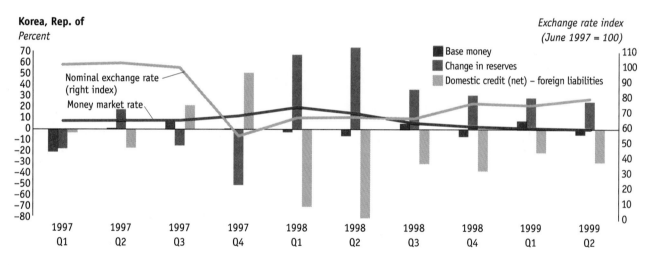

Korea, Rep. of
Percent

Exchange rate index
(June 1997 = 100)

Nominal exchange rate (right index)
Money market rate

Base money
Change in reserves
Domestic credit (net) – foreign liabilities

Note: Base money = change in reserves + domestic credit – foreign liabilities.
Source: World Bank data.

The large increases in net central bank credit mostly leaked out in losses of international reserves (figure 2.4).[15] These offsetting changes left the money base—and the money stock—roughly unchanged. For example, in Thailand in the first half of 1997, the central bank increased its credit to failing nonbanks by about 66 percent of the money base. Taking into account offsetting in the central bank balance sheet, the total increase would still have been 45 percent (see figure 2.4). Over the rest of 1997, after the stabilization program began, a similar amount of credit was provided. Thus, for the year as a whole, Bank of Thailand credit—

netting out credits offset by increased foreign liabilities—would have roughly doubled base money had international reserves not fallen.

The increase in Bank of Thailand credit was, in fact, almost completely offset by reserve losses. As a result base money rose only 16 percent for the year despite the massive increase in central bank credit. The reserve losses in the second half of the year occurred even as the exchange rate was allowed to depreciate substantially after June 1997—that is, the exchange rate was not floating freely. And the money market interest rate rose sharply despite the large increase in central bank credit

Figure 2.4 (continued)

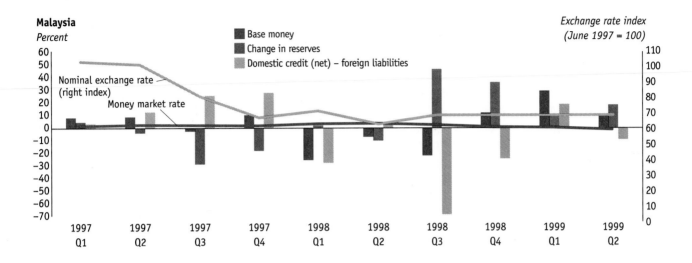

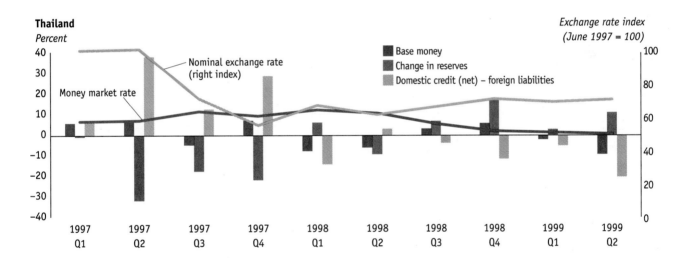

(see figure 2.4). Then in 1998, after a quarter in which the central bank reduced its net credit, the exchange rate appreciated and interest rates declined.

Other countries displayed a similar pattern during the crisis (see figure 2.4). At first central banks sharply increased domestic credit, largely to support weak financial institutions (and their depositors) when foreign credits and deposits were withdrawn and borrowers suspended debt service. But increased central bank credit was largely offset by reserve losses, so increases in base money were relatively small. Despite the large reserve sales, exchange rates depreciated. Indonesia saw the largest increase in base money and sharpest depreciation.

The link between financial crises and exchange rate crises is increasingly common worldwide (Kaminsky and Reinhart 1999). Nominal interest rates also rose in the countries. But adjusted for inflation or depreciation, the rise in interest rates was less than in many other financial crises, such as Mexico's in 1995 (Lane and others 1999). Nonetheless, the rise created cash-flow problems, adding to the large cash-flow problems from nonrenewals of externally financed loans, and many borrowers simply suspended debt service. Later, after a period of reduced outflows and tighter domestic credit, the exchange rate appreciated and interest rates fell.

Broad money (real) was roughly constant in all the countries, reflecting the limited rise in base money. In fact, broad money actually rose relative to (falling) GDP.[16] But credit conditions tightened sharply because of falling foreign loans to corporations and financial institutions and because of outflows of portfolio capital.

One explanation for these developments is that holders of assets, domestic and foreign, wanted to limit their holdings in the countries after the crisis broke. Attempts to increase domestic money and credit—even liquidity support to institutions—had to face that constraint. Loans and payments to cover runs by foreign lenders and domestic depositors would leak into the exchange market unless there was demand for the domestic currency assets being created. Indeed, large liquidity support to weak institutions may have contributed to investor concerns and thus exacerbated the outflows. Asset holders may have become concerned about whether the increase in central bank loans would eventually be covered by loan recoveries or would lead to substantial inflation or taxation. (See Dooley 2000 for a model of such behavior.)

If the exchange rate had been allowed to float more freely—that is, if less reserves had been sold—it might have been possible to increase nominal credit more. But the resulting additional depreciation would have made things even worse for externally indebted firms and financial intermediaries. Thus policymakers faced a dilemma. The situation stabilized in 1998, with stronger exchange rates and lower interest rates, only after central bank credit was tightened, higher interest rates prevailed for a time, outflows slowed, and expectations stabilized or improved.

This analysis also suggests a possible explanation for the correspondence between rises in interest rates and capital outflows shown in figure 2.4 (see also Furman and Stiglitz 1998; Kraay 1998; and Ohno, Shirono, and Sisli 1999). As the crisis developed, asset holders demanded much larger risk premiums to maintain their holdings. These premiums exceeded the increases in rates that governments could influence. Hence measured rates rose, but not enough to satisfy asset holders—yielding the empirical combination of rising interest rates and capital outflows.

A more fundamental question is, how much control did East Asian crisis countries have over monetary and credit conditions? In open economies financially integrated with the global economy, interest rates are heavily influenced by external influences and by risk premiums demanded by investors (see Tanner 1999 for examples). East Asia fit this pattern: private external loans and portfolio equity were equal to nearly 30 percent of GDP, and local depositors were sensitive to international conditions. With domestic interest rates heavily influenced by these factors, which are effectively determined offshore, it is likely that domestic monetary policy affects mainly exchange rates and reserves.

Even attempts to lower money market rates or channel credit to potentially productive uses or weak institutions run into the complication that the recipients will take the funds offshore if they consider the returns there more attractive—the demand for assets constraint noted above. Moreover, trying to support production with credit is difficult when even the smallest producer can become an exchange rate speculator in an economy with an open capital account. Domestic credit could have replaced more of the outflows if the exchange rate had really been floating, but this would have put even more pressure on those indebted offshore. Thus countries' attempts to provide liquidity support or loosen money mainly ended up putting pressure on the exchange rate and reserves, because of the fall in demand for financial assets (see also Tanner 1999 and Berg 1999).

Were capital controls an effective response?

As noted, Thailand and Malaysia tightened capital controls as part of policies to contain private outflows.[17] Thailand did so in mid-1997 on a small scale and had limited success in stemming outflows. Malaysia tightened its controls in September 1998 (after the crisis in the real sector had largely passed) and has maintained them, in modified form, ever since.[18] Malaysia's controls allowed it to narrow the spread between domestic and foreign interest rates. And Malaysia's recovery has been somewhat stronger than Thailand's. But that may also reflect Malaysia's lower initial debt, stronger macroeconomic situation, and tough initial response to the crisis.

Thailand's experience. In May 1997 Thailand tried to stem capital outflows by limiting transactions with and by nonresidents; the measures "did not apply to genuine transactions related to export and import of goods and services, direct investment or various types of portfolio investment" (IMF 1999a, p. 81). With the July float of the baht, a dual market in foreign exchange (onshore and offshore) was allowed to develop, and stricter conditions were later imposed on the surrender of export receipts (IMF 1999a, p. 82). In January 1998 the restrictions were lifted.

The restrictions were ineffective in stemming capital outflows. The balance of payments suggests that the largest outflows from Thailand occurred in the third and fourth quarters of 1997. In a way the ineffectiveness of the controls is not surprising. They were limited, especially in their inapplicability to residents, who could purchase foreign exchange with baht. Broad money was actually slightly less in nominal terms at the end of the second and third quarters of 1997 than in March 1997, and in real terms in the fourth quarter of 1997 as well. These declines suggest an outflow of residents' deposits, particularly taking into account the substantial increase in domestic dollar deposits (in baht terms) during this period of depreciation and the large increase in central bank credit.

Malaysia's experience. Before the crisis Malaysia was less vulnerable than Indonesia, Korea, and Thailand. Reserves were relatively high. External and short-term debts were relatively low, at least partly reflecting controls on short-term borrowing (IMF 1999a, p. 98). And banks were in better shape, with the lowest reported share of nonperforming assets and among the highest capital adequacy ratios among the crisis countries.[19]

There were weaknesses, however. In 1996 the balance of payments deficit was fairly high at 5.6 percent of GDP (though it was down from 8.4 percent of GDP the previous year, making Malaysia the only one of the four crisis countries to have a lower current account deficit in 1996 than in 1995). Like the other countries, Malaysia had experienced a massive building boom, partly related to state-related megaprojects. And like the other countries, Malaysia's capital-output ratio was rising, reflecting rising investment and increasing property investment.

Malaysia suffered from the initial impact of the crisis, with GDP falling 10 percent between the second quarter of 1997 and the second quarter of 1998. But capital outflows were much smaller than in the other three countries—in the first three quarters of 1998 private short-term outflows were $4.5 billion, compared with nearly $14.0 billion in Thailand. Monetary policy was similar to yet tighter than that in the other countries (see figure 2.4), partly reflecting Malaysia's better initial position. Malaysia also maintained tighter fiscal policy than the other countries. Malaysia did not borrow from the IMF, and it received less official support than the other crisis countries.

Malaysia, like the other countries, wanted to reverse the economic downturn. Its banks and corporations were particularly vulnerable to higher interest rates because of the large share of private sector credit in GDP. But it was difficult to lower domestic interest rates with Singapore's nearby market offering ringgit transactions and trading in Malaysian shares.

In September 1998, with international financial markets getting battered by the Russian crisis, Malaysia decided to impose capital controls in an effort to weaken the link between internal and external financial markets. The controls and related policies involved three main elements. First, the controls targeted assets with maturities of a year or less, requiring such investment to remain in the country until September 1999. Second, the government used the controls to appreciate the ringgit–U.S. dollar exchange rate by about 10 percent and fix it at that level. Third, the controls sought to limit the offshore financial activities in Singapore by banning offshore trading in ringgit instruments (including shares), by preventing Malaysian banks from offering credit facilities to nonresident banks and stockbrokers, and by requiring that all foreign trade transactions be settled in foreign exchange. The domestic conversion of ringgit to foreign currency was not prohibited, however, and domestic dollar accounts continued to be allowed under certain conditions (and remained small).

The government took advantage of the respite provided by the controls to lower interest rates and tried to encourage lending by recommending an 8 percent increase in credit to the private sector, lowering the margin on bank loans over the base rate, reducing the statutory reserve requirement from 8.0 to 4.5 percent, and easing the recognition of nonperforming loans from three to six months (IMF 1999b, p. 99). Government fiscal policy was also loosened. In February 1999 the

September 1998 controls were converted into taxes on repatriated short-term flows, applied at a graduated scale inverse to maturity. Malaysia's capital controls ran counter to orthodoxy, and many observers predicted severe consequences. But the results were actually rather positive:

- Interest rate spreads over the U.S. federal funds rate fell (figure 2.5). Malaysia's sovereign spread on eurobonds increased, however (Goldman Sachs, *Portfolio Strategy*, 22 March 1999).

- Foreign exchange reserves increased $10 billion between September 1998 and October 1999, a rise second only to Korea's among the crisis countries—and the largest in percentage terms.

- Offshore activities, especially in Singapore, dried up—reducing the potential pressure from an organized offshore parallel market, but leaving an overhang of offshore stocks to be resolved.

- The stock market generally, and financial stocks particularly, reacted positively, rising immediately after the controls were introduced and outperforming Thailand's index.

The controls provided breathing room to restructure financial institutions (chapter 4). Moreover, Malaysia's

credit rating improved despite the controls. Malaysia was able to raise $1 billion in European bond markets in May 1999, and was oversubscribed three times. However, the issue was scaled back from the planned $2–3 billion, and the 3.3 percentage point spread over U.S. Treasury bills exceeded Korea's 2.25 point spread. Moreover, the impact of capital controls is probably felt in spreads on private loans, and cannot be judged solely from spreads on government debt.

Capital outflows were only about $330 million in the quarter after controls were lifted on 1 September 1999—far less than predicted. This may partly reflect the graduated tax format and partly the expectation that the Malaysian market index would be restored to the Morgan Stanley Capital International index. Since then, however, additional foreign capital has been repatriated. And the large stock of shares frozen in the Singapore market has yet to be resolved.

Overall, the Malaysian economy turned the corner well. But it is difficult to attribute the improvements in performance solely or even primarily to the controls. Growth also recovered in Korea and Thailand in the fourth quarter of 1998, with Korea doing much better than Malaysia and Thailand nearly as well. Controls may have helped Malaysia's performance, but so did its better initial conditions and strong policy actions in the early days of the crisis. Most of Malaysia's turnaround reflects fiscal loosening and sharp improvements in the trade balance, which have little to do with the controls.

The stock market performed better in Malaysia than in Thailand, though that may reflect factors other than controls, such as Thailand's large debt overhang. Malaysia succeeded in reducing spreads between internal and external interest rates, an outcome common to most other episodes of controls (Dooley 1996). In Thailand the spread actually dropped more precipitously and to a lower level than in Malaysia (see figure 2.5). Given Malaysia's lower initial external debt, it might have been able to loosen monetary policy initially with less concerns about depreciation.

Controls did play a role, however. The external and internal situation in August 1998 appeared to be worsening fast. Given the risks, the government decided to resort to unorthodox measures. Investors—especially domestic investors—may have regarded Malaysia's short-run response as reasonable given the risks, even if those risks did not materialize and even if the response

Figure 2.5

Interest rate spreads have narrowed in Malaysia and Thailand

Money market rates and U.S. federal funds rate
Percent

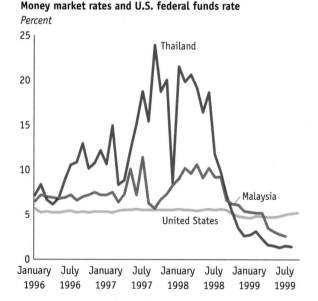

Source: World Bank data.

violated contracts in an unpredictable way. The fact that controls were phased out rather quickly and were consistent with other aspects of macroeconomic policy provided limited incentive and opportunity for investors to circumvent them, a major problem in many other countries (Dooley 1996). While the controls may have slowed capital outflows and may hinder short-term inflows, they may be discouraging longer-term inflows. Controls also may have a lingering effect on risk premiums. Thus more time needs to pass before the final chapter on Malaysia's experiment may be written.

The third phase: the road to recovery

East Asia has recovered since the end of 1998 (chapter 1). International reserves have been built up substantially, partly with the support of official inflows, decreasing vulnerability (see figure 1.7). Capital outflows continued to slow in 1999, while gross foreign direct investment and portfolio investment rose. With no further massive portfolio shifts out of the crisis countries, new policies and institutions will begin to dominate investor expectations. Thus the stage is set for a return of long-term private capital flows.

The countries' recent increased growth followed a period of tight money policy—as measured by varia-tions in domestic credit—with interest rates begin-ning to fall soon after.[20] Money and the money base remained relatively constant in real terms. Although domestic credit from the central bank was cut back, the money stock was maintained by increases in reserves arising from current account surpluses and official inflows in excess of (slowing) private outflows (table 2.3). Domestic interest rates started to fall in the second quarter of 1998 and are now fairly low (see figures 1.3 and 2.4 and Claessens, Djankov, and Klingebiel 1999).

The real exchange rate remains depreciated relative to mid-1997. This is despite the nominal exchange rate appreciation that has occurred—small at first in Korea, Malaysia, and Thailand but substantial in Indonesia.[21] The depreciated exchange rate has helped export performance, as has the recovery in the international electronics market. Korea, where investments during the boom were more oriented toward tradables, has benefited the most from the rebound in electronics. But Malaysia and Thailand have also received a boost. Indonesia has benefited from the rise in international oil prices.

Nonetheless, investment remains depressed, albeit from excessive levels, particularly in property. Investment finance, onshore and offshore, remains limited by weak

TABLE 2.3
Capital accounts in the crisis countries, 1996–2000
(billions of U.S. dollars)

Indicator	1996	1997	1998	1999 [a]	2000 [b]
Current account balance	−53.9	−25.2	69.6	60.5	47.7
Capital account	68.8	−31.1	−50.1	−15.0	−21.5
Private	70.2	−42.7	−60.0	−22.6	−27.8
Net direct investment	11.1	12.4	13.6	15.4	17.8
Gross portfolio investment	28.8	16.4	−4.1	8.5	15.6
Net long-term debt	36.0	27.7	−3.9	−5.5	4.3
Other [c]	−5.7	−99.2	−65.6	−41.0	−65.5
Official	−1.3	11.6	9.9	7.6	6.3
Multilateral (net)	−1.5	5.5	7.1	5.0	—
Bilateral	0.2	6.1	2.7	2.1	—
Overall	14.9	−56.3	19.5	45.5	26.2
Reserves [d]	−14.9	56.3	−19.5	−45.5	−26.2
IMF credit	−0.3	17.1	12.2	−11.2	—

Note: Data are for Indonesia, Republic of Korea, Malaysia, the Philippines, and Thailand.
a. Estimated.
b. Projected.
c. Residual, including short-term private debt outflows.
d. − Indicates increase.
Source: IMF and World Bank data and staff estimates.

institutions and cautious external lenders. Working capital and investment are largely being financed internally, in part by nonpayment of debt service. Over the long term there is a danger that investment will remain dampened by the overhang of property investment excesses and the weaknesses of financial intermediaries.

In 1999 gross private inflows increased, with Korea being the largest beneficiary and receiving net inflows. Foreign direct investment has risen sharply in Thailand, probably because of its restructuring efforts, and in Korea since its liberalization of foreign direct investment (chapter 3). As noted, Korea and Malaysia issued eurobonds, albeit with spreads of 2.25 and 3.30 percentage points over U.S. Treasury bills. In addition, both countries saw inflows of new bank loans. Finally, Korea received a sharp upswing in equity flows in 1999 following its liberalization of portfolio and long-term capital flows.

A large portion of the inflows reflects mergers and acquisitions, and future flows of this type will be determined by the pace of restructuring. Moreover, the depreciated real exchange rate will continue to attract foreign direct investment. In this context, Korea's liberalization of portfolio and foreign direct investment is likely to pay dividends. At the same time, investors are likely to suffer write-downs of their equity or conversions of debt to equity, particularly in the property sector.

Over the next few years net capital inflows are unlikely to approach the magnitudes of the early 1990s. Nor will they be able to finance (in macroeconomic terms) a substantial rise in investment. First, recent high official flows—totaling nearly $50 billion, with more than half going to Korea—will need to be repaid, either through trade surpluses or other capital inflows.[22] Second, restructured debt is maturing soon, notably in Korea. Finally, the crisis countries are unlikely to allow as rapid a buildup of external liabilities to the private sector as they did before the crisis—and external investors are likely to remain cautious.

The situation in China

China escaped the immediate effects of the East Asian crisis. This reflected both its strong macroeconomic position—including a large current account surplus (4 percent of GDP), large international reserves ($143 billion), and low official short-term debt (about 20 percent of reserves)—and its capital controls. Were China to rapidly integrate with world financial markets, however, it would be susceptible to problems unless it first reformed its weak financial institutions, strengthened its regulatory and supervisory infrastructure, and broadened its macroeconomic policy instruments. Such reforms could also boost China's growth. Yet China has limited time for these reforms. Financial integration is proceeding even with the officially closed capital account, and World Trade Organization obligations suggest that further opening will occur.

Foreign direct investment is China's dominant capital inflow (figure 2.6). After the United States, China receives more foreign direct investment than any other country. Foreign direct investment accounts for 10–15 percent of domestic investment. Enormous foreign direct investment reflects China's performance and incentives—and to some degree, limits on foreign loans and portfolio investment. It also reflects round-tripping by local investors, to take advantage of incentives for foreign direct investment (World Bank 1997a). Foreign direct investment is restricted in certain sectors, however, including the financial sector.

Other capital flows are legally limited. The government limits portfolio investment in Chinese companies and prohibits foreign investment in domestic stock markets. (Access is available only through special offshore shares.) The government also limits external borrowing by Chinese companies and official agencies by restricting access to foreign exchange. Hence portfolio investment and private lending are low. Exchange controls, albeit porous, and limited futures markets not only restrict hedging but also limit speculation against the currency. Nonetheless, financial integration is taking place spontaneously despite controls—as indicated by the large errors and omissions and short-term outflows in the balance of payments (see figure 2.6). The recent bankruptcy of the Guangdong Investment Trust Corporation, where actual liabilities were twice what was originally reported, supports the view that short-term external debt is substantially underestimated.

China can benefit from further, more transparent financial integration. It can tap into the pool of global capital both as a recipient and an investor. Financial integration would allow savers and investors to diversify risks. Financial integration should also improve resource allocation through competition and knowledge spillovers—provided state guarantees continue to be strictly limited.

Figure 2.6

Foreign direct investment dominates China's capital inflows

Current and capital accounts
Billions of U.S. dollars

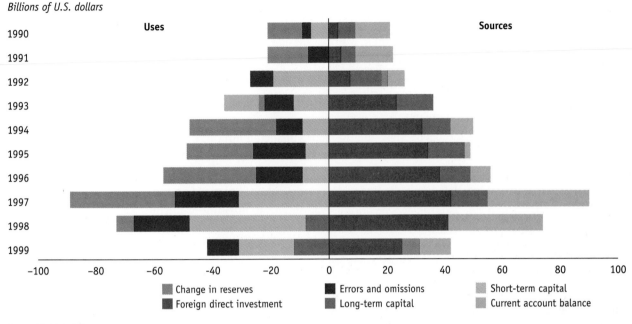

Source: World Bank data.

But the East Asian crisis illustrates the risks of large inflows before institutional and policy prerequisites are in place. China would be susceptible to systemic crisis if it were to open its capital account without further reforms. It still faces many problems similar to—and perhaps even greater than—those in the crisis countries:

- Corporations are weak: state enterprises have leverages of 2:1, commercial enterprises of 4:1.
- Financial institutions are also weak (nonperforming assets are estimated by some at 20–30 percent, even higher than in Indonesia before the crisis) and are subject to conflicting governance and incentives. These institutions could fail to use offshore borrowing productively, may get caught in maturity and currency mismatches, and be subject to moral hazard in lending.
- Financial information is inadequate, governance systems are weak (especially financial regulation and supervision systems, which lack the ability to close weak financial institutions), and legal frameworks make it difficult to execute collateral and carry out bankruptcy proceedings.

- Implicit contingent liabilities have built up in investment trust companies, state banks, and the like.

Moreover, though China has made major strides in using indirect, market-based instruments for macroeconomic policy, these instruments have not withstood the test of time and been proven fully effective.

China's capital controls will protect against exchange rate and debt crises only for a few more years, so the government must use this period to carry through with reforms now under way. Lack of progress on reforms would mean continuation of the large, surreptitious financial integration already occurring—with its adverse distributional consequences—and slower growth. Trade, foreign direct investment, mass communication, and unification with Hong Kong are opening new channels for residents to operate in international financial markets.

Future challenges for financial integration

Financial integration is increasing worldwide. In the 1990s developing countries took far more steps to liberalize capital controls than to tighten them, and current account invisible transactions were also liberalized substantially (IMF 1999b). Even after the East Asian crisis, Korea liberalized its capital account further (for long-term flows), Indonesia left its capital account open, and Chile, Malaysia, and Thailand eased restrictions on capital flows. Moreover, even countries with closed capital accounts, such as China, exhibit increasing financial integration. The real question, then, is not whether to integrate. It is whether integration will occur transparently or opaquely—and whether it will benefit the general public or only those with access to foreign markets who are willing to overstep laws.

Theory and some evidence suggest that financial integration can foster growth, diversify risk for individuals and firms, and smooth consumption. But definitive empirical evidence is lacking.[23] Foreign direct investment is particularly beneficial, and transfers technology and managerial skills and creates links with external markets. Evidence suggests that financial integration does not necessarily increase volatility (box 2.5). Thus, though financial integration poses risks, it can deliver benefits if it is well managed.

East Asia did not manage its financial integration well in the mid-1990s. Policies in Indonesia, Korea, Malaysia, and Thailand encouraged reliance on foreign capital, particularly short-term debt. The neglect of weaknesses in financial and corporate sectors led to imprudent uses of inflows. High and increasing leverage encouraged risk taking; relatively fixed exchange rates encouraged unhedged borrowing. International markets provided the funds because of these countries' history of sound policies and rapid growth—and probably with the expectation that, if problems arose, an exit could be made at relatively fixed exchange rates or government would take over the private debt (as happened in most countries).

Experience and theory suggest that no single package of policies will ensure financial stability. Country conditions matter, and policymakers face different constraints. Still, there is broad agreement on several policies for improving the management of financial integration and reducing vulnerabilities, both through actions by individual countries and upgrades in international financial architecture (see box 2.5)

Maintaining sound macroeconomic policies

The importance of sustainable, noninflationary fiscal and monetary policy is clear from the Latin American debt crisis of the 1980s. Monetary and exchange rate policies need to be consistent. A flexible exchange rate absorbs shocks from capital inflows and outflows. Higher reserves, relative to short-term debt and monetary liabilities, provide stability—particularly when the exchange rate is not allowed to move flexibly. All East Asian economies have increased their reserves relative to short-term liabilities and domestic money stocks (see figure 1.3). But the issues go well beyond traditional macroeconomic policy concerns.

Enhancing information

Policymakers, investors, financial markets, and market discipline all depend on timely, accurate information on financial institutions, firms, and the macroeconomy. Several international agencies are working to improve common standards. The IMF's macroeconomic data system provides a good base. The East Asian crisis countries participate in the system and publish these data on the Internet.

At the firm level, supervisors and regulators need to ensure that corporations and financial institutions publish timely, accurate information in line with generally accepted accounting standards.[24] But information, particularly on short-term debt, is difficult to collect in unregulated markets. Moreover, profits are made from obtaining and using information well, and firms may not want to reveal their strategies by disclosing information. Finally, information is not enough—it must be used prudently.

Managing external liabilities

Accurate, timely information on external positions is essential to policymakers and investors. Incentives for excessive and unhedged foreign borrowing must be reduced by, for example, equalizing taxation and reserve, liquidity, and other requirements on foreign and domestic loans. Countries must avoid attempting to prolong unsustainable booms by encouraging short-term capital inflows. Clear policies need to be set up and followed for guarantees of private external debt.

Higher capital requirements on financial institutions' external liabilities may be desirable to reflect the risks and potential social cost of foreign liabilities.[25] Extending this argument, some authors have suggested taxing or restricting capital inflows, particularly short-term inflows. But others have questioned the benefits of such policies, arguing that controls increase incentives for corruption, may be hard to enforce, and are ineffective in the medium run. Analyses of the experiences of East Asia and Chile provide only weak support for the use of such capital controls (see Gallego, Hernandez, and Schmidt-Hebbel 1999 and Ariyoshi and others 2000).

Strengthening the domestic financial sector

Regulations and supervision in line with international standards—such as the Basle capital accord, the Basle core principles for supervision, and the recommendations on capital markets offered by the International Organization of Securities Commissions—encourage prudent lending, limit excessive leverage, exposure, and related lending, and provide regulators and investors with more timely, accurate information on compliance. Above all, policymakers need to avoid regulatory forbearance and take quick action to deal with weak institutions.[26]

The central bank's lender of last resort function needs to be focused on maintaining the payments mechanism and reconsidered in light of the economy's openness. Permitting entry of well-known, well-capitalized

---

BOX 2.5

Does globalization increase volatility?

Are countries with open capital accounts more prone to crises? Open capital accounts may have two different, and opposite, implications for financial sectors in particular and economies in general. Financial integration tends to produce deeper and more stable financial sectors. But open capital accounts may increase the risk of sudden capital outflows and market and output volatility.

Several recent articles examine these issues from different angles. All conclude that sound regulation and supervision are needed to reap the benefits of capital account and financial liberalization. Easterly, Islam, and Stiglitz (1999) study the effects of open capital accounts on output. Their work suggests that the two opposite implications mentioned above cancel each other out. They find no significant relationship between the degree of capital account liberalization and economic volatility. But financial liberalization is associated with financial deepening, and deeper financial markets (relative to GDP) exhibit more stable growth (see box figure). Levine (1997) and King and Levine (1992) suggest that financial liberalization also helps growth.

At the same time, Kraay (1998) finds no evidence that capital flows are more variable in countries with open capital accounts. Kaminsky and Schmukler (1999) examine stock market cycles in 28 countries, including members of the G–7 and countries in Europe, East Asia, and Latin America. They examine the claim that financial cycles are more protracted after domestic and external financial liberalization. Interestingly, they find that financial liberalization does not necessarily lead to financial bubbles. Over time, liberalized capital markets become more stable.

Rossi (1999), in what he calls preliminary work on a panel of 15 countries, finds that restrictions on capital outflows increase the risk of banking crises (perhaps by driving activity offshore), do not have much effect on currency crises, and may support better economic performance. Restrictions on inflows seem to reduce the risk of currency crises—but not banking crises—and have significantly negative effects on growth. Finally, recent work suggests the importance of sound regulation in avoiding crises, both with capital account liberalization (Rossi 1999) and financial liberalization (Demirgüç-Kunt and Detragiache 1998).

Taken together, these studies suggest that empirical evidence on the relationship between financial openness and business cycles is not axiomatic. Policymakers should not fear that financial openness will automatically lead to instability. The benefits of capital account liberalization and domestic liberalization increase with a sound regulatory and legal framework and stable macroeconomic policies.

Growth volatility and private sector credit

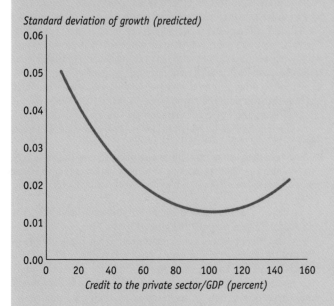

Standard deviation of growth (predicted)

Credit to the private sector/GDP (percent)

Source: Easterly, Islam, and Stiglitz 1999.

foreign banks may provide a buffer to runs on the currency, but it also encourages destabilizing shifts of deposits from domestic private banks (as does the existence of public banks). Developing private bond markets and fully funded pensions would not only support broadly based development, it would also provide long-term, local currency funding.

Notes

1. Explanations for the crisis include rogue speculators, inconsistent macroeconomic policies, weak financial systems, poor governance, and corruption. See Alba and others (1999); Berg (1999); Corsetti, Presenti, and Roubini (1998); Furman and Stiglitz (1998); Goldstein (1998); Kawai (1998); Krugman (1998); Lane and others (1999); Radelet and Sachs (1998); Sachs and Woo (1999); and World Bank (1998).

2. The use of private nonguaranteed and short-term debt as indicators of financial integration attempts to abstract from the impact of large fiscal deficits and explicit government guarantees. In 1990 the four East Asian crisis countries' ratio of total debt to GDP was 38 percent, about 20 percent less than large Latin American countries' 49 percent. The difference mainly reflects East Asia's much smaller fiscal deficits and public sectors. The ratio of debt to GDP reflects the importance of offshore financial intermediation. In terms of the more common ratio of debt to exports, East Asia ranked lower than Latin America because of its higher ratio of exports to GDP.

3. By 1996 the four countries' ratio of debt to GDP was 45 percent, compared with large Latin American countries' 41 percent.

4. In Thailand private nonguaranteed and short-term debt rose by 24 percent of GDP and total external debt by 17 percent of GDP between 1990 and 1996—and these figures may understate short-term debt. In Korea short-term debt rose by 8.5 percent of GDP in 1995 but fell by 2.0 percent of GDP in 1996.

5. This accounting of the finance for investment is based on the identity that the current account is the difference between investment and saving. Hence, if the current account worsens by less than the rise in investment, part of the rise in investment is financed by rising domestic saving. In all four countries the current account did not worsen as much as the investment rate rose; thus saving rates also rose in 1990–93.

6. Unaccounted-for outflows are estimated using the methodology in World Bank (1985); Dooley and others (1986); and Cuddington (1986). The estimate of unaccounted-for flows reflects differences in sources, methodology, and timing as well as difficulties in estimating the underlying data—particularly changes in short-term debt (see World Bank 2000).

7. Radelet and Sachs (1998) point out that there was no deposit insurance and that much of the lending went to nonbank financial corporations or nonfinancial corporations where there was little obvious likelihood of a bailout. However, bolder lenders probably lent with the idea that they could get out quickly (while the exchange rate was being defended) or somehow get the government to assume the debt—an assumption that was borne out in Korea and Thailand. The lenders may have done so despite the G–10's expressions of support for governments' resisting a takeover of private debt (Goldstein 1998, p. 38). None of the countries had formal deposit insurance. But in Thailand's 1983 crisis, depositors' losses were limited, even in nonbanks (Johnson 1991). In Indonesia large depositors lost substantial interest income in the first crisis in a major private bank in the early 1990s, but not in the second.

8. Chile's crisis, like East Asia's, reflected large private flows, not the increased public borrowing that characterized other Latin American countries.

9. The IMF's *International Financial Statistics* indicates that Thailand's international reserves still exceeded $30 billion at the end of June 1997, net of the monetary authorities' foreign liabilities. The Bank of Thailand was reported to have had large short-term forward contracts to support the baht, which left its net position near zero in June 1997 (as shown in Lane and others 1999). As discussed below, Thailand intervened in the foreign exchange market substantially after it announced its float, using official support.

10. Except in Thailand, there was little indication of problems in interest rate spreads or pressures on exchange rates (Eschweiler 1997). Indeed, the Indonesian rupiah was trading at the appreciated end of its exchange rate band at the end of June 1997. Furman and Stiglitz (1998) show that standard indicators were not good predictors of the East Asian crisis, though they did point to high short-term debt (see also IMF 1998 and Berg 1999). Nonetheless, there were indications of concern in terms of shortening maturities and capital outflows, as well as declines in stock markets (except in Indonesia).

11. A large and sophisticated literature is developing on contagion across the crisis countries and herd behavior of investors during the crisis. The crisis hit Thailand, Indonesia, Korea, and Malaysia within months, and sometimes weeks, of each other. Correlations of the countries' stock markets and exchange rates are high (Kawai, Newfarmer, and Schmukler 1999). But contagion is difficult to define except in the simplest way—contemporaneous shocks not explained by fundamentals, which begs the question of what fundamentals are. As noted, standard fundamentals were not good predictors of the crisis, and investors, foreign and domestic, fled the region almost simultaneously. Not surprisingly, even unsophisticated statistical analyses find contagion and herding. The difficulty is that the data cannot distinguish between irrational herding and the alternative hypothesis that investors responded to Thailand's collapse by suddenly becoming much more concerned about the problems discussed in the first section of this chapter (and the concern that other investors might exit) and the risk of an outcome similar to that in Thailand (Goldstein 1998, pp. 18–19). This is especially an issue given the political changes that were occurring in the three other countries (Berg 1999).

12. The IMF provided large support in installments, with front loading. The World Bank and Asian Development Bank provided large initial support through fast-disbursing loans issued in installments. Japanese loans to Thailand were disbursed in parallel with the IMF loans; in the other countries bilateral funding was a second line of defense that was not used much.

13. The ratio to GDP is calculated as the average for the two quarters. Quarterly GDP is measured in dollars at the average exchange rate.

14. Countries using crawling peg exchange rates, supported by reserve sales, are another example of an exchange rate regime where the exchange rate changes—sometimes daily—but is not floating freely.

15. Figure 2.4 is calculated using the monetary authorities' balance sheets (drawn from the IMF's *International Financial Statistics*). The increase in net central bank credit is calculated as the difference between the increase in the money base and the increase in gross reserves in foreign currency converted into domestic currency (or foreign assets in domestic currency in Indonesia, where foreign assets differ substantially from gross reserves multiplied by end-period exchange rates). This approach involves two important points. First, increases in foreign liabilities are in effect treated as offsets to increases in domestic credit. This approach implicitly assumes that the central bank uses borrowed foreign exchange to buy local currency

to support the exchange rate and does not allow a decrease in the money base. (To the extent that foreign borrowings are used to build up reserves, the negative relation between domestic credit and reserves is exaggerated.) Second, the calculation of changes in reserves excludes profits (losses) on foreign exchange assets and liabilities—that is, it is calculated at the average exchange rate for the period. This approach takes into account the possible use of profits from revaluation of reserves to expand credit, which is often neglected by focusing on specific types of lending by the central bank. Failure to adjust for these profits (losses) is obviously important given the large depreciations that occurred. Finally, Thailand's data do not clearly show the central bank's forward contracts.

16. The existence of foreign currency deposits in all the countries, particularly Indonesia and Thailand, complicates the interpretation of the money stock and credit conditions. The rise in the local currency value of foreign currency deposits, because of the large devaluations, tended to increase the broad money stock as measured in local currency, and there were shifts into foreign currency deposits as well. These shifts put pressure on banks because of the lack of demand for foreign currency loans, and probably contributed to pressures in credit and foreign exchange markets as banks tried to liquidate local currency loans and hedge their dollar deposits. Of course, any initial currency mismatches between deposits and loans, or an inability of borrowers to cover the large increase in local currency values of foreign currency loans, also put severe pressures on banks.

17. Indonesia also increased controls on banks' foreign exchange trading and positions, but reduced restrictions on foreign direct investment (see IMF 1999a, pp. 78–79). Pressures in the foreign exchange markets suggest that the controls were ineffective.

18. In 1994 Malaysia introduced prudential controls on external borrowing, including a ceiling on banks' net foreign liability positions. Indonesia had such limits well before the crisis and tightened them in March 1997. Although these controls may have contributed to Malaysia's low short-term debt, they do not seem to have had much effect in Indonesia, which had very high short-term debt, in many cases taken directly by nonfinancial corporations.

19. In addition, Malaysia's savings rate and budget surplus were higher than those in the other three countries, and Malaysia's growth had not declined much relative to the early 1990s.

20. Following the well-known analysis in Mundell (1968), changes in domestic credit are perhaps a better measure of policy intentions in an economy with an open capital account than either interest rates (which are heavily influenced by international rates and shifts in risk premiums, which in turn reflect expectations of future developments) or real money growth (which largely reflects money demand that is influenced by the internationally determined interest rates; the price level and the inflation rate, which in turn partly reflect exchange rate pressures and exogenous agricultural shocks; and, through these two variables, GDP). These issues, as well as the simultaneity of high interest rates and currency depreciation, make it difficult to identify the effects of a high interest rate policy. For example, in the crisis countries the highest average quarterly interest rates coincide with the most depreciated exchange rates, but thereafter interest rates fall, while the exchange rate appreciates. See Furman and Stiglitz (1998); Lane and others (1999, pp. 46–47); and Tanner (1999).

21. Indonesia's nominal rate has appreciated to about 7,500 rupiah to the U.S. dollar, compared with average monthly rates of more than 13,000 rupiah in mid-1998—and occasional spikes of more than 15,000 rupiah.

22. As noted, during the crisis official inflows financed the reduction in private asset holdings (outflows) by domestic and foreign residents, along with some increases in reserves. Return of those outflows would permit repayment of much of the official loans in macroeconomic terms. But these repayments would mean that the inflows would not be available to fund new investment (current account deficits)—they would merely return the ownership of the countries' obligations to their precrisis levels.

23. See Hanson (1994) for the theoretical arguments. Aside from casual empiricism, such as associating the high financial integration in East Asia before 1990 and the region's high growth, empirical evidence on the growth benefits of financial integration is hard to find. Rodrik (1998) suggests no link between the absence of capital account controls and growth in developing countries, but considers the average growth over a period and the number of years without capital flows—that is, an all-or-nothing definition of liberalized capital flows. Some countries may have benefited from fairly liberal flows but either kept a few restrictions (such as limits on foreign direct investment in certain industries or limits on company ownership by foreigners) or failed to enforce them. For example, the IMF considers Indonesia and Korea to have had pervasive capital controls in mid-1997 (IMF 1999a), but both countries had accumulated massive short-term debt. Indonesia, despite its Commercial Offshore Loan Team, was unable to control private offshore borrowing—and Rodrik (1998) appropriately considers Indonesia open. Regarding diversification of risk, its measurement, let alone its benefits, remains an open question.

24. More and better information is no panacea. Although exact data on Thailand's support for financial intermediaries and the exchange rate were not available, the support was widely reported in the financial press. Similarly, the high leverage and other problems of corporations and financial institutions were widely known—for example, ratings of Indonesian public banks were consistently low, and the banks depended on government backing. And more information is not an unmitigated blessing—revealing central banks' forward positions may encourage speculative attacks on currencies. More fundamentally, better information can reduce problems, but information asymmetries are inherent in lending by financial institutions, in developing country markets, and in international capital flows. Runs reflect such asymmetries, even in the most developed markets.

25. Indonesia's experience raises a concern, however, that such measures may encourage offshore booking of loans, especially by foreign banks.

26. After the U.S. savings and loan crisis in the 1980s, the U.S. banking law was revised to require supervisors to intervene in well-defined ways (to avoid regulatory forbearance) and to close a weak bank before its capital is exhausted. See Benston and Kaufman (1997) for a discussion of the law and its rationale.

References

ADB (Asian Development Bank). 1998. "Emerging Lessons and Prospective Challenges." Paper presented at an ADB–World Bank senior policy seminar on Managing Global Financial Integration in Asia, 10–12 March, Manila.

Alba, P., S. Claessens, and S. Djankov. 1998. "Thailand's Financing and Governance Structures" Policy Research Working Paper 2003. World Bank, Washington, D.C.

Alba, P., L. Hernandez, and D. Klingebiel. 1999. "Financial Liberalization and the Capital Account: Thailand, 1988–97." Policy Research Working Paper 2188. World Bank, Washington, D.C.

Alba, P., A. Bhattacharya, S. Claessens, S. Ghosh, and L. Hernandez. 1999. "The Role of Macroeconomic and Financial Sector Linkages in East Asia's Financial Crisis." World Bank, Washington, D.C.

Ariyoshi, A., K. Habermeier, B. Laurens, I. Otker-Robe, J. Canales-Kriljenko, and A. Kirilenko. 2000. *Country Experiences with the Use and Liberalization of Capital Controls*. Washington, D.C: International Monetary Fund.

Benston, G., and G. Kaufman. 1997. "FDICA after Five Years." *Journal of Economic Perspectives* 11 (3): 139–58.

Berg, A. 1999. "The Asia Crisis: Causes, Policy Responses, and Outcomes." IMF Working Paper 99/138. International Monetary Fund, Washington, D.C.

Claessens, S., and T. Glaessner. 1997. *Are Financial Sector Weaknesses Undermining the East Asian Miracle? A Directions in Development book*. Washington, D.C.: World Bank.

Claessens, S., S. Djankov, and D. Klingebiel. 1999. "Financial Restructuring in East Asia: Halfway There?" Financial Sector Discussion Paper 3. World Bank, Washington, D.C.

Claessens, S., S. Djankov, and L. Lang. 1998. "East Asian Corporates: Growth, Financing, and Risks over the Last Decade." Policy Research Working Paper 2017. World Bank, Washington, D.C.

Cole, D., and B. Slade. 1992. "Indonesian Financial Development: A Different Sequencing?" In D. Vittas, ed., *Financial Regulation: Changing Rules of the Game*. Washington, D.C.: World Bank, Economic Development Institute.

———. 1996. *Building A Modern Financial System*. Cambridge: Cambridge University Press.

Corsetti, G., P. Presenti, and N. Roubini. 1998. "What Caused the Asian Currency and Financial Crisis? Part II: The Policy Debate." NBER Working Paper 6834. National Bureau of Economic Research, Cambridge, Mass.

Cuddington, J. 1986. "Capital Flight: Estimates, Issues and Explanations." Princeton Studies in International Finance 58. Princeton University, Princeton, N.J.

Demirgüç-Kunt, A., and E. Datragiache. 1998. "Financial Liberalization and Financial Fragility." Policy Research Working Paper 1917. World Bank, Washington, D.C.

Dooley, M. 1996. "A Survey of Literature on Controls over International Capital Transactions." *IMF Staff Papers* 43 (4): 639–87.

———. 1999. "Responses to Volatile Capital Flows: Controls, Asset Liability Management, and Architecture." University of Santa Barbara, Santa Barbara, Calif.

———. 2000. "A Model of Crises in Emerging Markets." *Economic Journal* 110 (1): 256–73.

Dooley, M. P., W. Helke, R. Tyron, and J. Underwood. 1986. "An Analysis of External Debt Positions of Eight Developing Countries Through 1990." *Journal of Development Economics* 21 (May): 283–318.

Easterly, W., R. Islam, and J. Stiglitz. 1999. "Shaken and Stirred: Explaining Growth and Volatility." World Bank, Washington, D.C.

Eschweiler, B. 1997. "Emerging Asia: The Fallout after the FX Crisis." *Asian Financial Markets*. JP Morgan, Singapore.

Fernald, J., and O. Babson. 1999. "Why Has China Survived the Asian Crisis So Well? What Risks Remain?" International Finance Discussion Paper 663. U.S. Federal Reserve, International Finance Division, Washington, D.C.

Furman, J., and J. Stiglitz. 1998. "Economic Crises: Evidence and Insights from East Asia." *Brookings Papers on Economic Activity 2*. Washington, D.C.: Brookings Institution.

Gallego, F., L. Hernandez, and K. Schmidt-Hebbel. 1999. "Capital Controls in Chile: Effective? Efficient?" Central Bank of Chile Working Paper 59. Santiago.

Goldstein, M. 1998. *The Asian Financial Crisis: Causes, Cures and Systemic Implications*. Washington, D.C.: Institute for International Economics.

Gray, D. 1999. *Assessment of Corporate Sector Value and Vulnerability: Links to Exchange Rate and Financial Crises*. World Bank Technical Paper 455. Washington, D.C.

G–10 (Group of 10). 1996. *The Resolution of Sovereign Liquidity Crises: A Report to the Ministers and Governors*. Basle: Bank for International Settlements.

Hanna, D. 1994. *Indonesian Experience with Financial Sector Reform*. World Bank Discussion Paper 237. Washington, D.C.

Hanson, J. 1994. "An Open Capital Account: A Brief Survey of the Issues and the Results." In G. Caprio, I. Atiyas, and J. Hanson, eds., *Financial Reform: Theory and Practice*. Cambridge: Cambridge University Press.

———. 1995. "Opening the Capital Account: Costs, Benefits, and Sequencing." In S. Edwards, ed., *Capital Controls, Exchange Rates, and Monetary Policy in the World Economy*. Cambridge: Cambridge University Press.

———. Forthcoming. "Indonesia and India: Credit Allocation, Interest Rate Repression, and Contrasting Styles of Financial Liberalization." In P. Honahan, G. Caprio, and J. Stiglitz, *Financial Liberalization, How Fast, How Far?*

IMF (International Monetary Fund). 1998. *World Economic Outlook*. May. Washington, D.C.

———. 1999a. *Exchange Rate Arrangements and Currency Convertibility: Developments and Issues*. Washington, D.C.

———. 1999b. *International Capital Markets*. Washington, D.C.

Johnson, B. R. 1991. "Distressed Financial Institutions in Thailand: Structural Weaknesses, Support Operations, and Economic Consequences." In V. Sundararajan and T. Balino, eds., *Banking Crises: Cases and Issues*. Washington, D.C.: International Monetary Fund.

Kaminsky, G., and C. Reinhart. 1999. "The Twin Crises: The Cause of Banking and Balance of Payments Problems." *American Economic Review* 89 (3): 473–500.

Kaminsky, G., and S. Schmukler. 1999. "On Financial Booms and Crashes: Regional Patterns, Time Patterns, and Financial Liberalization." World Bank, Washington, D.C.

Kawai, M. 1998. "Evolving Patterns of Capital Flows and the East Asian Crisis." East Asia and Pacific Working Paper 98-04. World Bank, Washington, D.C.

Kawai M., and K. Iwatsubo. 1998. "The Thai Financial System and the Baht Crisis: Processes, Causes and Lessons." University of Tokyo, Institute of Social Sciences.

Kawai, M., R. Newfarmer, and S. Schmukler. 1999. "Financial Crises and Contagion in East Asia: Analysis, Policy Responses, and Lessons." World Bank, Washington, D.C.

King, R., and R. Levine. 1992. "Financial Indicators and Growth in a Cross Section of Countries." Policy Research Working Paper 819. World Bank, Washington, D.C.

Kraay, A. 1998. "In Search of the Macroeconomic Effects of Capital Account Liberalization." World Bank, Washington, D.C.

Krugman, P. 1979. "A Model of Balance-of-Payments Crises." *Journal of Money Credit and Banking* 11 (3): 311–25.

———. 1998. "Saving Asia: It's Time to Get Radical." *Fortune Investor*, 7 September.

Lane, T., and others. 1999. "IMF Supported Programs in Indonesia, Korea, and Thailand: A Preliminary Assessment." IMF Occasional Paper 178. International Monetary Fund, Washington, D.C.

Levine, R. 1997. "Financial Development and Growth: Views and Agenda." *Journal of Economic Literature* 35 (3): 688–726.

Montes, Manuel F., and Vladimir V. Popov. 1999. "The Asian Crisis Turns Global." Institute of Southeast Asian Studies, Singapore.

Mundell, R. 1968. *International Economics*. New York: Macmillan.

Obstfeld, M., and K. Rogoff. 1995. "The Mirage of Fixed Exchange Rates." *Journal of Economic Perspectives* 9 (4): 73–96.

Ohno, K., K. Shirono, and E. Sisli. 1999. "Can High Interest Rates Stop Regional Currency Falls? The Asian Experience in 1997–98." Asian Development Bank Working Paper 6. Manila.

Radelet, S., and J. Sachs. 1998. "The East Asian Financial Crisis: Diagnosis, Remedies, Prospects." *Brookings Papers on Economic Activity 1*. Washington, D.C.: Brookings Institution.

Rodrik, D. 1998. "Who Needs Capital-Account Convertibility?" In S. Fischer and others, eds., *Should the IMF Pursue Capital-Account Liberalization?* Princeton Essays in International Finance 207. Princeton, N.J.: Princeton University, Department of Economics, International Finance Section.

Rossi, M. 1999. "Financial Fragility and Developing Economies: Do Capital Controls, Prudential Regulation and Supervision Matter?" IMF Working Paper 99/66. International Monetary Fund, Washington, D.C.

Sachs, J., and W. T. Woo. 1999. "The Asian Financial Crisis: What Happened and What Is To Be Done?" In World Economic Forum and Harvard Institute for International Development, *The Asia Competitiveness Report 1999*. Geneva: World Economic Forum.

Stulz, Rene M. 1999. "Banks, the IMF, and the Asian Crisis." Ohio State University, Columbus, OH.

Tanner, E. 1999. "Exchange Market Pressure and Monetary Policy: East Asia and Latin America in the 1990s." IMF Working Paper 99/114. International Monetary Fund, Washington, D.C.

Warr, P. 1998. "Thailand: What Went Wrong?" In J. Witte and S. Koeberle, eds., *Competitiveness and Sustainable Economic Recovery in Thailand*. vol. 2. Bangkok: Office of the National Economic and Social Development Board and World Bank Thailand Office.

World Bank. 1985. *World Development Report 1985*. New York: Oxford University Press.

———. 1993. *The East Asian Miracle: Economic Growth and Public Policy*. A Policy Research Report. New York: Oxford University Press.

———. 1994. "Indonesia: Stability, Growth and Equity in Repelita VI." Report 12857-IND. East Asia and Pacific Region, Country Department III, Washington, D.C.

———. 1995a. *The Emerging East Asian Bond Market*. Washington, D.C.

———. 1995b. "Indonesia: Improving Efficiency and Equity: Changes in the Public Sector's Role." Report 14006-IND. East Asia and Pacific Region, Country Department III, Washington, D.C.

———. 1996a. *The Chinese Economy: Fighting Inflation, Deepening Reforms*. A World Bank Country Study. Washington, D.C.

———. 1996b. *Global Economic Prospects and the Developing Countries 1996*. Washington, D.C.

———. 1996c. "Indonesia: Dimensions of Growth." Report 15383-IND. East Asia and Pacific Region, Country Department III, Washington, D.C.

———. 1997a. *China Engaged: Integration with the Global Economy*. China 2020 Series. Washington, D.C.

———. 1997b. *Global Economic Prospects and the Developing Countries 1997–98*. Washington, D.C.

———. 1997c. "Indonesia: Sustaining High Growth with Equity." Report 16433-IND. East Asia and Pacific Region, Country Department III, Washington, D.C.

———. 1998. *East Asia: The Road to Recovery*. Washington, D.C.

———. 1999. *China: Weathering the Storm and Learning the Lessons*. A World Bank Country Study. Washington, D.C.

———. 2000. *Global Development Finance 2000*. Washington, D.C.

MAINTAINING TRADE AND INVESTMENT COMPETITIVENESS

Hong Kong brothers Victor and William Fung built one of Asia's most successful trading houses by reacting quickly to changes in the way their multinational clients do business. The secret to the brothers' success, and what sets them apart from many other Asian businessmen, is their belief that the global marketplace contains at least as many opportunities as threats. They realized in the early 1990s that to remain competitive they would have to change—so they did. What five years ago was a China-centric sourcing company is now a global network of factories on contract making a kaleidoscope of products for some of the biggest names in retailing. Li & Fung (Trading) now has 45 offices in 29 countries, up from 27 offices just four years ago.

—Far Eastern Economic Review, 22 July 1999, p. 10

Over the past 30 years East Asia has become increasingly engaged with the global economy. In the region's nine main economies, exports and imports of goods and nonfactor services rose 11.5 percent a year in 1970–95—more than twice the average world trade growth of 5 percent.[1] In the same period the region's share of world trade jumped from 4 to 16 percent.

These quantitative trends were linked with deep structural changes. For example, the region's trade shifted from exports of primary commodities and resource-intensive manufactures toward labor-intensive manufactures, and the region's more developed economies are now shifting toward capital- and technology-intensive manufactures. Since the 1980s the rapid growth and structural transformation of the region's trade have been boosted by fast-growing foreign direct investment flows to, and in some cases from, countries in the region. The region's share of global foreign direct investment inflows rose from about 3 percent in 1980 to 8 percent in 1990—then surged to more than 20 percent in 1994.

With the recent financial crisis, however, East Asia's once-lauded economic policies and performance have come under scrutiny. An enormous increase in corporate and financial sector debt—especially short-term foreign debt—was among the core vulnerabilities contributing to the crisis. A sharp drop in export growth in 1996–97 was among the factors that triggered a sudden loss of confidence in the region's financially fragile firms and financial intermediaries (table 3.1; figure 3.1), precipitating large capital outflows and the onset of the financial crash in 1997. Sharp declines in export revenues in 1998 heightened concerns about whether the weakness in export performance reflected cyclical factors or indicated deeper structural problems.

Although there were signs of a strong rebound in export revenues in the second half of 1999, these did not eliminate concerns about the presence of longer-term competitive difficulties. Foreign direct investment flows to the region largely held up in nominal dollar terms in 1998–99, helping to moderate the depressing effect of large outflows of bank lending and portfolio capital. Still, in 1999 foreign direct investment to the region represented only about 8 percent of the world total—less than half the 1994 peak. In 1998, for the first time in 10 years, Latin America received more foreign direct investment than did East Asia.

Information and communication technology—the knowledge economy—will likely be an important source

TABLE 3.1

Changes in East Asian and world export revenues, volumes, and prices, 1971–98

(percent)

	1971–80	1981–90	1991–95	1996–98	1995	1996	1997	1998
Dollar revenues								
East Asia	27.0	11.4	16.6	1.7	22.3	8.0	5.8	−8.7
China	19.3	15.8	21.1	12.4	23.5	16.6	20.7	−0.1
Hong Kong, China	22.2	15.2	15.7	0.2	14.0	5.3	3.3	−7.9
Indonesia	39.6	2.1	12.3	2.9	14.3	10.4	2.4	−4.1
Korea, Rep. of	34.2	14.1	15.2	2.2	31.6	4.0	7.5	−5.0
Malaysia	25.3	9.5	20.7	0.6	25.8	9.6	1.6	−9.3
Philippines	19.6	5.2	17.4	3.0	24.3	15.5	9.1	−15.7
Singapore	30.1	12.1	16.7	−4.1	22.6	5.2	0.2	−17.6
Taiwan, China	29.8	13.7	11.2	0.3	19.4	4.2	6.3	−9.6
Thailand	22.9	14.9	19.3	−1.9	25.3	1.5	1.6	−8.9
World	21.0	6.5	8.2	2.3	18.6	5.0	3.9	−1.9
Real volumes								
East Asia	13.0	10.0	13.0	7.4	14.3	6.3	12.4	3.5
China	14.3	12.3	16.2	12.4	13.2	5.5	23.1	8.7
Hong Kong, China	9.7	3.6	13.4	2.0	11.0	5.5	5.1	−4.6
Indonesia	9.5	1.5	11.1	6.2	7.9	8.2	7.8	2.5
Korea, Rep. of	21.4	11.2	14.9	16.6	24.0	13.0	23.6	13.3
Malaysia	8.1	11.0	15.5	6.7	17.6	7.2	10.8	2.0
Philippines	10.3	4.0	9.5	12.6	12.0	8.6	20.9	8.3
Singapore	16.1	11.3	13.1	2.4	14.9	5.6	6.9	−5.3
Taiwan, China	17.3	10.7	8.7	6.0	12.8	6.8	8.7	2.6
Thailand	9.9	14.1	14.3	2.9	15.5	−1.8	6.6	3.9
World	5.7	4.6	6.7	6.9	8.9	6.1	10.3	4.3
Dollar prices								
East Asia	12.4	1.3	3.2	−4.8	7.0	1.4	−4.1	−11.6
China	5.9	3.3	4.1	0.2	9.1	10.5	−1.9	−8.1
Hong Kong, China	11.5	1.3	2.1	−1.8	2.7	−0.2	−1.7	−3.5
Indonesia	27.5	1.3	1.2	−3.1	6.0	2.0	−5.0	−6.4
Korea, Rep. of	10.8	2.5	0.1	−10.2	6.1	−6.0	−8.0	−16.5
Malaysia	15.2	−1.5	4.6	−5.7	7.0	2.3	−8.3	−11.1
Philippines	9.6	1.4	7.2	−8.6	11.0	4.0	−7.8	−22.0
Singapore	7.8	0.6	3.2	−2.4	6.7	−0.4	6.3	−13.0
Taiwan, China	11.3	2.6	2.3	−5.5	5.9	−2.5	−2.2	−11.9
Thailand	12.4	0.5	4.4	−4.6	8.5	3.4	−4.7	−12.3
World	14.5	1.7	1.4	−4.3	8.9	−1.0	−5.8	−5.9

Note: Data refer to national income account exports of goods and nonfactor services. Philippines data for 1996–98 are for goods only. East Asia data are a simple average for the nine economies in the table.
Source: World Bank data; Datastream.

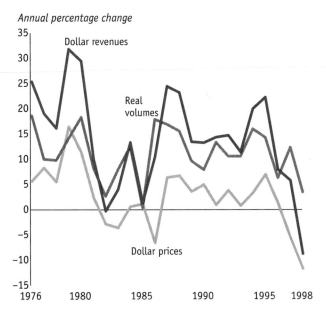

Figure 3.1

East Asia's export growth slumped during 1996–98

Annual percentage change

Source: World Bank data.

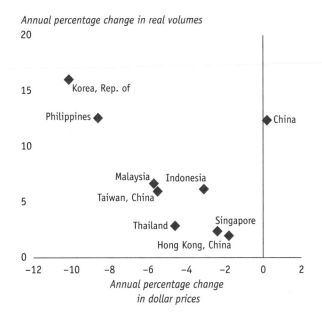

Figure 3.2

Despite lower prices, a few economies were able to sustain rapid export growth in 1996–98

Annual percentage change in real volumes

Source: World Bank data.

of future productivity gains. Is the region poised to make the most of these trends? Before the crisis hit, Hong Kong (China), the Republic of Korea, Singapore, and Taiwan (China) had already lost significant export market shares in high-technology sectors like electrical machinery, telecommunications equipment, office machinery, electric power machinery, and scientific instruments (Yeats 1999)—raising concerns about productivity trends over the long term. The region's economies need to take stock of changes in the global economy and assess how well they are positioned to latch on to dynamic sectors of world trade and productivity gains.

Cyclical changes in trade

Several cyclical factors in the global economy slowed East Asia's export growth in 1996 and the first half of 1997—just before the financial crisis. Once started, the crisis itself was another powerful force dampening trade.

Lower export revenues, volumes, and prices

In dollar terms, East Asia's annual export revenue growth slumped from 17 percent in 1991–95 to 2 per-

cent in 1996–98 (see figure 3.1 and table 3.1).[2] For most East Asian economies, dollar export revenues were flat or falling in 1996–98, with nearly all experiencing a sharp drop in 1998.

Most of the decline in export revenue growth was explained by a drop in dollar prices for the region's exports. In 1996–98 dollar prices fell about 5 percent a year, compared with a 3 percent annual increase in 1991–95. Average growth in export volumes also fell, by about half, though the 7 percent annual increase in 1996–98 was low only relative to the double-digit pace in the first half of the 1990s. While most countries experienced both an absolute fall in export prices and a decline in export growth, there were important exceptions to the general pattern (figure 3.2).

Korea, for example, maintained more than a 15 percent annual increase on average in export volumes during 1996–98, but most of the potential gains in revenue were eroded by huge drops in dollar export prices. Thus the 2 percent average gain in Korea's dollar export revenues in 1996–98 was not much greater than in Thailand, which experienced much more sluggish export growth but also smaller price declines. China, on the other hand, maintained high volume growth without any apparent decline in export prices.

A stronger dollar and weaker world demand

Weaker export volumes and prices in 1996–98 were not entirely unprecedented. They can be largely explained by three cyclical developments in the global economy: a sustained rise in the effective value of the dollar, slower growth in many of the markets for East Asian exports, and a severe downswing in the global semiconductor industry.

East Asia's export revenues, volumes, and prices had also suffered a significant decline in the early 1980s, when annual dollar export growth slumped to 6 percent—down from nearly 30 percent in 1971–80 (see table 3.1). Both the earlier and the more recent episode of export weakness were accompanied by a strong rise in the value of the dollar against other world currencies, resulting in lower dollar prices for tradables worldwide. Annual movements in world and East Asian dollar export prices are closely linked (with a correlation coefficient of 0.9 in 1970–98), and there is a strong inverse association between both sets of export prices and the effective exchange rate of the dollar (figure 3.3). In the second half of 1995 the dollar began a sustained rise

that continued into 1999 and only began to be reversed in the later part of that year.

In 1996 and the first half of 1997 East Asian currencies, with their effective pegs to the dollar, tended to rise with the dollar against the yen and other currencies. Thus even while mounting competition squeezed Asian export prices down along with world prices, export prices tended to fall less than world prices. This loss of price competitiveness in world markets also contributed to slowing export volume growth in 1996.

Weaker dollar export prices and export volume growth from 1996 probably heightened creditors' concerns about East Asian countries' capacity to service their fast-rising short-term debt and so contributed to the panic and reversal of capital flows in 1997. With the outbreak of the financial crisis, the severe devaluations of regional currencies cut further into dollar export prices in the latter part of 1997 and in 1998, causing them to substantially outpace the fall in world export prices (see figure 3.3).

Despite the large improvement in relative price competitiveness after the devaluations of 1997–98, significant increases in export volume growth did not appear until 1999. Indeed, in 1998 export volume growth for the region fell to 3–4 percent, among the lowest levels

Figure 3.3

A stronger dollar meant weaker export prices

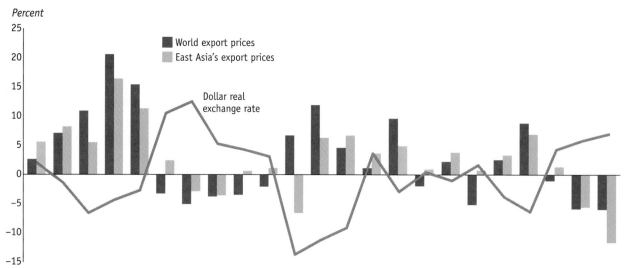

Source: World Bank data.

region's exports, but it may be beginning to operate with the easing of credit constraints.

Greater complementarity of trade structures in some respects, however, appears to be accompanied by greater similarity of export composition and competition in others. The second tendency increases the extent to which currency devaluation in one East Asian economy provokes competitive devaluations in others—contributing to steep terms of trade declines like those in Korea. Since 1985 most East Asian countries have seen large declines in manufactured exports based on natural resources and become increasingly concentrated on high-technology exports (almost entirely electronics). Low-income countries like China and Indonesia have continued to increase export shares in low-technology sectors, but the rest of the region is starting to exit these sectors (Lall, Albaladejo, and Aldaz 1999).

The increasing similarity of export structures is highlighted in table 3.5, which shows cross-country correlations of export structures at the three-digit SITC level. Since 1985 there has been a striking increase in the number of correlations of 0.4 or more, especially between the export structures of East Asia's middle- and high-income economies. China, which is often mentioned as an emerging competitive threat, has a rather limited number of high correlations—though one is with Thailand, often noted as the country facing the most significant threat from Chinese competition.

The region's more uniform export structures—and the attendant danger of exaggerated price competition among regional producers—may partly reflect market-based cyclical factors, such as the tendency toward speculative overinvestment in new, high-growth industries such as semiconductors. But this trend is also likely to have been exacerbated by policy and institutional distortions. Weaknesses in corporate governance and in financial regulation and policy may, for example, have dulled incentives for suppliers of capital to curb firms from laying excessively speculative and concentrated bets in a limited number of sectors. In addition, distortions in trade and foreign direct investment policies may have contributed to excessive investment in export-oriented high-tech sectors.

Developments in trade policy

Over the past 15 years East Asian countries have liberalized their trade policies using a variety of unilateral, regional, and multilateral approaches. Most countries in the region are members of the World Trade Organization, and China's recent progress on acceding to the organization will likely be a significant step in the region's advance toward free trade (box 3.1). Countries have also undertaken trade liberalization through regional venues such as the Association of Southeast Asian Nations and the Asia-Pacific Economic Cooperation group. The region's robust move toward freer trade was confirmed by the unwillingness of policymakers to retreat into protectionism in response to the recent crisis.

East Asia's average tariff and nontariff barriers have been halved since the mid- to late 1980s (table 3.6). But during the same period other developing regions—notably Latin America and the transition economies of

TABLE 3.5
Correlations of East Asian manufactured export structures, 1985 and 1995

Economy	China	Hong Kong, China	Indonesia	Korea, Rep. of	Malaysia	Philippines	Singapore	Thailand	Taiwan, China
China	1	0.163	0.510	0.390	0.146	−0.037	0.748	0.139	0.154
Hong Kong, China	0.592	1	0.068	0.254	0.101	0.205	0.224	0.290	0.549
Indonesia	0.355	0.172	1	0.043	0.310	0.386	0.394	0.027	0.032
Korea, Rep. of	0.218	0.407	0.100	1	0.147	0.071	0.205	0.121	0.401
Malaysia	0.176	0.432	0.183	0.737	1	0.732	0.324	−0.003	0.092
Philippines	0.318	0.512	0.218	0.664	0.823	1	0.147	0.276	0.147
Singapore	0.200	0.367	0.078	0.667	0.749	0.620	1	0.042	0.186
Thailand	0.571	0.547	0.217	0.524	0.597	0.581	0.705	1	0.262
Taiwan, China	0.352	0.445	0.097	0.640	0.673	0.566	0.817	0.765	1

Note: Correlations for 1985 are shown above the diagonal. Correlations for 1995 are shown below the diagonal. Correlations above 0.4 are highlighted.
Source: Lall, Albaladejo, and Aldaz 1999.

BOX 3.1

Progress on China's accession to the World Trade Organization

In November 1999 China reached agreement with the United States on the terms of its accession to the World Trade Organization (WTO). (China has also reached accords with at least 16 other WTO members, including Japan and Korea, and is in discussions with others, including the European Union.) China's offer commits it to abide by the discipline of the international trading rules embodied in the WTO and to provide market access to many sectors that are now partly or wholly closed.

China's average industrial tariffs will be cut from 25 percent in 1997 to 9 percent in 2005. Tariffs on major agricultural products of interest to the United States will be cut from 32 percent to 15 percent by 2004. All tariffs will be bound at the time of accession, helping increase investor and consumer confidence about the reforms. The share of imports covered by administrative barriers will fall from 33 to 11 percent.

China's offer on services includes opening up distribution and retail systems and telecommunications and financial services in ways unimaginable a few years ago. Foreign investors will be able to invest in joint ventures in these areas for the first time. Competition from foreign suppliers is expected to spur more efficient resource allocation between sectors of the Chinese economy, as well as productivity improvements within these sectors. Perhaps even more important, the agreement commits China to further market reforms well into the new century.

TABLE 3.6

Tariffs and nontariff measures in East Asia and Latin America, 1984–98

(percent)

Region/country	Average unweighted tariffs		Core nontariff frequency ratio	
	1984–88	1994–98	1989–94	1995–98
East Asia	19.4	10.4	26.5	14.2
Hong Kong, China	0.0	0.0	2.1	2.1
Indonesia	28.4	13.2	53.6	31.3
Korea, Rep. of	21.0	8.5	50.0	25.0
Malaysia	14.1	10.3	56.3	19.6
Philippines	28.0	16.8	11.5	—
Singapore	0.3	0.4	1.0	2.1
Taiwan, China	22.4	11.2	1.0	2.1
Thailand	41.2	23.2	36.5	17.5
Latin America	29.5	11.4	20.0	8.8
Argentina	28.1	11.6	3.1	2.1
Bolivia	17.8	9.7	0.0	—
Brazil	48.6	12.1	16.5	21.6
Chile	22.0	11.0	5.2	5.2
Colombia	37.8	11.6	55.2	10.3
Mexico	18.7	12.9	27.8	13.4
Uruguay	33.7	11.2	32.3	0.0
East Asia/ Latin America	0.7	0.9	1.3	1.6

Note: Tariffs are simple average bound tariffs. Core nontariff frequency ratios are the portion of Harmonized Standard 2 (HS2) product lines affected by nontariff measures.
Source: World Bank data; Michalopoulos 1999.

ratio for nontariff measures—that is, the portion of product lines affected by one or more core nontariff measures—fell faster in Latin America than in East Asia.[3] The move toward freer trade in other developing regions, and the shift of resources in those regions to uses where they have the greatest comparative advantage, represents a potential source of significant welfare gains for East Asian countries—as it does for all participants in the world trading system. These shifts will increase competition for East Asian producers in certain industries and sectors while creating new opportunities in others.

In response, the policy imperative for East Asian countries is to accelerate the removal of impediments that hinder East Asian firms from seeking out and shifting resources into areas of their greatest comparative advantage and opportunity. Continued reductions in trade barriers and other policy distortions are important in this respect. East Asian countries also need to address a longstanding tendency toward discretionary and selective use of protective measures to promote industrial development strategies or to protect specific interest groups.

Average tariffs are much more dispersed in East Asia than in Latin America (Michalopoulos 1999). This is important because efficiency losses tend to be higher for a dispersed tariff structure than for a uniform one. In the mid-1990s the average coefficient of variation of tariffs in Korea, Malaysia, the Philippines, and Thailand was 1.6, compared with 0.3 in Latin America. Tariffs in East Asia actually became more dispersed between the mid- to late 1980s and mid- to late 1990s

Eastern Europe—have made even faster progress on trade liberalization. In the mid- to late 1980s average unweighted tariffs were about 40 percent lower in East Asia than in Latin America, but in the mid- to late 1990s they were only 10 percent lower. Similarly, the frequency

(ADB 1999). Sectors that tend to receive special protection include agriculture, food processing, and manufacturing sectors catering to domestic markets, such as automobiles. Many services sectors, especially the financial sector and telecommunications, have been heavily protected by restrictions on foreign direct investment (see below).

Import protection creates a bias against exports in several ways—by raising the cost of imported intermediates used in export production, by drawing primary factors of production away from the export sector into the import substitution sector, and by drawing resources away from and raising the price of nontradables, some of which are important inputs in export production. East Asian countries have used a range of devices to offset the antiexport bias induced by import protection, including export subsidies and exemptions or refunds of duties on imports used in export production. Import duty exemptions are deepest in Korea and Malaysia, where they are available not only to direct exporters but also to indirect exporters—that is, domestic producers of inputs for direct exporters. Exemptions are shallower in countries like Indonesia and Thailand.

Because multilateral rules on the use of export subsidies have been considerably tightened by the World Trade Organization, countries will likely place even more emphasis on duty exemptions as a means of reducing antiexport bias (Bora, Lloyd, and Pangestu 1999). But these schemes provide only partial relief from antiexport bias, since they only offset the high costs of imported intermediates. They do not address the more indirect problem of higher costs for nontraded inputs.

Thus duty exemptions tend to create a bias in favor of industries, such as electronics, that rely on imported components and inputs, and provide less relief to industries that rely on domestic nontraded inputs. As a result the widespread use of these exemptions may have contributed to the growing similarity of export structures and focus on import-intensive processing and assembly. These distortions need to be addressed not by reducing the exemptions but by reducing the barriers to imports at the root of the problem.

Prospects remain positive for continued trade liberalization in the region. In earlier periods a crisis like that in 1997–99 could have provoked a retreat into protectionism—even though experience and economic theory suggest that this hinders recovery. But East Asia resisted protectionism. Thailand temporarily increased tariffs for revenue purposes, and raised rates on automobiles and a few other products, but this was a fairly modest retreat. Moreover, Indonesia and Korea reduced protection to make their exports more competitive.

Many East Asian countries are also pursuing trade reform in a regional context. For example, Thailand has announced wide-ranging tariff cuts in the context of the Association of Southeast Asian Nations' free trade area (AFTA)—the region's main free trade area. The AFTA was established in 1992 with a common effective preferential tariff to lower tariffs on manufactured and processed agricultural products to 0–5 percent within 15 years. In 1994 the timeframe was shortened to 10 years (by 2003) and unprocessed agricultural products were added. ASEAN members have made substantial commitments to the scheme: 98 percent of tariffs will fall between 0–5 percent by 2003 (2006 for Vietnam and 2008 for Lao PDR and Myanmar).

But the discriminatory nature of free trade areas carries the risk that ASEAN countries' trade will be diverted from their most efficient trading partners. While the trade creation associated with entering a regional trading bloc increases welfare, the associated trade diversion often offsets these benefits (Fukase and Martin 1999a, b, and c; Fukase and Winters 1999; Lewis and Robinson 1996). As a result this type of import liberalization often yields small benefits. But it may be a useful stepping stone to further liberalization because it exposes domestic industry to more competition and creates a situation where there are substantial benefits from reducing the trade diversion associated with discriminatory liberalization. For instance, Indonesia and the Philippines intend to build on their AFTA concessions to advance their unilateral most-favored-nation–based liberalization.

The other main regional group, Asia-Pacific Economic Cooperation (APEC), aims to realize a free and open trade and investment area in the region by 2010 for industrial members and by 2020 for developing members, following a unilateral and nondiscriminatory approach to trade liberalization. While there has been some disappointment in the group's ability to achieve liberalization beyond that achieved by the World Trade Organization, it has complemented the WTO's work in areas such as information technology.

The group has also fostered participation and accession by its non-WTO members. APEC has adopted several common positions for the current WTO negotiations, including calling for the inclusion of manufactures trade and the abolition of agricultural export subsidies (Fukase and Martin 1999d).

Trends in and issues for foreign direct investment

Global foreign direct investment (FDI) flows rose more than tenfold between 1985 and 1998—from $56 billion to $644 billion, or from 0.5 to 2.3 percent of world GDP. Preliminary data indicate that global FDI surged by more than one-quarter in 1999, to over $820 billion.

Viewed against this backdrop, growth in FDI to East Asia has not been especially notable. FDI to the East Asian countries in table 3.7 quadrupled between 1985 and 1990—but this only kept pace with world flows, so these countries continued to account for 7–8 percent of the total. East Asia's share of global FDI then surged to reach 21 percent in 1994. But nearly all of this was explained by the enormous increase to China, while the share of other East Asian countries increased far more modestly.

FDI flows to the region in 1998–99 were broadly stable at about $70 billion, and flows to the five crisis countries—Indonesia, Korea, Malaysia, the Philippines, and Thailand—stayed around $17–18 billion. The stability of FDI during the crisis helped moderate the depressing effect of large outflows of bank lending and portfolio capital flows. Since 1994, however, East Asia's

share of global FDI flows has fallen (figure 3.7). FDI flows to China fell about 10 percent in 1999, to $40 billion, while those to Indonesia, Korea, Malaysia, the Philippines, Singapore, and Thailand rose about 10 percent, to $27 billion. In both cases, however, the flows represented further declines in shares of world FDI flows.

FDI flows to Latin America, on the other hand, rose through the 1990s—and in 1998 exceeded those to East Asia for the first time in a decade. In 1999 FDI to Latin America rose by more than 30 percent, to $97 billion. The share of FDI flows to the transition economies of Eastern Europe also jumped in the 1990s (see figure 3.7).

Before the crisis

Several factors have fostered the growing importance of FDI in the global economy: the move toward more liberal investment and trade policies, declines in transport and communications costs, and the growing importance of knowledge and other intangible assets in production (see World Bank 1997, ch. 2). Trade liberalization and falling transport costs have encouraged greater subdivision of production processes according to comparative advantage, with design, manufacture, assembly, and finishing occurring where they can be accomplished at least cost.

In theory this international fragmentation or globalization of production processes could be undertaken through arm's-length international trade. But such an outcome is unlikely for the technologically sophisticated and differentiated products that are increasingly important in world demand. Here profitable produc-

TABLE 3.7
Foreign direct investment flows to East Asia and the world, 1980–98
(billions of dollars)

Region/economy	1980	1985	1990	1993	1994	1995	1996	1997	1998
East Asia	—	4.1	16.2	42.8	52.6	56.9	65.5	71.5	69.9
China	—	1.7	3.5	27.5	33.8	35.8	40.2	44.2	45.5
Indonesia [a]	0.2	0.3	1.1	2.0	2.1	4.3	6.2	4.7	-0.3
Korea, Rep. of	0.0	0.2	0.8	0.6	0.8	1.8	2.3	2.8	5.1
Malaysia	0.9	0.7	2.3	5.0	4.3	4.2	5.1	5.1	3.7
Philippines	-0.1	0.0	0.5	1.2	1.6	1.5	1.5	1.2	1.7
Singapore	1.2	1.0	5.6	4.7	8.6	7.2	7.9	9.7	7.2
Thailand	0.2	0.2	2.4	1.8	1.4	2.1	2.3	3.7	7.0
Crisis countries [b]	1.2	1.4	7.2	10.6	10.2	13.8	17.5	17.6	17.2
World	46.3	55.7	203.1	219.4	253.5	328.9	358.9	464.3	643.9

a. Indonesia data contain an undetermined amount of debt incorrectly recorded as foreign investment.
b. Indonesia, Republic of Korea, Malaysia, the Philippines, and Thailand.
Source: UNCTAD 1999; World Bank data.

Figure 3.7

East Asia is receiving a smaller share of global foreign direct investment

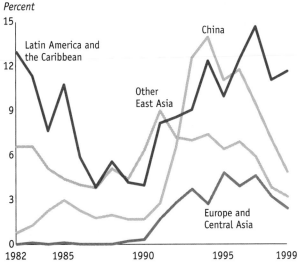

Note: "Other East Asia" are Indonesia, Republic of Korea, Malaysia, Philippines, Singapore, and Thailand.
Source: World Bank data.

tion depends on specialized intangible assets such as research and development (or knowledge more generally) and skills in design, styling, promotion, management, marketing, and sales.

Information and other market failures often make it difficult to buy and sell these intangible, firm-specific assets through arm's-length trade. Thus firms find it easiest to exploit the locational cost advantages of producing in different countries by establishing foreign affiliates that retain access to their intangible assets—that is, through "efficiency-seeking" FDI. Such investment facilitates the classical gains from trade associated with specialization according to comparative advantage. Its rising importance, especially in global manufacturing FDI, is evidenced by the rising shares of intrafirm trade in world trade and of exports in the total sales of multinational firms' foreign affiliates—as well as by the growing weight of components and intermediates in world trade noted above (see also UNCTAD 1999).[4]

Efficiency-seeking FDI can be distinguished from "market-seeking" FDI, which is motivated by a desire to gain access to markets protected from imports by trade barriers. Market-seeking FDI tends to substitute for trade and may exacerbate the efficiency losses asso-

ciated with trade protection. Market-seeking FDI may in turn be distinguished from the situation in many services industries, where cross-border trade is prevented not by trade barriers but by the nature of the product itself. Here FDI to establish a commercial presence in a given market is one of the primary means of conducting international trade. Developing countries increasingly look to FDI in services to increase the productivity and efficiency of their economies, by making available critical business services such as telecommunications and financial services at lower cost and better quality.

As in other regions, FDI flows in East Asia have been influenced by a mix of macroeconomic, policy, and other factors. Sharp increases in effective exchange rates and relative wages in Japan and the first-tier newly industrialized economies—Hong Kong (China), Korea, Singapore, Taiwan (China)—contributed to a wave of efficiency-seeking intraregional FDI flows from these countries to China and the second-tier newly industrialized economies—Indonesia, Malaysia, the Philippines, Thailand—from the mid- to late 1980s onward. These flows relocated labor-intensive production processes to low-cost production areas and were a powerful engine in the emergence of a regional production economy linked through trade in inputs. About three-quarters of the enormous flows of FDI to China in the 1990s came from Japan and the first-tier newly industrialized economies. By the mid-1990s about half of the FDI in East Asia was intraregional (Diwan and Hoekman 1998).

Before the crisis, FDI policies varied considerably across the region. Korea maintained tight restrictions on most FDI inflows, relying on direct purchases of technology by its own firms for acquisition of technology. FDI inflows averaged less than 0.5 percent of GDP and in the 1990s were outpaced by FDI outflows until 1998. FDI policies in the second-tier newly industrialized economies, on the other hand, have been more open. Indonesia, Malaysia, the Philippines, and Thailand have had fewer restrictions on entry and on equity participation in manufacturing. Indeed, they have competed vigorously for export-oriented (especially high-tech) FDI by offering significant fiscal incentives (such as tax breaks) that exceed world norms.

Just how effective these fiscal incentives have been in attracting FDI is still in dispute. Many studies conclude that such incentives are not effective once the fundamentals that affect FDI are taken into account. Others find evidence that incentives have an effect, especially for export-oriented FDI, even if they are not the key factor. But even if fiscal incentives do attract FDI, the high costs they impose may not be sufficiently offset by the benefits associated with FDI. Such costs can include the loss of revenue to the government, the economic distortions induced by the incentives, and in some cases inducements for corruption and rent seeking.

Potentially costly government intervention may be justified by the expectation that businesses and residents will garner significant technological externalities or spillovers from the presence of multinational firms. But the existence and size of spillovers associated with FDI are hotly debated (see Caves 1996; Moran 1998; Hoekman and Saggi 1999; and Rodrik 1999). Given these uncertainties, it may be appropriate for policymakers to take a more cautious attitude toward using substantial fiscal incentives to attract FDI. It may also be appropriate for countries to reform fiscal incentives at a regional level, as this may alleviate fears of being strategically undercut by continued large incentives in neighboring countries.

As noted, many countries have tried to attract FDI to export-oriented manufacturing. FDI in domestic-oriented sectors has faced tighter access restrictions and, where permitted, has concentrated in sectors with significant import protection (Bergsman and Bora 1999). Throughout the region, FDI in services has faced the tightest restrictions (table 3.8).

East Asia's FDI policies have been especially restrictive in financial and telecommunications services. The consequences of excessive restrictions on FDI in services, on the one hand, and of promotion of FDI in manufacturing, on the other, are apparent in the sectoral distribution of FDI in the region (figure 3.8). The share of FDI going to services in East Asia in 1997 fell far short of the share in the developed world or in Latin America, while the share going to manufacturing dwarfed those in the other regions. This distribution of FDI may have contributed to structural weaknesses in the region's economic performance—such as the growing similarity of regional export structures. Low FDI in services tends to hamper productivity improvement in critical business services, and so crimps efficiency improvements in the economy at large (box 3.2).

After the crisis

As noted, FDI inflows to the five crisis countries remained relatively stable in 1997–98, at $17–18 billion (see table 3.7). But the experiences of individual countries varied widely. In 1998 inflows to Korea and Thailand surged about 80 percent and to the Philippines, about 40 percent. Korea maintained the strongest performance in the region in 1999, when flows rose another 55 percent, to $8.5 billion. Flows to Malaysia, on the other hand, fell

---

TABLE 3.8

Foreign direct investment restrictiveness before the crisis for services in East Asia, Mexico, and developed countries

Region/country	Average	Business	Communications	Distribution	Financial	Transport
East Asia	59	51	70	46	72	57
China	47	36	82	28	45	46
Indonesia	56	56	64	53	55	53
Korea, Rep. of	67	57	69	63	88	57
Malaysia	31	32	42	8	61	12
Philippines	73	48	76	48	95	98
Thailand	81	78	84	78	88	78
Mexico	44	29	74	33	55	28
Developed countries	24	11	43	13	35	17
Australia	29	18	44	18	45	20
Canada	31	23	51	20	38	24
Japan	19	6	35	5	36	11
New Zealand	19	9	43	8	20	13
United States	12	1	35	0	20	3

Note: Index value of 100 represents maximum restrictiveness.
Source: Hardin and Holmes forthcoming; Findlay and Warren 1999.

Figure 3.8

Manufacturing accounted for most foreign direct investment in Asia

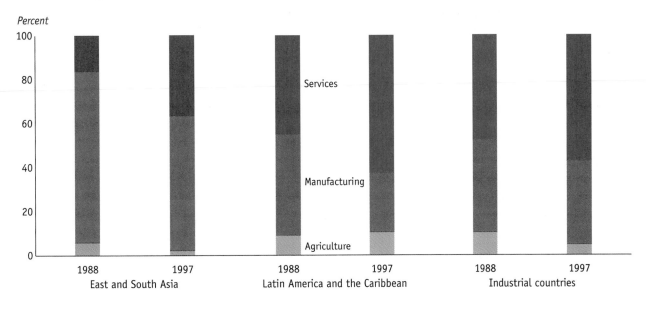

Source: World Bank data.

BOX 3.2

How much would East Asia gain from liberalizing services?

A recent study attempts to estimate the economic gains from eliminating the barriers to trade that remain after implementation of the Uruguay Round agreements (Dee and Hanslow 1999). The study tries to calculate the gains from eliminating barriers to trade not just in agriculture and manufacturing but also in services—particularly those deriving from restrictions on FDI in services. The study looks at so-called static gains from trade (that is, those deriving from the reallocation of resources to sectors with greater comparative advantage) and from the elimination of monopolistic rents (due to greater competition). Like most studies of this type, it does not attempt to calculate

the dynamic gains from trade (such as increases in productivity due to freer trade), which could be much larger than the static gains.

Full trade liberalization would lead to a median GDP increase of 3.9 percent among major developing East Asian countries. China stands out with an enormous 18 percent increase, deriving mainly from the benefits of opening up its highly restricted services sector. Indonesia is another country where liberalizing services would generate most of the gains. In other East Asian countries most of the gains would come from liberalizing agriculture and manufacturing.

	Real GDP change (percent) from liberalization in			Real income change (billions of dollars) from liberalization in		
Region/economy	Agriculture and manufacturing	Services	Total	Agriculture and manufacturing	Services	Total
East Asia						
China	3.4	14.8	18.2	13.7	91.3	105.0
Indonesia	0.5	3.4	3.9	1.2	4.0	5.2
Korea, Rep. of	1.5	0.1	1.6	8.8	1.7	10.5
Malaysia	3.7	0.8	4.5	3.4	1.2	4.6
Philippines	5.5	0.3	5.8	1.8	1.1	2.9
Taiwan, China	2.7	0.2	3.0	11.6	0.4	12.0
Thailand	2.7	0.2	2.9	4.2	1.5	5.8
Other						
European Union	0.1	0.0	0.1	6.8	-7.6	-0.8
Japan	0.3	0.0	0.3	20.2	7.6	27.7
United States	0.2	-0.1	0.1	23.2	-2.2	21.1

Source: Dee and Hanslow 1999.

about 30 percent in 1998 and were flat in 1999. Flows to Indonesia since the financial crisis have been negligible.

All the crisis countries have relaxed restrictions on FDI. Liberalization has been most marked in Korea, which had the least open stance before the crisis. Malaysia, which enjoys among the highest levels of FDI relative to GDP, has undertaken the fewest additional measures (Bergsman and Bora 1999). Most countries have eased restrictions on foreign ownership, with the most notable change being the opening of banking and financial sectors. In Korea almost all sectors, including banking, have been opened to 100 percent foreign ownership, though some restrictions persist.

Restrictions on cross-border mergers and acquisitions and foreign land ownership have also been relaxed. Indonesia had increased the number of sectors open to total foreign ownership in 1994. The list of sectors allowing no or only minority foreign ownership was further shortened in the wake of the financial crisis (mostly in transportation, communications, and trade). Ceilings on foreign ownership in the financial sector were also increased, from 49 to 100 percent.

In Thailand most manufacturing activities had few restrictions before the crisis, and several that had been restricted (steel, petrochemicals) have been opened to foreign mergers and acquisitions investment. Majority foreign ownership of financial institutions has also been permitted, though it still requires approval from the Board of Investment. In Malaysia FDI in export-oriented sectors has traditionally been unrestricted, while access to domestic-oriented and service sectors has been tightly controlled, usually at 30 percent foreign ownership. Here FDI liberalization has been more limited. Some restrictions on ownership in manufacturing have been relaxed, but restrictions in banking have not.

FDI flows in the wake of the crisis have been buoyed by cheaper asset prices and by the need for heavily indebted local firms to restructure their balance sheets. These factors, along with the significant excess capacity in many industries, have stimulated cross-border mergers and acquisitions relative to new "greenfield" investment. By 1998 investment through mergers and acquisitions, relatively unimportant before the crisis, had increased to more than half of FDI in the five crisis countries (figure 3.9). Much of the new mergers and acquisitions activity appears not to have been of the "fire sale" variety predicted by some analysts. Rather, it

was undertaken by multinational corporations to increase ownership and infuse fresh capital in firms that were already affiliates.

Increased cross-border mergers and acquisitions can provide significant new equity for corporate and financial restructuring in the region. In the longer term, expanded foreign investment and ownership can also intensify competition and so spur wider gains in efficiency and innovation—of special importance in services, which otherwise do not face competition from cross-border imports. An increased foreign presence can help revitalize the financial sector in the wake of a financial crisis (chapter 4). But while formal restrictions on FDI in the financial sector have been relaxed, movement on actual transactions has been mixed. Thailand has made the most progress, with six banks at various stages of sale to foreign buyers. But in Korea only one bank has been sold, and Malaysia has not put any on the block.

Finally, most countries in the region have maintained and in some cases increased the use of complex fiscal incentives for FDI. Indonesia had eliminated these incentives in the mid-1990s but returned to their use before the financial crisis—and added to them after it. China also reinstated fiscal incentives it had earlier removed, such as exemptions of

Figure 3.9

Mergers and acquisitions have become important sources of foreign direct investment

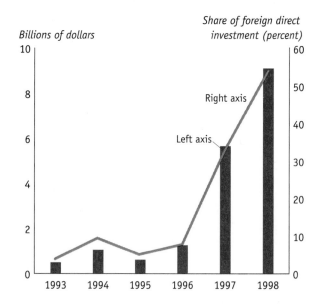

Note: Data are for Indonesia, Republic of Korea, Malaysia, Philippines, and Thailand.
Source: World Bank data.

prevalent in Indonesia, Malaysia, and the Philippines. Controlling ownership in banks by Korea's *chaebol* (conglomerates) is prohibited by legislation, but the largest chaebol influenced bank lending through the government and have preferred access to credit through their control of nonbank financial institutions. The controlling owners of Thailand's major private banks do not form part of broader conglomerates and so are not subservient to nonfinancial enterprises. As in the other countries, however, Thai bank owners are politically well-connected.

Recent empirical work supports the observation that structural factors deepened the crisis. Weaknesses in legal institutions for corporate governance—in particular, ineffective protection and enforcement of creditor and minority shareholder rights—had more significant effects on the exchange rate depreciations and equity price declines of 1997–98 than did standard macroeconomic variables. The reason? Controlling owners may treat outsiders fairly as long as prospects are favorable and external financing is needed. But when prospects deteriorate, expropriation of outsiders rises if investor protection is weak. Deficiencies in corporate governance did not constrain the impressive precrisis performance of East Asia's emerging market economies—but they amplified the subsequent market downturns.

Policy flaws and market exuberance

Though structural weaknesses among banks and corporations appear to have exacerbated the crisis, these deficiencies were not unique to the region and so do not fully explain why the crisis was deeper in East Asia than in most other emerging market economies. Moreover, many of the same weaknesses prevail in East Asian economies that did not succumb to the crisis.

Policy flaws also made the crisis worse. Foreign exchange policies provided stable exchange rates for extended periods, reducing the perceived risks of borrowing and lending in foreign currency—and so encouraging the growth of foreign currency–denominated debt (given higher domestic interest rates) and discouraging the use of hedging instruments. The use of substantial foreign exchange reserves (accumulated prior to the crisis) delayed adjustments to changes in investor sentiment, prolonging costly but ultimately futile efforts to maintain exchange rate stability.

Governments also fostered foreign currency intermediation directly, through arrangements such as the Bangkok International Banking Facility (where foreign bank loans grew from $8 billion in 1993 to $50 billion in 1996; Kawai 1997), and indirectly, through higher taxation of local relative to foreign currency intermediation. More generally, the liberalization of domestic financial systems and capital flows since the late 1980s occurred without parallel strengthening of prudential regulation and supervision, facilitating greater risk-taking by financial institutions.

The region's long history of growth lulled governments and creditors (foreign and domestic alike) into complacency. Warning signs in the mid-1990s—such as rapid credit growth increasingly financed by short-term foreign borrowing—were ignored or downplayed (table 4.2). Large current account deficits were more easily tolerated because they were privately generated and financed. High saving rates (primarily by households), supplemented by heavy foreign borrowing, were intermediated primarily by banks, leading to high corporate leverage and facilitating the tendency toward leverage implicit in ownership and legal structures. Easy access to credit contributed to speculative price bubbles within real estate and excess capacity in other sectors, and coincided with declining investment efficiency (figure 4.1).

Once the crisis broke in mid-1997, the enormous reversal in capital flows had major repercussions. The net swing from inflows to outflows between 1996 and 1997 totaled $100 billion for the region's five crisis countries—Indonesia, Korea, Malaysia, the Philippines, and Thailand—or 11 percent of their GDP before the crisis. Moreover, these flows mask much more volatile intrayear gross portfolio flows, which wreaked havoc in regional financial markets.

Before the crisis, an unusual feature of the four hardest-hit crisis countries—Indonesia, Korea, Malaysia, Thailand—was the coexistence of structural weaknesses and uninterrupted growth. High domestic savings, extensive use of foreign capital, and open capital accounts fueled excess investment and asset price inflation, which deepened the crash once it was triggered. But the Philippines, which also suffers from corporate governance deficiencies and was subjected to comparable financial market volatility, avoided a systemic financial crisis—illustrating the important role of excess private debt in deepening the

TABLE 4.2

Precrisis financial depth and debt indicators, 1996

(percent)

Indicator	Indonesia	Korea, Rep. of	Malaysia	Philippines	Thailand	China[a]
Savings/GDP	27.5	33.7	36.7	19.6	33.1	41.3
Investment/GDP	30.7	38.4	41.6	24.0	41.0	38.3
Bank credit to private sector/GDP	55.4	57.6	89.8	49.0	100.0	45.8[b]
Stock market capitalization/GDP	40.0	28.6	310.0	97.3	55.0	24.6
Outstanding bond issues/GDP	1.8	45.0	45.4	16.8	11.0	12.2[c]
Corporate debt/equity[d]	310	518	150	160	250	200–400[e]
Short-term external debt/reserves	176.6	193.0	41.0	79.5	99.7	19.3
Short-term external debt/M2	27.7	31.1	11.9	17.7	25.8	2.2
Public debt/GDP	22.9	8.8	36.0	105.1	15.7	19.0
Public debt/GDP, 1999	91.5	29.5	52.0	105.0	50.3	29.0

a. Estimates are for 1998 unless otherwise noted.
b. Includes collective-owned, individual, joint stock, shareholding, foreign funded, and other nonstate-owned sectors.
c. Data are for 1997; includes state bonds, financial bonds, corporate bonds, and bonds issued by government investment company.
d. End-1997 data for Indonesia, Korea, and Malaysia. September 1998 data for Thailand.
e. Lower end represents industrial and state enterprises, higher end represents commercial enterprises.
Source: World Bank and IFC data.

Figure 4.1

Investment became less efficient before the crisis

Incremental capital-output ratio
Five-year rolling average (percent)

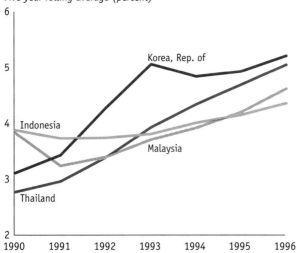

Source: World Bank data.

crisis in neighboring countries. The Philippines's lower domestic savings and history of crises had reduced external creditworthiness, preventing a huge buildup of corporate leverage. Managers of major private banks were more wary of market risks, and so maintained capital levels well above the 10 percent minimum required for Tier 1 capital—far more than most other countries in the region (World Bank 1999d; Okuda 1999).

Macroeconomic responses to the crisis are discussed in chapter 2. From a banking perspective, perhaps the most damaging was the way 16 private banks in Indonesia were closed in November 1997—prior to the provision of an explicit deposit guarantee, and at a time when the public was aware that insolvency was not limited to the banks selected for closure. This action undermined confidence in private banks (even though insolvency among public banks appears to have been much deeper). With foreign banks cutting interbank and trade credit lines to their local counterparts, the subsequent depreciation of the rupiah far outpaced currency declines in neighboring countries. As a result Indonesian corporations, which held foreign currency debt of some $65 billion in 1997, suffered extensive damage (World Bank 1999c).

Financial restructuring since the crisis

By early 1998 large segments of the financial and corporate sectors in Indonesia, Korea, Malaysia, and Thailand were severely distressed or insolvent. Equity prices and currencies had collapsed, private credit lines had been cut, and output was plummeting. The subsequent restructuring—involving conflicts over the recognition and allocation of losses among shareholders, creditors, managers, workers, and taxpayers—took on political dimensions, further complicating the resolution effort (Haggard 1999).

Financial dimensions of the crisis and resolution efforts are summarized in table 4.3. The data have several shortcomings, however. Despite audits and better accounting, estimates of losses involve considerable guesswork. Loans are often rolled over as they come due, often to avoid declaring them in default, so it takes time for bank supervisors (and banks) to detect them. Estimates of nonperforming loans tend to rise over time (as sequential rollovers become more difficult), but it would be wrong to interpret such increases as a worsening of the underlying situation. Furthermore, nonperforming loans may be backed by liens and other collateral whose value depends on the performance of the real economy. Hence estimates of banks' net worth are especially prone to error.

Governments initially provided liquidity support to avert runs on banks. As bank runs became more serious, governments guaranteed all deposits—and in some cases, other financial liabilities—making bank losses a government responsibility. Across the region, some 70 banks and more than 250 financial institutions have been closed.

Nonetheless, many of the banks left open remain undercapitalized. Most have received injections of public capital,[1] but in the four hardest-hit countries an estimated $80 billion in additional capital is needed (assuming adequate provisioning; Claessens, Djankov, and Klingebiel 1999a). Governments own nearly 80 percent of banking assets in Indonesia, more than half in Korea, and a third in Thailand (see below). How these assets are sold back to the private sector will have important implications for financial regulation and supervision.

The four crisis countries have taken different approaches to recapitalizing banks and resolving nonperforming assets. Indonesia, Korea, and Malaysia have injected public funds into undercapitalized banks while transferring a portion of nonperforming loans to centralized, publicly owned asset management corporations. These corporations are responsible for recovering assets and restructuring the financial liabilities of overindebted debtors. Thailand, by contrast, has tied the provision of public funds to more stringent conditions imposed on bank owners. Thailand has not created a centralized asset management corporation to dispose of nonperforming loans because it wants banks to recapitalize themselves and devise their own asset disposition strategies.

Korea

Korean banks were rescued from defaulting to foreign creditors in late 1997 when the government (partially) guaranteed banks' foreign debt service to facilitate rescheduling of their foreign liabilities. The government then assumed a central role in recapitalization. With the December 1997 election of a new president unbeholden to the corporate and banking establishment, the newly created Financial Supervisory Commission was able to force change, making more credible the government's initial response to the crisis (Cho 1999; Haggard 1999).

In April 1998 the government committed 64 trillion won ($47 billion) to bank recapitalization, and by November 1999 it had spent nearly 60 trillion won.[2] As a result capital ratios in most banks were raised to 8 percent (using the prevailing backward-looking loan classification criteria). Banks still need additional capital, however, reflecting:

- The shift to forward-looking loan classification criteria in 2000.
- The losses incurred by banks from the Daewoo crisis and bond market decline (see below).
- The pressures from ongoing corporate workouts that have progressed more slowly.

Restructuring Korea's largest chaebol has proven more difficult, partly because of their ready access to financing from investment trust companies. The investment trust industry almost tripled in size between the end of 1997 and mid-1999, nearly reaching the size of commercial bank deposits. The near-collapse of Daewoo—the second largest chaebol, with liabilities of about $75 billion—in August 1999 prompted investors to withdraw funds from the investment trust companies, which sold their bond holdings to finance the withdrawals, depressing bond prices. At the government's behest, banks bought some 20 trillion won of bonds, but bond prices remain vulnerable to rising interest rates and to prospects for investment trusts.

Malaysia

Among the four hardest-hit countries, Malaysia was perhaps best positioned to confront the crisis. Foreign debt and corporate leverage were relatively low, the latter reflecting a deeper domestic capital market.

TABLE 4.3
Financial restructuring in East Asia

Action	Indonesia	Korea, Rep. of	Malaysia	Thailand	China
Initial government response Liquidity support	$21.7 billion (18 percent of GDP)	$23.3 billion (5 percent of GDP)	$9.2 billion (13 percent of GDP)	$24.1 billion (20 percent of GDP)	None; banks liquid
Nonperforming loans Nonperforming loans/ total loans[a] (percent)	31.4 (9/99)	17.9 (9/99)	24.0 (12/99)	41.1 (12/99)	25.0[b]
Nonperforming loans/ total loans after transfers to asset management corporations (percent)	12.4	10.1	17.5	38.5	12.9[b]
Financial distress resolutions Bank closures	66 of 237	None	None	1 of 15	1 commercial bank
Closures of other financial institutions	None	More than 200	None	57 of 91	40 urban credit cooperatives and 5 trust and investment companies
Mergers	9 nationalized or state banks are being merged	8 of 26 absorbed by other banks	58 to be merged into unspecified number by December 2000	3 banks and 12 finance companies	Multiple urban credit cooperatives and 2 banks
Banks temporarily nationalized	12	4	1	4	
Bank recapitalization strategies Public funds for recapitalization	Bonds equivalent to $40 billion issued in 1999; $20 billion to be issued in 2000	Government injected $50 billion into 9 commercial banks; 5 of 6 major banks now 90 percent controlled by the state	Danamodal injected $1.7 billion into 10 institutions	Government injected about $9 billion into private banks and about $11 billion into public banks	Government injected 270 billion yuan ($32.6 billion) in mid-1998 into the 4 state banks. Banks now being recapitalized as loans are transferred to asset management corporations
Majority foreign ownership of banks	1 pending	1 announced, 1 pending	Not allowed. Foreign bank share is significant, however	4 completed, 2 pending	Allowed, but not for domestic currency operations
Weak financial institutions still in system	Many weak commercial banks	Many weak nonbank financial institutions	Difficult to assess	Some weak public and private commercial banks	Many weak banks and nonbank financial institutions

a. Includes nonbanks and loans transferred to asset management corporations.
b. People's Bank of China estimate as of mid-1999; private estimates are higher.
Source: Claessens, Djankov, and Klingebiel 1999a; World Bank data.

Malaysia's restructuring program has been tightly orchestrated by the government, emphasizing mergers and avoiding closures of financial institutions or sales to foreign institutions. Initially, 16 billion ringgit ($4.2 billion) was allocated for bank recapitalization, and by July 1999 the newly created Danamodal had injected 6.4 billion ringgit ($1.7 billion) into 10 financial institutions. Several of these institutions have repaid the capital, however, and by November 1999 the amounts due to Danamodal had fallen to 4.6 billion ringgit ($1.2 billion). As a result estimates were lowered of the capital outlays required by Danamodal.

By September 1999 the asset management agency, Danaharta, had acquired 39 billion ringgit ($10.3 billion) in nonperforming loans from financial institutions. At one point the government wanted all financial institutions to merge into six financial groups. But that directive was withdrawn in October 1999, and the deadline for reorganization of the financial sector was extended to December 2000.

Indonesia

Indonesia's financial sector faces the most daunting challenges. The banking system was the region's weakest before the crisis. Heavy debt owed by domestic firms to foreign creditors has complicated corporate debt resolution. The currency suffered a deep depreciation after the crisis. Bank recapitalization poses a huge fiscal burden, reflecting higher public debt before the crisis and more extensive banking losses. And there was little political consensus on reform, at least until the October 1999 presidential election. Reforms also stalled because of concern and political controversy stemming from the allegation in mid-1999 of kickbacks by Bank Bali to the then-ruling Golkar party.

The slow progress is not for lack of new institutions and instruments created in the wake of the crisis: the Indonesian Bank Restructuring Agency to lead restructuring of the most insolvent banks, an Asset Management Unit within the restructuring agency to acquire nonperforming loans from frozen or merged banks, the "Jakarta Initiative" to facilitate voluntary corporate restructuring, a new bankruptcy law, and the Indonesian Debt Restructuring Agency (under the "Frankfurt Agreement") to enable debtors and creditors to protect against exchange risk.

Thailand

Thailand closed two-thirds of its finance companies, and the Financial Restructuring Agency has auctioned off most of the assets acquired from them. As noted, stringent requirements on government provision of capital have been used to encourage banks to raise capital on their own (box 4.1). Though banks have done so, several remain undercapitalized.

Bank holdings of nonperforming loans have fallen from their mid-1999 peak, however, aided by faster repayment and restructuring and by the transfer of bad loans to newly created, bank-owned asset management corporations. The establishment of bank-owned asset management corporations was encouraged by the removal of tax disincentives and by a regulation allowing private banks to transfer loans to their majority-owned asset management corporations at book value, less provisioning required under a phased-in forbearance program. Excluding asset sales from the Financial Restructuring Agency, restructured debt totaled 1.07 trillion baht ($28 billion) by the end of 1999, accelerating considerably in the second half of the year. But initial debt negotiations appear to have produced inadequate restructuring to allow for debt service to be sustained by operational cash flows, requiring rounds of subsequent restructuring.

Governments in the region's smaller economies have also taken steps to address financial and corporate weaknesses (box 4.2).

How have firms fared?

Regardless of their indebtedness, all firms in the region needed to adapt to reduced demand and the shift in relative prices stemming from exchange rate depreciation. Such operational restructuring—as opposed to financial restructuring, which changes the liability side of a firm's balance sheet—seems to be occurring, although the inability to service debts has elicited more attention.

Operational restructuring: limited but encouraging evidence

Operating cash flows are a common measure of firm performance. Subtracting the cost of goods sold (direct and indirect material and labor)—but not noncash expenses like

Recapitalization schemes for Thai banks

The Thai authorities created the Financial Restructuring Agency to manage the assets of the finance companies that were closed in 1997, by quickly selling the claims. A series of auctions has sold about $4 billion in assets, at an average price of about 25 percent of face value. The buyers deal with the debtors without the government's involvement.

Banks were treated differently, both because they had more bad loans and because (having encountered political dissent on which finance companies to close) the government did not want to become the creditor even temporarily. Two recapitalization schemes, announced in August 1998, were intended to give bankers an incentive to collect on their nonperforming loans and operate their banks efficiently. Neither scheme has elicited much interest, however, although banks have until November 2000 to apply.

Under the Tier 1 scheme, the government takes a (preferred) equity stake in a bank that immediately adopts the accounting, provisioning, and capital adequacy rules that are to be phased in by the end of 2000. The government first eliminates any negative net worth (without taking equity), then raises equity to 2.5 percent of risk-adjusted assets by injecting tradable government bonds. The government also matches every dollar of new private equity up to the requisite 4.5 percent. Thus the government would have a majority stake in any bank with capital under 2.5 percent, but its stake would be minor in banks closer to the requisite 4.5 percent capital. Although private investors have a call option to buy out the government's stake, until these are exercised, the government has the right to replace the bank's managers. Although the threat is only intended for use against egregious misconduct, it has kept all but two quasi-private banks from volunteering for the scheme.

The Tier 2 scheme also injects government funds, except that instead of (preferred Tier 1) equity, the government holds the bank's subordinated debt up to 2 percent of the bank's risk-weighted assets. The amount declines over time to make its early use more attractive. Furthermore, this injection is tied to the amount of corporate debt that the bank (as creditor) restructures in agreements with indebted firms. This facility has not been used because banks lack Tier 1 capital, not Tier 2.

Instead of using the schemes, many banks have issued new equity to private investors. But it would be incorrect to infer that their net worth is therefore positive. The new equity is inseparably tied to subordinated debt with a yield high enough to attract bank depositors. So although there may now be sufficient "private equity" at risk in these banks, the government may not be able to resist political pressures to protect unwary investors from subsequent losses.

Revitalizing banks and enterprises in the region's small economies

Some of East Asia's small economies face acute corporate and banking stress, similar in scope to that in the main crisis countries. In Mongolia in September 1999, for example, nonperforming loans were estimated at about half of loans to state enterprises and the private sector. In Lao PDR the banking system was declared insolvent during audits in 1996 and 1997, with estimates of nonperforming loans ranging from 25 to 70 percent and recapitalization costs estimated at $70 million. The regional crisis has likely increased banking losses in Lao PDR. Data on nonperforming loans for Cambodia are not readily available but likely fall in a similar range.

Thus the reform agenda in Cambodia, Lao PDR, and Mongolia includes disposing of bad assets, restructuring corporations and state enterprises, strengthening corporate governance, and improving regulatory and supervisory frameworks and institutions. Cambodia is adopting a new Financial Institutions Law, restructuring the majority state-owned Foreign Trade Bank prior to its privatization, and strengthening bank supervision. In Lao PDR the seven state-owned commercial banks have been consolidated into three, and efforts have been made to improve supervision and prudential regulations. Managerial and operational improvements (primarily in credit risk appraisal, collateral valuation, debt recovery, and liquidity management) are also being addressed. Mongolia has created an asset management corporation to oversee the liquidation of two banks and the restructuring of a third. Several other Mongolian banks are undergoing restructuring prior to divestiture.

Elsewhere in the region, Papua New Guinea has embarked on an ambitious privatization program that targets public utilities and commercial enterprises as well as the country's largest financial conglomerate, which accounts for some 40 percent of bank assets.

depreciation, or financing costs like interest payments—shows whether a firm could operate without additional cash infusions. Even "loss making" firms can run a cash surplus, but a cash-deficit firm is often an economic catastrophe (because output is worth less than the inputs used) and ripe for liquidation. Viable firms may operate briefly with a cash deficit—as with a start-up with tremendous potential—but this is not the case for most firms.

Figure 4.2 shows operating cash flows scaled by the book value of the firm's assets (a rate of return) for a "balanced" sample of manufacturing firms for which precrisis and postcrisis data were available.[3] Most firms had a positive rate of return both before and after the crisis (table 4.4). A few firms had a precrisis surplus but a postcrisis deficit—perhaps those that failed to adjust—but this share is only slightly larger than that of firms with a precrisis deficit and postcrisis surplus. There is some evidence that precrisis rates of returns were low in some countries (Korea) and high in others (Philippines, Indonesia), but accounting differences among countries make such comparisons tricky. Regardless of whether firms could have been more profitable before the crisis, they coped surprisingly well with the crisis—with a positive mean return in 1998.

Operational restructuring was forced by hard budget constraints. A firm with an operating cash deficit cannot pay its workers and suppliers without new cash infusions (as distinct from a rollover of loans falling due), and such infusions were not forthcoming during the crisis. But operational restructuring is limited by the technology embedded in machinery, and so differs by sector. Manufacturing and services coped with the crisis the best, and construction the worst (Xu 1999). This is not surprising because construction was most affected by the real estate collapse, and a vacant building cannot be put to alternative use.

Aggregate data do not allow one to examine how firms restructured or if they could—or should—have done more than they did. While average returns are somewhat lower (and their variance greater) after the crisis in every country, this may have been firms' best response. Although labor is often an important variable

cost, it may be rational not to release underused workers—especially if they have firm-specific skills and the downturn is thought to be temporary.

So, firms may have wisely retained some idle workers but paid them just enough to keep their operating cash flows at a slight surplus rather than myopically raise short-term returns. The rise in unemployment was not commensurate with the decline in output—a relief for governments worried that the crisis would cause massive unemployment. Wages and benefits fell, and most firms operated with a slight surplus, though the surpluses were often insufficient to service mushrooming debts.

A need for progress on corporate debt

Although most firms may have adapted their operations to generate a modest cash surplus, many cannot service their debts, which rose as currencies depreciated and interest accrued at higher rates. By 1998 debt-equity ratios were considerably higher for the sample of firms considered in figure 4.2.

There is also evidence that in 1999 more than one-quarter of Korean, Malaysian, and Thai firms and nearly two-thirds of Indonesian firms could not cover their interest payments from operational cash flows (Claessens, Djankov, and Klingebiel 1999a). These data refer to firms listed on stock exchanges. If distress is higher for unlisted firms, the portion of unserviced debt may be higher than these numbers indicate.

While some of these nonperforming loans may be repaid as economies recover and firms' operations improve, some firms may have more debt than they will

TABLE 4.4

Firms' returns on assets and leverage before and after the crisis

(percent)

| Economy | Number of firms | Average operating cash flow as a share of book value | | Share of firms with higher postcrisis leverage |
		Precrisis	Postcrisis	
Indonesia	97	14.6	11.9	91.5
Korea, Rep. of	236	9.6	9.1	83.3
Malaysia	312	12.2	9.6	64.1
Philippines	67	15.1	10.2	77.2
Thailand	194	11.5	10.6	80.6
China	71	9.0	7.7	54.4
Hong Kong, China	273	10.7	9.9	41.0

Source: Xu 1999.

Figure 4.2

Even with the crisis, most manufacturing firms continued to see positive returns

Return on assets for a sample of firms (percent)

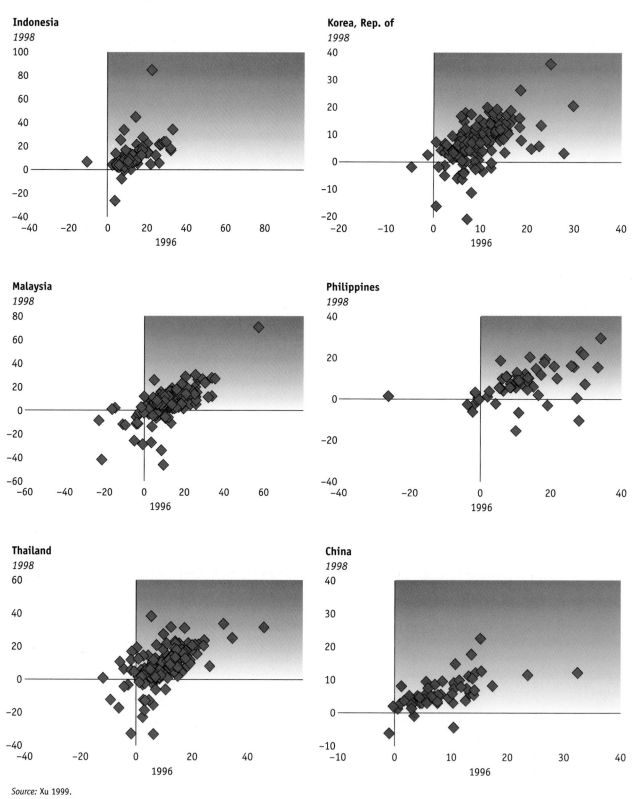

Source: Xu 1999.

itate a reduction in claims, but without some link that may not happen.[6]

Adjusting deposit insurance

During the crisis governments did not allow depositor losses even though explicit deposit guarantees were not in place. But guaranteeing all bank deposits is fiscally costly. It has regressive distributional implications because deposits tend to be highly concentrated. And it makes even large, sophisticated depositors less likely to examine the quality of their banks.

All the crisis countries plan to limit explicit deposit guarantees as the crisis ebbs. Eliminating implicit guarantees is more difficult. For that to happen, large depositors would have to bear losses when banks fail—and that seems unlikely in the short term.

Links to economic recovery and growth

With economic recovery—sparked by fiscal stimulus, stronger external demand, and private consumption—under way in Korea, Malaysia, and Thailand, to what extent will financial and corporate distress constrain future growth? Starting with excess capacity, firms have been able to meet rising demand with relatively little new bank credit,[7] and large firms have had access to alternative sources of capital such as bond and equity markets. But sustaining robust recoveries will require new investment as capacity use rises—including by unconnected firms that must rely primarily on bank credit to finance such investment.

It is not clear how able or willing banks will be to finance new investment. If firms are overindebted and liability restructuring is protracted, access to new credit may be limited. For a given credit quality, the propensity to lend will depend on the extent to which regulations impinge on banks' business instincts.

Even without private debt overhang and restructuring problems, a number of factors suggest slower growth in East Asia's emerging markets relative to before the crisis. First, the increase in public debt since 1997 will, other things being equal, raise interest rates and tax rates, with adverse effects on private investment. Second, private capital flows are unlikely to reach their precrisis levels for some time, adding to interest rate pressures as private demand recovers.

Slower growth makes it more difficult for firms to overcome their overindebtedness. Considering the adverse incentives of overindebted firms, the susceptibility of insolvent banks to taking excessive risk, and the need for substantial new funding for banks, it would be premature to interpret the recovery in East Asia as a vindication of restructuring efforts to date—or to minimize the scope of the additional effort that will be needed.

Although further progress on bank recapitalization and corporate debt restructuring will facilitate a return to robust growth, it should be recognized that the restructuring process is itself endogenous to the pace of growth. If the increase in demand in 1999 is sustained, the pressure on creditors and debtors to resolve their differences will likely intensify as the cost of inaction rises. And the collateral value of nonperforming assets can be expected to increase as incipient recoveries become more broadly based—in which case asset sales by banks and asset management corporations would become more palatable, producing more resources for bank recapitalization. Such a virtuous cycle would be aided by the fact that firms appear to have initiated operational restructuring, and so may be favorably positioned to use new investment productively once their debts have been restructured.

Corporate governance and ownership

Governments in the region need to address shortcomings revealed by the crisis in regulation, supervision, corporate governance, and ownership of the region's banks and corporations. A first step is to recognize the interrelatedness of these elements.

External vulnerabilities persist

As noted, structural weaknesses in the financial and corporate sectors aggravated the crisis. The integration of global capital markets poses another concern because the level and volatility of private capital flows could return to precrisis dimensions as memories of the crisis fade. The stronger the recovery from the crisis, the faster this can be expected to occur. Despite extensive discussions on limiting capital inflows to discourage volatility and reduce reliance on short-term flows, the practical applicability and effectiveness of that approach remain in doubt, and few governments in the region are eager to adopt such instruments.

While most crisis countries are unlikely to rely on fixed exchange rates, the precrisis proclivity toward exchange rate stability apparently remains intact. In the first half of 1999, for example, reserves were built up sharply as intervention held back the market-driven tendency of local currencies to appreciate against the dollar. In a situation of sustained positive investor sentiment toward East Asia, it is difficult to envisage a scenario of purely market-determined exchange rates, because concerns for export competitiveness would weigh strongly as in the past. If investor sentiment were to then adversely shift, currencies would likely again be defended to protect foreign currency debtors.

These considerations indicate that the instability posed by the external environment can be expected to recur. In the near term, new shocks may not disturb financial markets to the extent seen in 1997 because asset prices have been deflated and borrowers and investors may be more cautious. But banks and corporations have been weakened by the crisis, so it would take less volatility in financial markets to inflict serious damage to balance sheets. Moreover, public debt has grown significantly, limiting the ability of governments to mount future rescues on comparable scales.

Will better prudential standards suffice?

The need to address shortcomings in supervision, regulation, accounting, auditing, and legal standards has been widely emphasized in the aftermath of the crisis. Each of the crisis countries has adopted measures to improve prudential standards—while tolerating some regulatory forbearance to facilitate recovery (table 4.6).

Korea has probably gone furthest in strengthening bank supervision. The newly created Financial Supervisory Commission has consolidated regulatory functions that had been shared by the finance ministry and the central bank, enhancing regulatory credibility over the banks. But weaker oversight of investment trust companies has allowed the companies to grow explosively since the crisis while continuing to finance loss-making chaebol affiliates. Moreover, banks have been obliged to support the investment trust companies following the Daewoo crisis, undermining efforts to improve credit evaluation and risk management.

Most prudential measures will take time to implement, if only due to human resource constraints. And their effectiveness, implemented in isolation, may be limited. Even in OECD countries, supervisors are seldom at the cutting edge of market developments. Banks can fail before their problems are detected even when prudential, accounting, and legal frameworks are more sophisticated than what East Asia can realistically strive for in the medium term. Further, the effectiveness of prudential standards (as well as efforts to improve protection of outside investors) is closely intertwined with corporate ownership structures, which in turn reflect the preferences of the dominant forces within govern-

---

TABLE 4.6
Changes in prudential standards in East Asia

Standard	Indonesia	Korea, Rep. of	Malaysia	Thailand
Loan classification (days elapsed before considered past due)	No change—180 days	Lowered from 180 to 90 days	No change—180 days	Lowered from 360 to 90 days
Loan loss provisioning: substandard/doubtful/loss (percent)	From 0/50/100 to 10–15/50/100	From 20/75/100 (backward-looking) to 20/50/100 (forward-looking)	No change—0/50/100	From 0/50/100 to 20/75/100
Interest accrual	Lowered from up to 6 months to up to 3 months; no clawback	Lowered from up to 6 months to up to 3 months, with clawback	No change—up to 6 months, with clawback	Lowered from up to 6 months to up to 3 months; no clawback

Source: Claessens, Djankov, and Klingebiel 1999a; World Bank data.

ment and the private sector—and may be slower to change.

The crisis has shaken up relationships among corporations, banks, and governments. How these evolve or are rebuilt will have significant repercussions on how effectively prudential standards are implemented, as Korea illustrates. Better prudential standards are essential for enhanced financial governance (box 4.5). But their effectiveness will not be determined in isolation.

Strengthening protection of outside investors

Recent work on corporate governance has found large differences across countries in the ownership concentration of publicly traded firms, in the breadth and depth of capital markets, and in the access of firms to external finance. A common element explaining these differences is the quality of legal protection of outside investors—both shareholders and creditors—from expropriation by the managers and controlling shareholders of firms (box 4.6; La Porta and others 1999). Rajan and Zingales (1999), however, suggest that political factors may be more important to financial development than legal systems.

East Asia's market economies do not rank much below other emerging market economies in terms of equity protection or creditor rights. There are, however, deficiencies in enforcement of investor rights, reflecting judicial shortcomings (La Porta, Lopez-de-Silanes, and Shleifer 1998). Moreover, valuations of firms controlled by inside shareholders are below those of comparable firms with broader ownership in some East Asian countries, suggesting that expropriation of outside investors may be significant (Claessens, Djankov, and Lang 1999).

Most assessments have pointed to the need to strengthen the rights of outside investors, and progress has been made on this front (table 4.7). Still, the effectiveness with which rights are enforced remains an issue. In most countries better enforcement of recent and prospective changes will require sustained efforts to strengthen the courts.

Enhancing transparency through more stringent disclosure requirements—based on international accounting and auditing standards—will be essential to strengthen investor protection. The participation of credit rating agencies, securities analysts, professional watchdogs, and the financial media will also enhance transparency (Leechor 1999). While there may be pow-

---

BOX 4.5

Using markets to detect banking vulnerabilities

East Asian countries are strengthening bank supervision. But supervision alone cannot detect all problems. Allowing markets to play a complementary role in uncovering problems can strengthen the prudential framework.

Deposit insurance and guarantees have eroded normal market incentives in the region. Depositors now look to insurance rather than heed the soundness of the bank they entrust their deposits with—and capital requirements will not inhibit owners from taking on excessive risk. Such moral hazard could be overcome by risk-based premiums, but rules cannot measure risk accurately, and supervisors should not be given too much discretion. So, the insurance premium reflects the average risk of banks rather than their individual risk. Rules to reduce risk (adequate capital, provisioning for likely loan losses, prompt corrective action) can be bypassed in myriad ways. And supervisors primarily monitor compliance, rather than assess true risk, so the incentive to take excessive risk at the taxpayers' expense remains.

Two broad alternatives have been suggested to correct this problem. The first is a revival of Henry Simon's ideas (of the 1930s) on "narrow banking," which requires banks that offer riskless deposits to invest only in marketable assets (traded commercial paper, treasury bills, and so on) so that losses cannot be hidden. But there is a fixed cost to issuing securities, which is a large proportion for small borrowings, so having narrow banks raises the question of how to fund the plethora of small firms that normally borrow from banks.

The second alternative is the Calomiris (1997) proposal, where banks must fund a small fraction of their assets (say, 2 percent) through subordinated debt (uninsured certificates of deposit) that is then traded. If the yield exceeds 0.5 percent over comparable riskless instruments, the bank is closed. The Calomiris proposal essentially forces every bank to issue tradable paper so that markets (which have better incentives than rule-bound supervisors) uncover its risk. These proposals will not cure all the ills of East Asian banking, but they offer alternatives to relying exclusively on the abilities of bank supervisors to detect problems.

Source: Calomiris 1997.

Corporate governance in Western theory and East Asian practice

Corporate governance can be defined as addressing the ways principals (investors) oversee their agents (managers of the firm). Thus corporate governance and corporate finance are closely related—how firms are governed is inextricably linked to how they are financed.

Until recently much of the economic literature in the West has focused on the problems arising from the separation of ownership and control, or how firms' financiers prevent expropriation or waste by firms' managers. This literature stems from the image of a typical firm that has widely dispersed ownership with control delegated to professional managers. In practice, however, a small portion of firms conforms to this image. And most are concentrated in a few advanced markets, especially in the United Kingdom and United States.

In most countries—certainly in East Asia outside Japan—most firms are closely owned or privately held. The main shareholders of closely held firms typically play an active role in management and have the deciding vote in major decisions. In publicly held firms highly concentrated shareholdings and a predominance of controlling ownership are the norm. Under these circumstances the agency problem between ownership and control becomes irrelevant. Moreover, concentrated ownership brings potential advantages, such as the ability of a controlling owner to provide more focused strategic direction and to facilitate restructuring and long-term commitment.

Where ownership is concentrated and the principal shareholders also manage the firm, the main concern is that the firm's operations could be structured to serve the insiders' interest to the detriment of overall profitability. For example, if business transactions are not at arm's length, profits can more easily be diverted to insiders through side deals with related parties conducted for the profit of the insiders at the expense of the noncontrolling shareholders. The central issue for corporate governance under these conditions is how to prevent insiders from expropriating the assets of noncontrolling shareholders.

Source: Leechor 1999; Prowse 1998; Shleifer and Vishny 1997.

TABLE 4.7

Equity rights, creditor rights, and judicial efficiency in East Asia, mid-1999

Indicator	Indonesia	Korea, Rep. of	Malaysia	Thailand
Equity rights				
One-share one-vote	0	1	1	0
Proxy by mail	0	0	0	0
Shares not blocked	0	+1	0	+1
Cumulative voting	0	0	0	1
Equity rights score (sum)	0	2	1	2
Improvement over 1996	None	+1	None	+1
Creditor rights				
Restrictions on reorganizations	1	1	1	1
No automatic stay on assets	+1	0	0	1
Secured creditors paid first	0	1	1	0
Management does not stay on in reorganizations	+1	1	1	1
Creditor rights score (sum)	3	3	3	3
Improvement over 1996	+2	None	None	None
Judicial efficiency				
Timetable to render judgment	+1	+1	0	+1
Existence of a specialized bankruptcy code	+1	1	0	0
Judicial efficiency score (sum)	2	2	0	1
Improvement over 1996	+2	+1	None	+1

Note: A 1 indicates that equity and creditor rights are in the law, that there are time limits to render judgment, or that specialized bankruptcy courts exist. A + indicates an improvement over the law in place before the crisis—that is, in 1996.
Source: Claessens, Djankov, and Klapper 1999; La Porta and others 1998 as cited by Claessens, Djankov, and Klingebiel 1999a.

erful vested interests protecting the status quo, the pressure from foreign investors for convergence of regulatory standards should not be underestimated as capital markets integrate. The crisis has increased awareness about the importance of corporate governance. Countries and corporations unable or unwilling to address investor demands risk becoming increasingly ostracized, which can be an important motivator for reform.

If countries succeed in improving outside investor protection, the rationale for interlocking ownership structures and financing arrangements would diminish as the benefits of greater choice in trade and finance partnerships begin to outweigh the comforts of traditional relationships. Continued integration of trade and capital flows would further loosen such nontransparent ties.

Addressing corporate structure and conglomerate influence

A growing body of work has characterized the East Asian conglomerate as one in which a large number of firms—typically including at least one bank and nonbank financial institution—are controlled by a single family. Family control can reach high levels even for publicly traded firms. Control is often enhanced and further concentrated through pyramid structures and deviations from one-share one-vote rules (Claessens, Djankov, and Lang 1999), and company boards tend to be composed of those with allegiance to the controlling family.

Such conglomerates account for large shares of market capitalization and have preferred access to credit provided on a relationship basis and facilitated by their ownership of financial institutions. The top 10 families control more than half of listed corporations in Indonesia and the Philippines and nearly half in Thailand. The concentration of ownership falls with the level of development, however: the top 10 families in Japan account for just 2.4 percent of market capitalization (see table 4.1). Legal and regulatory systems have been influenced by the concentration of corporate resources and its links to government, suggesting that prospective reforms in these areas will also be influenced by changes in ownership structures.

Across East Asia, the structure of corporate ownership—both the dominance of conglomerates and the closely held structure of individual firms—has evolved in response to the business environment, the concentration of wealth, the quality of the legal framework and the judiciary, the methods of dealing with government officials, and even the ethnic composition. The crisis could have an influence on corporate ownership, but it is difficult to speculate on its nature and timing.

Among the region's four hardest-hit countries, conglomerates appear to have become more dominant since the crisis. Firms unconnected to the conglomerates and small and medium-size enterprises have had less access to credit and capital than firms within conglomerates. In Korea in 1998, for example, the top five chaebol raised more than two-thirds of the resources raised through stock and bond issues. A recent study by the Korea Stock Exchange concluded that through capital injections from one affiliate to the other, the top 10 chaebol had increased their control over subsidiary firms since the crisis.

It would be premature, however, to draw conclusions on the direction of ownership change based on developments to date. That change can be significant even if it is slow to develop—as illustrated by Japan, where the dominant role of the *keiretsus* may be changing fundamentally some 10 years after the collapse of Japanese property and stock markets. The largest keiretsus are grouped around a large bank and consist of firms from each large industrial sector, with keiretsu members holding up to 60 percent of each other's shares and the bank financing up to 40 percent of the group's borrowing needs.

The shakeup of the keiretsus has been triggered by the mergers of some of the country's largest banks—which make maintaining previous connections more difficult and cumbersome. But regulatory pressure (for example, more stringent disclosure requirements on asset holdings), the need for banks to search for higher returns on capital, and the benefits from unconstrained access to supplies for firms also appear to have been strong motivating factors (*Financial Times*, 9 November 1999). At the same time, in 1999 Japanese firms were raising funds through capital markets instead of banks at a record pace.

Several of the forces shaping the Japanese keiretsus are also present in the East Asian crisis countries. In Malaysia government-encouraged mergers of financial institutions could strain prior relationships in the conglomerates to which these institutions belong. In Indonesia, through the Bank Restructuring Agency, the public sector effectively owns a substantial share of the formerly private corporate sector, and is seeking ways to re-privatize. Elsewhere in the region, private sector–driven bank consolidation is occurring. Disclosure requirements are also being upgraded in most countries.

If countries are successful in improving prudential standards and protection of outside investors, the rationale for concentrated ownership of firms and the prevailing scale of interlocking ownership patterns would diminish and wider equity ownership would become more attractive. Continued competition from trade and capital flow integration would loosen intra-conglomerate relationships as both the cost of confinement and the benefits of greater choice from trade and finance rise. In this context the growing importance of knowledged-based industries could become an important force accelerating the pace of ownership change.

Who owns the banks? Who should?

In industrial countries the (inconclusive) debate on cross-ownership has focused on whether major ownership stakes by banks of nonfinancial firms can strengthen oversight of the banks' corporate clients. By contrast, the cross-ownership pattern in much of East Asia—where banks and other financial institutions are part of the conglomerate (and subservient to it)—offers no meaningful opportunity for banks to provide effective oversight to their corporate clients. Moreover, this ownership structure appears to have distorted credit allocation in favor of firms affiliated with the conglomerate (despite formal limits on connected lending) both before and after the crisis.

Continued financing of firms affiliated with conglomerates has slowed operational restructuring in these firms

(Cho 1999). As noted, nonaffiliated firms and small and medium-size enterprises have a harder time obtaining credit. Finally, if firms within the conglomerate have ready access to credit from their affiliated financial institutions, they have less incentive to seek alternative sources of financing (such as bonds and equity), reinforcing the concentration of financing toward banks and bank credit.

Diluting this cross-ownership structure therefore appears worthwhile. The crisis provides an opportunity to accelerate the process since, through their intervention in failing banks, governments have acquired large portions of banking assets—particularly in Indonesia, Korea, and Thailand (table 4.8). How these stakes are sold is important.

Foreign banks are an obvious source of new capital and better oversight and management. East Asian banking systems have among the lowest foreign ownership among developing regions. In a number of countries elsewhere—Chile, Hungary, Poland—increased foreign bank presence following financial crises has fostered financial development. Thus increasing foreign ownership and management of the financial system offers the most direct means of improving credit evaluation.

But selling banks to foreigners will likely be a long process. First, the record on sale to foreigners is sobering, and reflects protracted negotiations over allocating the losses and gains from the resolution of nonperforming assets. In Korea one bank was sold to a foreign group, but negotiations for a second bank have dragged on. In Indonesia a single proposed sale became caught in a wider controversy. Malaysia has not offered any banks for sale to foreigners. Thailand has made the most progress in this area; four banks have been sold and two other sales are pending.

TABLE 4.8

Government ownership of financial system assets in East Asia, mid-1999

(percent)

Indicator	Indonesia	Korea, Rep. of	Malaysia	Thailand
Share of assets carved out	23	3	4	10[a]
Share of assets held by state-owned and nationalized financial institutions	55	55	14	22
Share of banking assets held by the state	78	58	18	32
Assets held by the state as a share of GDP	79	124	62	48
Share of assets held by foreign banks	17[b]	8	23	13

a. Finance companies' assets transferred to the Financial Restructuring Agency.
b. Includes joint banks.
Source: Claessens, Djankov, and Klingebiel 1999a; Bongini, Claessens, and Ferri 1999; World Bank data.

Even if foreign sales pick up, on its own foreign ownership is unlikely to fundamentally alter the ownership structure of financial institutions. Foreign interest could dwindle after the first few sales—foreign institutions have traditionally focused on multinational and blue-chip firms and trade financing, and may not be inclined to inherit extensive branch networks. Moreover, opposition to foreign domination would grow if foreign ownership were to grow rapidly. Hence re-privatization of intervened banks that attempts to break the precrisis links to corporate ownership will have to involve more than sales to foreigners.

Widely dispersed ownership of banks may not provide effective oversight to banks until enforcement of prudential regulations is adequate. Hence selling off intervened bank shares fully to the public also may not be a viable option for the re-privatization effort. Another option is to sell shares widely to the public but also encourage fee-based representation of the dispersed owners to oversee bank management. Firms with banking experience would represent the public in this process.

Finally, to the extent that government-intervened banks are resold to conglomerates, an effort could be made (or legislation could be passed) to limit the ownership stake by a single influential group. Instead, re-sales could come in smaller packages to a larger number of conglomerates. A combination of these schemes could significantly dilute the precrisis ownership pattern between conglomerates and financial institutions.

As governments sell intervened banks back to private or foreign investors, legislation needs to be considered to limit the share of financial institutions that can be owned by conglomerates and to disallow controlling ownership. The sequencing of these measures and their political feasibility will vary by country.

It may seem inadvisable to tackle the complexities of ownership reform when governments are preoccupied by financial and corporate restructuring. Yet some of the issues are integral to the restructuring process and cannot be put off. For example, the manner in which re-privatization of government-intervened banks is conducted will affect ownership patterns. Moreover, the web of cross-ownership affects—and can slow—the application of technical solutions to the financial restructuring of corporations. If, for example, an under-capitalized bank is a major creditor to an overindebted firm from the same conglomerate, restructuring negotiations involving third parties are compromised.

Links to capital market development

Banks dominate financial intermediation in East Asia, a factor that may have contributed to the buildup of systemic risk, given cross-ownership patterns. The combination of deeply stressed banks with a lack of alternative financing sources for most firms may have deepened the subsequent crisis.

Since the crisis, capital markets have been called on to play a larger role in corporate finance, as banks struggle to regain their footing. The development of these markets on a sustained basis can help institutionalize arm's-length financial relationships (buttressed by independent credit rating agencies), lessen the role of relationship-based deals, and provide the missing "spare tire" in the face of future banking crises (Greenspan 1999).

A number of factors could strengthen bond and equity markets in the aftermath of the crisis, but these will depend on policy implementation. If efforts to dilute conglomerate ownership of financial institutions are successful, the demand for alternative sources of financing should increase among conglomerate-affiliated firms. Better protection of minority shareholders and enhanced transparency would strengthen the supply of equity and bond finance. Since public deficits and debt have increased in the wake of fiscal stimulation and bank recapitalization, government bond markets can be expected to provide more reliable benchmarks for corporate bond issues—which were often missing in fiscally conservative East Asia prior to the crisis.

To avoid distorting bond and equity market development, it will be important to ensure that tax policies do not bias the financing choices of suppliers and firms. Also important will be to avoid biasing risk perceptions. In the short run the blanket guarantee of bank deposits has tilted this balance in favor of banks. How governments limit the explicit and implicit guarantees on bank deposits will also affect the development of nonbank capital markets. Finally, strengthening regulatory capacity while developing capital markets will be essential if the costs of poor bank regulation are not to be repeated.

The crisis and China

Long before the East Asian crisis, China had started to reform its troubled state-owned enterprises and financial institutions. State enterprises were being subjected to more competition and, more recently, to harder budget constraints. Banks were to transform themselves from fiscal agents into commercial entities. These changes were occurring in a sequenced manner; mass privatization was eschewed, partly to avoid the wrenching disruption experienced in some transition economies of Central and Eastern Europe.

Aided by a booming private sector, the share of state enterprises has fallen to less than 40 percent of production from nearly 90 percent two decades ago. State enterprises still account for some 85 percent of the value of bank loans, however. Moreover, continued enterprise restructuring will likely be more difficult because it will involve displacing some 20 million state enterprise employees—in an economy where urban unemployment is already 8 percent and 10 million new workers enter the labor force each year.

The regional crisis has lent urgency to China's efforts to tackle systemic weaknesses. It has highlighted the risks of supervisory and regulatory inadequacies, perverse incentives imposed on the productive sector, and weak corporate governance. The fragility of major conglomerates in neighboring economies has raised questions about the wisdom of promoting a similar path for Chinese corporations. And prospective accession to the World Trade Organization has highlighted the need to ready Chinese banks to compete with their foreign counterparts within two years of accession (at which point foreign banks are to be permitted to offer services in local currency to Chinese enterprises) and to make Chinese regulations and legal systems more compatible with international norms.

Vulnerabilities and strengths after the crisis

Most of China's problems in the financial and corporate sectors are indigenous to its transition, though a number of weaknesses resemble those in neighboring market economies (World Bank 1999a). But important differences from these market economies have contained the risk of crisis in China.

Banks are weak. Because of unreliable accounts, the share of nonperforming loans is difficult to estimate, resulting in a wide range of estimates—for example, JP Morgan (1999) estimates nonperforming loans at 40 percent in mid-1999, though official estimates are much lower (see table 4.3). Banking skills are weaker than in neighboring economies. Until 1998 most bank lending responded to directives from central or local authorities rather than to evaluations of commercial lending opportunities.

Financial regulation remains inadequate. Expansion of China's financial system has outpaced regulation and supervision of the financial system. This is evident not only for banks but also for the many nonbank financial institutions, such as trust and investment companies, that have taken on excessive risks.

Many enterprises serving the domestic market are not competitive. Several large enterprise groups have focused on investment and size rather than profitability and efficiency. Most medium-size and large enterprises are under financial stress, with a significant share losing money in 1998. Price deflation and slowing growth since 1997 have exacerbated the problems. Small enterprises, including collectively owned enterprises and township and village enterprises—which had been the most dynamic part of the Chinese corporate sector since reform started two decades ago—are having trouble transforming into efficient enterprises. Little of the domestic economy has been influenced by the efficiency and competitiveness that characterize export-oriented ventures.

Corporate leverage is high. Equity contributions from government and tapping of equity markets have been minor, leading to high leverage. The average debt-equity ratio is about 2:1 for industrial and state enterprises and about 4:1 for commercial enterprises. A 1995 survey found that debts exceeded assets in nearly 40 percent of nonfinancial state enterprises (Wu Jinglan 1998).

Corporate governance and management are weak. Entrepreneurial ability is lacking in large enterprises, and ownership responsibility and accountability are poorly defined. Foreign capital cannot be a universal solution (although it can play an important role)—leaving aside geopolitical considerations, the economy is too large.

Incentives are changing but are subject to revision. Although enterprises are facing tighter budget constraints, the incentives for managers and employees of banks have changed only gradually, as have the behavior of enterprises and local governments. And there have been mixed messages to banks—for example, to stop lending to risky clients but also to support the domestic fiscal stimulus with greater lending to infrastructure, and to stop lending to loss-making enterprises but also to be mindful of social stability.

Significant challenges remain. With such significant structural problems, a robust transition will require China to improve the health of the financial system, realign incentives toward commercial objectives, and break the dependence of loss-making state enterprises on state banks. Still, a number of important differences between China and the East Asian crisis economies lessen the risk of an externally driven crisis.

First, in contrast to those economies, China has enjoyed a strong external position, with net creditor status for most of the 1990s. Foreign savings are largely in the form of direct investment and long-term loans. Other than window companies—whose primary function is to raise external finance for local firms—most enterprises have little foreign currency–denominated or external debt. Second, China is more insulated from capital account instability. Its currency cannot be converted on the capital account (for example, offshore borrowing and short-term capital flows are restricted), providing an additional buffer against destabilizing external financial flows. As a result foreign reserves are large relative to short-term debt and capital flows, which lends credibility to the prevailing policy of a fixed exchange rate.

Finally, many of the problems to be tackled are within a closed, state-owned circle. The government is the largest trade creditor, creditor bank, and owner for problematic state enterprises. China's main commercial banks are owned by the central government, which increases depositor confidence in this part of the banking sector. This transitional state provides an alternative framework and system of control for many legal and incentive issues.[8]

While these factors have sheltered China from the regional crisis, financial crises are usually triggered by factors not properly recognized in advance. Unreliable accounts and inadequate supervision and control in financial institutions leave China vulnerable to problems that may be aggravated if the economy slows further. Recognizing the seriousness of the problem, the Chinese authorities have made financial sector reform a top priority.

Financial reforms since the crisis

Since 1993 the government has implemented a number of reforms in the financial sector, including the Central Bank Law and Commercial Bank Law of 1995. The Commercial Bank Law envisioned the transition of banks from fiscal agents to commercial entities, responding to market signals, responsible for their losses, and not dependent on government for signals on the allocation of credit or, indeed, their survival.

The internal controls of the main state banks were centralized, giving the newly formed Financial Working Committee the power to appoint and dismiss branch managers of state banks and to protect banks from local government intervention. To break the link between local government and central bank branches, the central bank (People's Bank of China) formed nine regional offices by combining provincial branches. The offices began operating on 1 January 1999. The Ministry of Finance implemented new national financial accounting standards in 1998. Other accounting standards are now being issued on an accelerated schedule.

The clean-up effort for trust and investment corporations—most of which were known to be insolvent for several years—accelerated in 1998 with the closure of several prominent ones, including the Guangdong International Trust and Investment Corporation, the country's second largest foreign debt–issuing trust and investment corporation. This high-profile and high-risk move represented a sea change in that it applied the rule of law to semiofficial activities, clarified the limits on sovereign responsibility, and enforced a hard budget constraint, thereby challenging previously held assumptions on the rules of the game.

Oversight responsibilities for capital markets were clarified and consolidated under the China Securities and Regulatory Commission, and a new agency was established to oversee the insurance industry. The widespread over-the-counter markets set up in various localities without a formal framework were closed. The long-delayed Securities Law was approved in December 1998 and included a clear definition of insider trading. The Securities and Regulatory Commission issued new rules calling for increased enforcement and disclosure for listed firms, including disclosure of assets, cash flows, changes in shareholder stakes, and performance of subsidiaries, representing initial moves toward aligning with international standards.

An initial strengthening of the capital base of state-owned banks took place in August 1998, on the order of $32.5 billion (about 3 percent of GDP). But this is only a fraction of the amount needed given inadequate classification and provisioning for nonperforming loans. In early 1998 the government announced a risk-based loan classification system that divides loans into five categories as recommended by the Bank for International Settlements. A pilot program was completed in one province in late 1998, and there are plans to extend the system.

The government plans to tackle the losses embedded in the banking sector (Zhang Chunlin 1999; Paulson and Wang Jun 1999), and in late 1998 adopted a good-bank bad-bank approach to cleaning the banking system. In April 1999 the first asset management corporation, Cinda, was established for the China Construction Bank, one of the four big state commercial banks. Three other asset management corporations, each with registered capital of 10 billion yuan (about $1.2 billion), were set up in October 1999 to handle the nonperforming loans of the Bank of China, Agricultural Bank of China, and Industrial and Commercial Bank of China. Their charge is to preserve asset value and to conduct a wide range of transactions—including debt collection, debt reorganization, debt-equity swaps and temporary equity holding, assets securitization, and sale of equity and debt holdings to domestic and foreign investors.

Such resolution of bad assets is necessary but must be accompanied by rigorous bank restructuring to stop the accumulation of new losses. If insolvent financial institutions continue to take deposits, and credit discipline is weakened by the expectation of implicit or explicit debt relief, the ultimate cost of bank recapitalization could rise substantially. The Chinese government is gleaning lessons from the East Asian crisis and other countries on how to avoid these dangers. The current emphasis is on debt-equity swaps to increase profitability through lower financial charges. Without capacity to match this with underlying restructuring of inefficient state enterprises, this approach will increase fiscal losses and extend the life of enterprises that should be liquidated or downsized, creating moral hazard in the corporate sector.

Corporate reforms since the crisis

Corporate reform in China is complex (box 4.7). Recognizing this, state enterprise reform was the focus of the September 1999 Party Plenum. The thrust of recent policy developments has been based on China's experiences, but certain reforms were reinforced with an eye to the East Asian crisis.

State enterprises were granted increased autonomy in production, trading, and pricing during the 1980s and 1990s. Wages and rents began to be liberalized through the introduction of labor and property markets. Protection was reduced through increased competition from private and foreign firms. Support from the budget was also reduced (to just over 1 percent of GDP in 1998). But these pressures increased state enterprise losses, which continued to be financed by state banks.

A lack of progress under earlier experiments with corporatization has shifted the focus toward more fundamental reform of the ownership structure of state enterprises, with a need for capable and well-motivated stakeholders. There is now a serious debate on enterprise manager selection, pay, and incentives. Several large state enterprises plan to enter international capital markets, and more are expected to be listed in the domestic stock market (Zhang Chunlin 1999). State enterprises have increasingly been allowed to raise equity through the stock market as a means of reducing leverage (and bank exposure), but also to allow equity investors to monitor their performance. Privatization of small state enterprises, mostly through the initiatives of regional governments, is also being accelerated.

The failures of conglomerates in the region have given more weight to bankruptcy relative to merger as a corporate restructuring measure, as confirmed in the decisions of the September plenum, and highlighted the role of corporate governance in developing a successful

The Shenyang Machine Tool Company: a state enterprise success story?

The Shenyang Machine Tool Company (SMTCL) symbolizes the challenge of state enterprise reform in China. Located in the industrial northeast, in 1993 the SMTCL had more than 23,000 workers producing antiquated machine tool technology from the 1960s. Management focused on producing to the plan, not profit, and workers were provided a range of benefits, from housing to medical facilities. But as a key enterprise in the core industrial sector of the "rust belt" city of Shenyang, the SMTCL had one main advantage: it had been designated as one of the "100" enterprises, and Shenyang as one of the "10" cities, under the Chinese enterprise reform experiment of 10,000–1,000–100–10. As a pilot, the SMTCL became the focus of the municipal government's commitment to state enterprise reform and a major beneficiary under the World Bank–financed Shenyang Industrial Reform Project.

The reform project touched on every aspect of SMTCL operations and structure, including organizational, physical, and technological restructuring. In 1994 the SMTCL was corporatized as a limited liability company, and two years later it was publicly listed on the Shenzhen exchange. The SMTCL rapidly shed its social and nonproductive assets. But in late 1995 a major threat to the reform process arose when the massive debt burden of one of its factories was revealed, threatening the financial viability of the entire company. In characteristic support for its state enterprise reform experiment, the municipal government split away the factory (including its debt) and placed it into bankruptcy.

Meanwhile, systems restructuring, product design, and technological upgrading continued in an effort to transform the SMTCL into a competitive, modern machine tool enterprise. The SMTCL's financial situation nonetheless deteriorated, reflecting a slump in the global machine tool market, heightened competition from imported sources, delays in acquiring technology, and persistent quality and service problems. In 1993–97 the SMTCL's financial statements resembled those of many other state enterprises in China, with declining sales, increasing accounts receivables, inventory representing more than one year of sales revenue, and spiraling short-term debt to cover working capital requirements. By 1997, as the company's financial situation became increasingly untenable, a further overhaul of the investment program and financial restructuring became necessary. Despite a workforce reduced to 14,000 in the first five years of project implementation, global competitiveness remained elusive.

In 1998 the company injected fresh capital by issuing new shares—on the stock market and to employees. The municipal government converted a long-term directed loan into equity. A plan was agreed to use $10 million of World Bank project resources for retraining and additional severance payments. Working together, the municipal government, management, and the Bank increased pressure on all aspects of SMTCL operations—to substantially improve its accounts receivables, inventory, and quality control management, and to push sales in traditional lines of machine tools while intensifying the development of new product lines.

These efforts appear to be paying off. Sales rose 40 percent in 1998, and sales and profits continued to rise in 1999. The SMTCL now dominates the domestic market in several product lines. The transformation of the SMTCL was evident in its exhibit at the October 1999 Chinese International Machine Tool Show in Beijing. The SMTCL exhibited seven new technologies, placing it at the top of the domestic competition and on a competitive footing in the international market. Orders from the show exceeded half of SMTCL sales in 1998. This strong demand has again put pressure on working capital requirements, given limited financing options and with short-term debt still too high to accommodate additional debt. China's restrictions on access to the stock market mean that an additional stock float is unlikely in the short term. Unlike previous rescues led by the municipal government, SMTCL managers have been told to find their own solutions. New initiatives being pursued include selling off the head office building to raise working capital.

The SMTCL experience illustrates the challenges facing state enterprise reform, in particular the extent of physical and labor restructuring involved, the evolving role of the local authorities, and the vital role of managerial initiative in leading the process. At the policy level the experience highlights the need to enable succeeding firms to raise capital more efficiently and to strengthen the social safety net so that state enterprise reforms may be invigorated.

modern enterprise system. While the nature of the transformation in the relationship among businesses, government, and political party is very different from that in other Asian countries, the separation of government and commercial functions is a key objective of the government reorganization initiated in 1998. By late 1998 nearly all party and government administrative organs were ordered to sever their links with enterprises they control, though remnants of these links may linger for some time.

The crackdown on corruption was partly influenced by the Asian crisis, including political developments in Indonesia. In July 1998 Chinese President Jiang Zemin reaffirmed the importance of combating serious economic crimes. Results of government audits were given more publicity, as with the nationwide audit of 120,000 state enterprises and government agencies in 1998. Government conduct is under greater scrutiny. A new law on tendering and bidding went into effect on 1 January 2000. Corruption and smuggling scandals led to an order to the police, military, and other security agencies to divest themselves of their considerable industrial, commercial, and financial assets. And the cleanup of various financial institutions and activities was accelerated, including efforts to address financial improprieties.

Finally, the significance of small and medium-size enterprises in providing employment and flexibility is being recognized. The Chinese constitution was amended in March 1999 to give private business an equal political and social status, and a new law on individually owned (sole proprietorship) firms was enacted in August 1999. Local governments have been encouraged to organize credit guarantee funds and supporting services for small and medium-size enterprises, and all state banks have been ordered to set up special credit departments for these enterprises. This may be a warranted response to concerns about urban unemployment, but it will be important to ensure that it does not lead to unsustainable increases in the contingent liabilities of local governments.

China's corporate reform is constrained by progress in addressing social concerns—in particular, excess employment in enterprises and the role of enterprises in providing social insurance, housing, and other social benefits. China has been making progress in introducing social welfare, pension reforms, and unemployment insurance and other employment-related assistance. The government is well aware of the importance for social and economic stability of further progress on these reforms. The East Asian crisis underscored the need to establish a social safety net and other instruments that can help households manage risks associated with a market economy that is increasingly integrated with the global economy.

Challenges ahead

While much progress has been made, the Chinese authorities face a number of challenges in implementing their reform agenda and readying financial and state enterprises for greater competition and market discipline. For example, rigorous restructuring of many major enterprises is envisaged through debt-equity swaps by the recently created asset management corporations. Monitoring and enforcing such restructuring will be a major challenge. Promoting efficient reallocation of corporate ownership and control represents another challenge, particularly since competitive sales to strategic private investors are generally not permitted. In this setting, the need for sufficient numbers of qualified agents of restructuring may constrain sustainable restructuring.

In the areas of oversight and ownership, management incentives need to be improved even as the party remains in charge of personnel decisions. The spread of nontransparent conglomerate structures is of concern given the dearth of information available to and relative inexperience of investors in the stock market. Privatizing collectives and township and village enterprises without stirring local resentment is an ongoing concern. Finally, building the institutions, policies, and culture to promote the rule of law and diminish the scope for patronage and extortion will become more important.

Notes

1. Recapitalizing banks removes one disincentive for them to renegotiate their claims on overindebted firms. An inadequately capitalized bank risks being closed by its regulator by admitting that loans are worth less than their book value—which is the implication of reducing the face value of their claims. An adequately recapitalized bank does not face this disincentive.

2. By late 1999 government commitments for financial sector restructuring reached 74 trillion won.

3. Xu (1999) describes the data and analysis. A "balanced" sample includes only those firms for which data exist in all the years used in the analysis. Claessens, Djankov, and Klingebiel (1999a) analyze data from the same source but form larger, unbalanced samples. What one gains in sample size may be lost in disparity of firms in the sample.

4. This section draws on Claessens, Djankov, and Klingebiel (1999b).

5. A bank with a negative net worth would be unable to attract new equity unless the government brings capital up to at least zero. Such recapitalization does not benefit the owners or the borrowers but merely avoids losses to the depositors, and need not—although it often does—involve the government taking a share in the bank's ownership.

6. The Thai recapitalization scheme includes such a feature, but corporate debt restructuring is linked to the provision of Tier 2 capital. But if banks lack Tier 1 capital and find the conditions attached to government funding for Tier 1 capital unattractive, they are unlikely to access government funding of Tier 2 capital (see box 4.1).

7. Through mid-1999 bank credit to the private sector declined in Malaysia and Thailand and declined significantly in Indonesia. But it expanded in Korea, where bank lending to small firms in the first nine months of 1999 grew rapidly.

8. This same factor implies that there may be fragility in other parts of the financial system where the implicit guarantee is perceived as less strong. Also, should depositor growth slow in other parts of

the state banking sector, it will be more difficult to cover the losses (see Paulson and Wang Jun 1999).

References

Bebchuk, Lucian A. 1988. "A New Approach to Corporate Reorganizations." *Harvard Law Review* 101 (February).

Bongini, Paola, Stijn Claessens, and Giovanni Ferri. 1999. "The Political Economy of Dealing with Bank Distress: Evidence in East Asia." Policy Research Working Paper 2265. World Bank, Washington, D.C.

Calomiris, Charles. 1997. *The Postmodern Bank Safety Net: Lessons from Developed and Developing Economies.* Washington, D.C.: AEI Press.

Cho, Yoon Je. 1999. "Korea's Financial Restructuring: Steps Taken and Remaining Challenges." Paper prepared for ASEM Regional Economist's Workshop: From Recovery to Sustainable Development, 15–17 September, Denpasar, Bali, Indonesia.

Claessens Stijn, Simeon Djankov, and Leora Klapper. 1999. "Resolution of Corporate Distress: Evidence from East Asia's Financial Crisis." Policy Research Working Paper 2133. World Bank, Washington, D.C.

Claessens, Stijn, Simeon Djankov, and Daniela Klingebiel. 1999a. "Financial Restructuring in East Asia: Halfway There?" Financial Sector Discussion Paper 3. World Bank, Washington, D.C.

———. 1999b. "How to Accelerate Corporate and Financial Sector Restructuring in East Asia?" Public Policy for the Private Sector Note 200. World Bank, Washington, D.C.

Claessens Stijn, Simeon Djankov, and Larry H. P. Lang. 1999. "Who Controls East Asian Corporations?" Policy Research Working Paper 2054. World Bank, Washington, D.C.

Claessens Stijn, Simeon Djankov, Joseph P.H. Fan, and Larry H.P. Lang. 1999. "Expropriation of Minority Shareholders." Policy Research Working Paper 2088. World Bank, Washington, D.C.

Crispin, Shawn W. 2000. "Capital Crunch." *Far Eastern Economic Review*, 17 February.

Greenspan, Alan. 1999. "Lessons from the Global Crisis." Remarks made to the World Bank Group and International Monetary Fund, 27 September, Washington, D.C.

Haggard, Stephan. 1999. "The Politics of Corporate and Financial Restructuring: Korea, Thailand and Indonesia Compared." University of California, San Diego.

Haggard, Stephan, Lee Chung, and Maxfield Sylvia, eds. 1993. *The Politics of Finance in Development.* Ithaca, N.Y.: Cornell University Press.

Hausch, Donald B., and S. Ramachandran. 1999. "Bankruptcy Reorganization through Markets: Auction-based Creditor Ordering by Reducing Debts (ACCORD)." Policy Research Working Paper 2230. World Bank, Washington, D.C.

IMF (International Monetary Fund). 1999. "The Asia Crisis: Causes, Policy Responses, and Outcomes." IMF Working Paper 99/138. Washington, D.C.

Johnson, Simon, Peter Boone, Alasdair Breach, and Eric Friedman. 1998. "Corporate Governance in the East Asian Financial Crisis, 1997–98." Massachusetts Institute of Technology, Cambridge, Mass.

JP Morgan. 1999. *Asian Financial Markets.* Fourth quarter.

Kawai, Masahiro. 1997. "Capital Flow Liberalization and Financial Market Opening in Asia-Pacific Countries." In Youn-Suk Kim, Ippei Yamazawa, and Woo-Hee Park, eds., *Economics of Triad: Conflict and Cooperation among the United States, Japan and Korea.* Seoul: Korea Institute for Economic Policy.

———. 2000. "Financial and Corporate Restructuring: Building Institutions and Resolution of the East Asian Crisis." World Bank, East Asia and the Pacific Regional Office, Washington, D.C.

Klingebiel, Daniela. 1999. "The Use of Asset Management Companies in the Resolution of Banking Crises: Cross-Country Experiences." Policy Research Working Paper 2284. World Bank, Washington, D.C.

La Porta, Rafael, Florencio Lopez-de-Silanes, and Andrei Shleifer. 1998. "Law and Finance." *Journal of Political Economy* 106: 1113–55.

La Porta, Rafael, Florencio Lopez-de-Silanes, Andrei Shleifer, and Robert Vishny. 1999. "Investor Protection: Origins, Consequences, Reform." Financial Sector Discussion Paper 1. World Bank, Washington, D.C.

Leechor, Chad. 1999. "Protecting Minority Shareholders in Closely Held Firms." Viewpoint Note 190. World Bank, Washington, D.C.

Okuda, Hidenobu. 1999. "The Financial Deregulation and the Production Technology of Philippine Domestic Commercial Banks: Estimation of Cost Functions in the Period of 1990–1996." Paper prepared for ASEM Regional Economist's Workshop: From Recovery to Sustainable Development, 15–17 September, Denpasar, Bali, Indonesia.

Paulson, Jo Ann, and Wang Jun. 1999. "Setting Priorities for Restructuring the Four Big State Banks in China." Background paper prepared for the People's Bank of China Workshop on Bank Restructuring, Beijing.

Prowse, Stephen. 1998. "Corporate Governance: Emerging Issues and Lessons from East Asia." Paper prepared for the Responding to the Global Financial Crisis seminar at the 1998 Annual Meetings of the International Monetary Fund and World Bank Group, 6–8 October, Washington, D.C.

Rajan, Raghuram, and Luigi Zingales. 1999. "The Politics of Financial Development." *International Monetary Fund Seminar Series* (International) 44: 1–82.

Shleifer, Andrei, and Robert W. Vishny. 1997. "A Survey of Corporate Governance." *Journal of Finance* 52 (2): 737–83.

World Bank. 1999a. *China: Weathering the Storm and Learning the Lessons.* East Asia and Pacific Region. Washington, D.C.

———. 1999b. *Global Economic Prospects and the Developing Countries.* Washington, D.C.

———. 1999c. *Indonesia: From Crisis to Opportunity.* East Asia and Pacific Region. Washington, D.C.

———. 1999d. *Philippines: The Challenge of Economic Recovery.* East Asia and Pacific Region, Poverty Reduction and Economic Management Sector Unit. Washington, D.C.

Wu Jinglan. 1998. *Strategic Restructuring of the State Sector.* Beijing: China Development Publishing House (in Chinese).

Xu, Colin. 1999. "Impacts of the East Asian Crisis on Corporations: Shocks, Institutions and Their Interactions." World Bank, Washington, D.C.

Zhang Chunlin. 1999. "Corporate Sector in China: The Decline of State Ownership." World Bank, Washington, D.C.

CHAPTER 5

RESPONDING TO THE GOVERNANCE CHALLENGE

In a development without parallel in Asia, more than 400 activist organizations have joined together to scrutinize the records of hundreds of politicians past and present. "We're under no delusion that we can change styles of politics overnight by removing graft and corruption," says Choi Yol, one of 10 co-chairmen of the Citizens' Coalition for General Election 2000, spearheading the anti-corruption drive. Alongside Choi's coalition is a more moderate grouping, the Citizens Coalition for Economic Justice. Together, the two umbrella bodies represent scores of public interest organizations, including social activists, trade unions, and professional organizations. They plan to organize voters in a drive to send tens of thousands of yellow cards to politicians deemed "undesirable" who run in the election, while those labelled "rejected" will receive red cards. "I'm all for this campaign," grins Kim Si Yol, a Seoul cab driver, who says he has even contributed cash to the effort. The size of these political targets is testimony to how far South Korea has come since the 1997 financial crisis put dissident leader Kim Dae Jung into government.

—Far Eastern Economic Review, 17 February 2000, p. 20

Whether East Asia can sustain an energetic recovery and achieve longer-term social and economic goals will largely depend on how well countries are governed. Governance in the region is undergoing profound change in response to new resource constraints and increased demands for accountability. Governments are being challenged to deliver better services at lower cost and to give more citizens more say in how public business gets done.

The drive for more efficient, effective, and accountable government emanates from three main sources. The first is the immediate fiscal strain brought on by the crisis—a dramatic rise in public debt is squeezing public spending just when recession compels governments to assume more responsibility for protecting low-income groups.

Globalization is the second source of pressure for governance reform. Facing global competition, governments throughout the region must ensure that the public policies regulating key economic activities—such as infrastructure or the financial sector—are effective at getting world-class performance. The state must also set the right conditions for effective provision of education and health services, crucial to the future competitiveness of the region's human resources.

The third driver of governance reform is socioeconomic and political transformation. The changing makeup of East Asian societies—by way of demography, urbanization, education, and income—is redefining what citizens want from government. Older, more urban, middle-class populations—perched more precariously since the crisis—have voiced louder demands for a range of public policies and services, such as new social safety net spending. These demands are being made in a radically different political context of greater pluralism and more activist, globally connected media. New, democratic, and more accountable governments have generated corollary demands for more probity and better performance of public officials.

How can East Asian governments cope with these mounting, complex pressures and move successfully into sustained economic recovery and social development? The answer lies in a new, redefined public sector with a more modest role for the state and a modernized approach to government administration—in short, a new public management that responds effectively to rapidly changing internal and external conditions. This chapter traces the emergence of the main drivers of governance change, outlines their effect on public institutions, and suggests government responses.

Crisis-driven pressures in public finance

The crisis put new fiscal pressures on government through macroeconomic adjustments and through contingent liabilities associated with the systemic crisis in the financial and corporate sectors.

Bigger budget deficits

The crisis increased budget deficits. Part of this was a natural consequence of declining revenues as the tax base shrank for income, value added, and import taxes. And unlike in less severe recessions of the past, government spending could not adjust quickly. Government spending on imports rose with currency devaluations, and this could only partly be offset through lower import volumes.

Moreover, the devaluations precipitated balance sheet losses on government books, and the interest burden (in local currency) on foreign debt rose roughly 30 percent (the amount of the nominal devaluation). Finally, as the depth of the recession became apparent, most governments further increased spending to stimulate the economy. As a result budget balances for the five crisis countries—Indonesia, the Republic of Korea, Malaysia, the Philippines, and Thailand—fell sharply into deficit (figure 5.1). These recession-induced effects will reverse as the region recovers. But they leave a legacy of public debt and higher spending.

China's public sector balance also deteriorated, though without the complications of devaluation and recession. Just before the crisis, the government had intended to eliminate the modest fiscal deficit of about 2 percent. But with the deterioration in China's external position—partly a consequence of the crisis—and structural tendencies toward deflation (chapter 1), the authorities became concerned that eliminating the deficit would slow growth too much. As a result the government abandoned its oft-stated objective of a balanced budget in late 1997 and enacted a substantial fiscal stimulus. When that produced only partial results, it enacted more in 1998 and 1999.

Financial restructuring and other contingent liabilities

The costs of financial sector restructuring and other contingent liabilities are a second new strain on public resources. During the crisis many governments intervened in their financial systems to protect depositors and investors (chapter 4). Since 1996 public debt as a share of GDP has more than tripled for Indonesia, Korea, and Thailand and has risen sharply in Malaysia. Recapitalization costs are the main culprit (table 5.1).

The future fiscal costs accruing to public sector balance sheets will depend on the design of recapitalization schemes and the success governments have in recovering assets from debtors during restructuring and bankruptcy processes. Future costs will also depend on the

Figure 5.1

Budgets have fallen into deficit

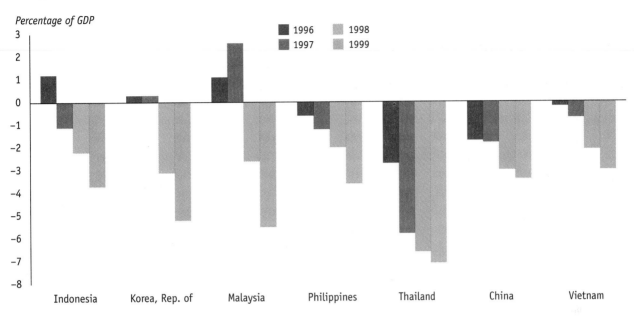

Percentage of GDP

Legend: 1996 · 1997 · 1998 · 1999

Note: Data for 1999 are projections.
Source: IMF and World Bank data.

value of government holdings in recapitalized banks if and when they are resold to the private sector.

Implicit guarantees to the financial sector were not the only contingent liability to come onto governments' balance sheets as a result of the crisis. Contingent liabilities in power and roads associated with government-guaranteed contracts have created new obligations for the public sector. Quantifying the magnitude of these liabilities is difficult, partly because they often involve "take or pay" contracts and because public purchasing entities—such as the Electricity Generating Authority of Thailand—are still negotiating with independent power producers over the distribution of losses.

With recapitalization costs and other new liabilities, interest payments are consuming a much larger share of revenues than before the crisis. These payments range from about 15 percent in Korea and Thailand to about 30 percent in Indonesia and the Philippines (figure 5.2). With interest payments on domestic debt projected to double in 2000, interest costs could eat up more than half of revenues in Indonesia and the Philippines. At the other extreme, China's interest share is relatively low. Although revenues will rise with recovery, spending will rise as well. Most countries have reduced real spending

on education and health by about 10 percent by holding wages below inflation (chapter 6). But wage demands will eventually push up social spending. In the next few years, then, spending will have to accommodate an increased burden of debt service. That means, among other things, that governments will have to become more efficient to provide current levels of service.

Is fiscal adjustment needed?

The region entered the crisis with low debt. So while postcrisis debt is high, it is not unmanageable. Still, governments will probably have to raise primary balances just to keep debt levels stable. For example, even if Thailand's growth rate were to equal its real interest rate over the next few years, it would have to eliminate the 4.8 percent imbalance between its revenues and noninterest spending—that is, lower its primary deficit to zero—to avoid further increasing public debt (table 5.2).

Because Thailand's low primary balance in 1999 was heavily affected by the recession, its cyclically adjusted primary balance was somewhat higher, at about –2.0 percent of GDP. Thus the recovery in economic activity

TABLE 5.1
Public sector debt, 1996–99

(percentage of GDP)

Country	1996	1997	1998[a]	1999[b]	Change, 1996–99	Recapitalization cost	
						To date	Expected additional cost
Indonesia	22.9	61.9	67.3	91.5	68.6	37.3	12.7
Domestic debt	0.0	0.0	16.3	52.5	52.5		
Foreign debt	22.9	61.9	51.0	39.0	16.1		
Interest/GDP	0.0	1.6	3.2	3.9[c]	3.9		
Korea, Rep. of	8.8	14.2	23.8	29.5	20.7	15.8	10.7
Domestic debt	7.6	9.5	12.4	22.2	14.6		
Foreign debt	1.2	4.7	11.4	7.3	6.1		
Interest/GDP	0.4	0.5	1.0	2.6	2.2		
Malaysia	36.0	32.7	37.0	52.0	16.0	10.9	5.5
Domestic debt	31.8	28.0	31.6	44.0	12.2		
Foreign debt	4.2	4.7	5.4	8.0	3.8		
Interest/GDP	2.7	2.3	3.6	3.2	0.5		
Philippines	105.1	114.5	108.9	105.0	−0.1	0	
Domestic debt	72.5	70.7	62.7	59.6	−12.9		
Foreign debt	32.6	43.9	46.2	45.4	12.8		
Interest/GDP	4.7	5.5	6.2	6.8	2.1		
Thailand	15.7	29.2	38.2	50.3	34.6	17.4	15.4
Domestic debt	7.0	6.8	23.1	31.3	24.3		
Foreign debt	8.7	22.5	15.1	19.0	10.3		
Interest/GDP	0.9	2.7	1.9	2.3	1.4		
China[d]	19.0	20.0	26.0	29.0	10.0	3.0	
Domestic debt	6.0	5.4	10.8	14.0	8.0		
Foreign debt	13.0	14.6	15.2	15.0	2.0		
Interest/GDP	0.7	0.8	0.9	2.0	1.3		

Note: The years indicated are fiscal years for Indonesia (April 1/March 30) and Thailand (October 1/September 30) and calendar years for China, Korea, Malaysia, and the Philippines.
a. Estimated.
b. Projected.
c. Does not include a 2.1 percent of GDP interest payment associated with a bank recapitalization bond.
d. National government debt only.
Source: World Bank and IMF data and staff estimates; Claessens, Djankov, and Klingebiel 1999.

would probably reduce any needed subsequent adjustment by about half. In the other crisis countries, if growth rates were to equal real interest rates, primary balances would have to be increased by anywhere from about 0.5 percent of GDP in Malaysia to about 2.0 percent in Korea and Thailand once the effects of revenue buoyancy are considered—and more if these countries wanted to reduce debt.

Global and domestic pressures for change in government

Before the crisis, East Asian governments were small for their income levels, except for the aid-dependent small countries (figure 5.3). Small size allowed for flex-

ibility in resource allocation during the early years of growth and undoubtedly contributed to the "miracle" years.

Global drivers

Globalization, the spread of market forces, and socioeconomic shifts are changing that. New, more enduring claims are being made on governments in three areas. First, there are calls for spending on a new social safety net that supports more flexible urban labor markets (chapter 6). During the recession, governments hurriedly cobbled together public employment programs, rural infrastructure programs, social funds, and income support mechanisms. But even as the economy recovers,

Figure 5.2

Interest payments are eating up more tax revenues

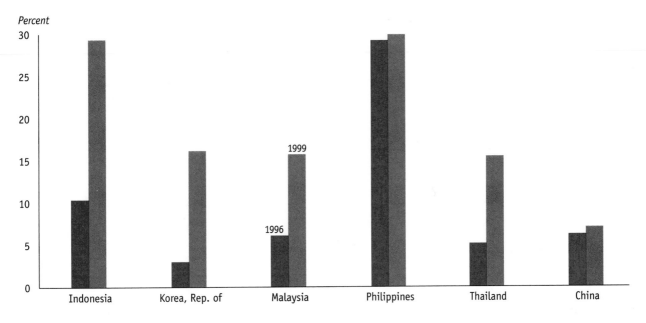

Source: World Bank data.

TABLE 5.2
Primary balances, 1994–99
(percent)

Country	Average 1994–96	Projected 1999	Cyclically adjusted[a] 1999
Indonesia	1.0	−1.1	−1.0
Korea, Rep. of	0.9	−2.6	−2.2
Malaysia	4.0	−2.3	−0.6
Philippines	4.1	1.7	1.8
Thailand	1.2	−4.8	−2.2
China	−1.0	−2.5	−2.4

a. See table note at the end of the chapter for a definition of cyclically adjusted primary balances.
Source: World Bank staff estimates.

governments are considering permanent programs that will protect workers in a market economy.

Second, governments are being asked to educate citizens in an era when knowledge is the key to growth. Third, competitive countries in the global marketplace need efficient ports, transport systems, and urban infrastructure. This demand extends to urban governments because cities are now competing for new jobs. Thus government must be more active in coordinating infrastructure development. While this need not take the form of

direct provision (especially in advanced and large market countries), it will require better planning and regulation.

Domestic drivers

As East Asian societies become wealthier, more urban, and older, they are placing new demands on government for better public facilities and services and better environmental quality. With more Asians living in urban areas, for example, public spending on environmental regulation will likely rise.[1] The result will be a range of programs, with more money for air quality monitoring, more attention to fuel standards, and more resources for managing forestry concessions and water pollution. New public investments will also be needed for sanitation and water supply and for environmentally friendly urban transport systems. Today the region's environmental spending is quite low (World Bank 1996).

Demands for more spending on pensions and health are being driven by an increasingly "gray" Asia. Populations in the region are aging, both because of a higher life expectancy at birth and a rising share of the population above 60 (Heller 1997; Bos and others 1994). Between 1990 and 2030 the share of people over

Figure 5.3

Before the crisis, East Asian economies were small for their income levels, 1989–98

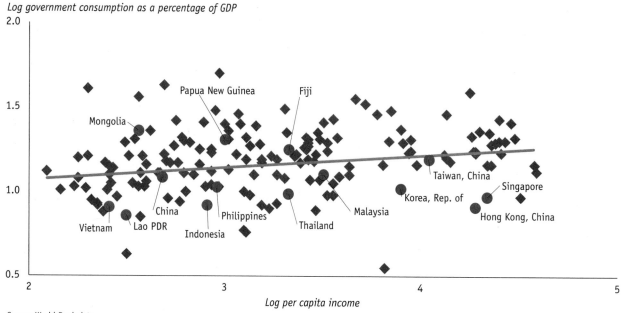

Log government consumption as a percentage of GDP

Log per capita income

Source: World Bank data.

60 will more than triple in Singapore (from 8.5 to 29.4 percent) and will triple in Thailand (from 6 to 18 percent). In other Southeast Asian countries the share will more than double. The same forces are at work in China (World Bank 1997a).

The elderly tend to have higher incomes and so demand more from public health systems. Aging individuals also tend to suffer more from environmental neglect, which contributes to chronic noncommunicable diseases such as cancer, cardiovascular diseases, and neuropsychiatric diseases (Heller 1997, p. 5)—substantially increasing demands for health care. In addition, technological changes may increase the unit costs of medical care. And because women live longer than men, their financing needs during old age merit special attention. The need for an appropriate mix of public and private pensions and health care has become even more urgent (Asher and Heij 1999). An effective response to these demands requires strong public institutions, larger government budgets, and creative ways to involve the private sector in areas where the state's presence is no longer necessary.

These adjustments will need to be made in the context of heightened demands for more effective and more accountable government. East Asia's 30 years of prosperity were accompanied by the emergence of an educated

urban middle-class clamoring for better services in areas like health and education, and by greater public participation in decisionmaking and greater public accountability. More East Asians live in cities, and many of those demanding a new political voice are close to national capitals. Managing these forces to promote better governance will require new initiatives to manage public institutions.

A shift toward openness

Much of East Asia experienced dramatic political change in the 1990s, with a decisive shift toward pluralism (Diamond and Plattner 1998). These trends have been reinforced by global connections—enhancing information on and standardizing demand for a range of products, services, lifestyles, and values. The combination of these global trends and the regional crisis has accelerated political change. Political regimes have changed in Indonesia, Korea, the Philippines, and Thailand. Even in China and Vietnam some political liberalization appears to have occurred.

Political liberalization has coincided with global advances in communications and with pressures for more transparent decisionmaking. A significant rise in media freedom and increased information flows have made citizens better informed and better able to participate in political processes and public management. Between 1980 and 1996 daily newspaper readership rose significantly throughout the region (except in Vietnam). Recent political openings in Indonesia and Thailand have been accompanied by a marked increase in press activity—both in volume and in editorial independence. True press freedom, however, comes when the media have legal protection and independence from vested interests. East Asian countries still face significant challenges in meeting these requirements.

Even in less open contexts, information flows are increasing through communication and technology advances such as the Internet. While still at a low base relative to advanced countries such as the Netherlands and the United States, Internet connectivity in East Asia has increased dramatically (figure 5.4). And since data show only direct Internet portals, actual exposure could be far higher, through Internet cafes and other mechanisms for communal access.

Indicators of effective governance

East Asian public institutions performed some crucial functions—macroeconomic management, promotion of export-led industrialization, poverty reduction—exceptionally well before the crisis (box 5.1). But the crisis has revealed serious shortcomings in public sector performance. Kaufmann, Kraay, and Zoido-Lobatón (1999b) develop aggregate indicators on governance in the region in 1997–98, combining perceptions of governance compiled by more than a dozen commercial risk rating agencies, international organizations, and other nongovernmental organizations.[2] These perceptions are grouped into six broad indicators: voice and accountability, political instability and violence, government effectiveness, regulatory burden, rule of law, and (absence of) corruption (figure 5.5).

Though it is difficult to measure governance precisely, governance ratings in East Asia are more or less average by international standards. Korea and Malaysia are generally among the top third of performers, while Indonesia and Myanmar consistently score among the bottom third. China, the Philippines, and Thailand fall in the middle. Thus a country's institutional quality is highly correlated with its level of development.

For the most part governance ratings for East Asian countries are roughly what one would expect given their per capita incomes. Only Indonesia consistently has inferior scores relative to countries of similar per capita

Figure 5.4

Internet use is exploding

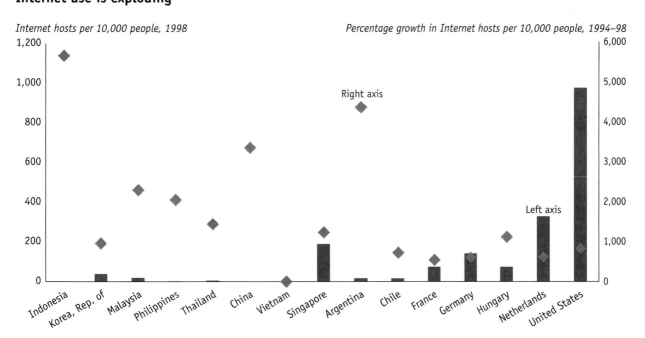

Source: World Bank data.

Figure 5.5

Governance in East Asia

Voice and accountability

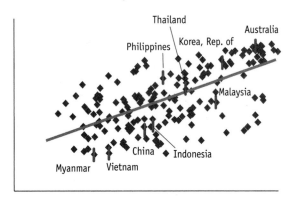

Log per capita PPP GDP

Political instability and violence

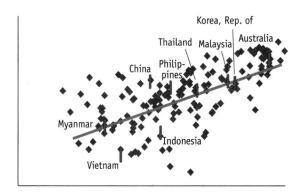

Log per capita PPP GDP

Government effectiveness

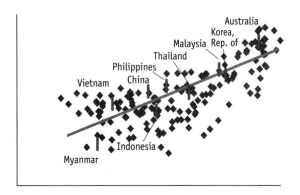

Log per capita PPP GDP

Regulatory burden

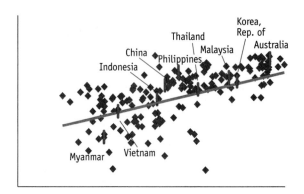

Log per capita PPP GDP

Rule of law

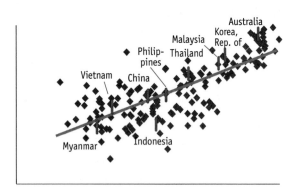

Log per capita PPP GDP

Absence of corruption

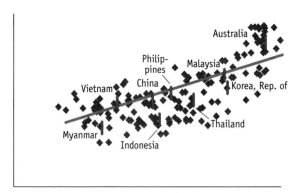

Log per capita PPP GDP

Note: The y axes represent the aggregation of up to 12 separate indices normalized to the same scale. The vertical line for each East Asian country shows the range of likely values of governance for that country. There is a 90 percent probability that governance in that country is within the indicated range. PPP stands for purchasing power parity.
Source: Kaufmann, Kraay, and Zoido-Lobatón 1999b.

BOX 5.1

Views of governance before the crisis—and since

Before the crisis, effective public institutions and governance were commonly believed to have fostered the impressive economic performance and high growth of the East Asian miracle countries (World Bank 1993). Since the crisis, however, views of East Asian governance have become less rosy. Corporate arrangements between the state and economic elites are now blamed for government favoritism that propped up failing businesses and banks. Korea's *chaebol* (conglomerates) and the state institutions that mediate their interests have been characterized as dysfunctional cronyism. And accusations of corruption have proliferated. What caused the change in perceptions of East Asian governance?

The conventional wisdom held that well-trained, enlightened technocrats provided the predictable and transparent policies needed for sustained growth with equity. Three institutional mechanisms were thought to be at work. A politically insulated (or, in military-backed regimes, protected), well-educated, technocratic team—the economic bureaucracy—was purportedly established to formulate and manage policy. East Asian governments (especially Korea and Malaysia) were credited with competent, uncorrupt professional bureaucracies, recruited and managed according to competitive, meritocratic rules and principles, operating with comparatively high efficiency. And deliberation councils supplied an interface between the state and society that gave business elites a say in policy and assured stability and predictability in macroeconomic and policy environments (Campos and Root 1996).

But these three tenets of the East Asian miracle were not entirely accurate. Technocrats were not completely insulated from patronage and political influence. Civil service practices suffered deficiencies—automatic promotion and seniority drove some Korean civil service practices, Malaysia introduced ethnic balance into civil service hiring, opportunities for rent seeking undermined bureaucratic neutrality and performance in Indonesia, and political and informal patronage were legitimized in the Philippine civil service. Even where civil service models stressed merit, they focused on compliance with rules rather than performance and responsiveness. Finally, the virtues of deliberation councils may have been overstated. The councils gave voice to elite policymakers and so may have provided incentives for rent seeking and corruption. And while elite interest groups may articulate the concerns of key private actors and build consensus for government policies, they cannot supplant broadly based, formally legitimized political institutions.

income. Given these findings, it is hard to argue that either of the extreme views on the East Asian state is valid. In hindsight, unqualified praise for government institutions is surely overstated. But postcrisis claims that "crony capitalism" is more pernicious in East Asia than in other regions of comparable income are no less misguided.

Moreover, East Asian countries have done better on some governance indicators than on others, providing possible target areas for reform efforts. For example, East Asia appears to have performed better than its per capita income would predict on government effectiveness, the regulatory burden, and, except for Indonesia, the rule of law. The region performs less well on measures of voice and accountability, and its corruption record is middling. Thus governments still have ample room for improvement.

What can be done to improve public institutions?

Several steps can be taken to strengthen East Asia's public institutions. Government can reposition itself—undertaking fiscal adjustment to do more with less, taking on new roles and shedding old ones, and decentralizing revenue, spending, and services to local levels. Public resources, financial and human, can be managed more effectively. And efforts can be made to enhance accountability and counter corruption.

Repositioning government

Fiscal adjustment: doing more with less. Even with the recovery, the four hardest-hit crisis countries—Indonesia, Korea, Malaysia, Thailand—will likely have to raise taxes, cut spending, or both simply to hold debt levels constant. The needed adjustment could run 1–3 percent of GDP. Other countries suffering from slower growth may also have to adjust. The actual adjustment required will depend on the policy headroom desired to manage future risk (see below) and on economic performance.

Although such adjustments are manageable and politically feasible, they are made more difficult by the jump in interest spending, which will put pressure on spending as public wages recoup losses to inflation. Tight budgets will also place greater demands on government for more careful financial management, and on human resource management to ensure that pay and employment practices result in the best possible services.

With new constraints on public spending, increased global competition, and more vocal citizen demands for participation and public service, public administrations in the region must reconsider basic assumptions about which tasks government should perform and how it can best perform them.

New roles for government—and the private sector. The crisis has accelerated the demise of the old East Asian state. Governments are playing a smaller role in allocating resources through planning, incentives, and implicit or explicit guarantees. Direct production through state enterprises is also likely to diminish. At the same time, states everywhere are shouldering broader mandates to protect low-income groups and intensify regulation and supervision of financial intermediation. Public institutions will also play a more active role in enforcing competition, protecting the environment, and ensuring that the elements needed to compete globally—education, infrastructure, efficient cities—are in place.

But the state's role in providing public services will become increasingly narrow and indirect. As governments shed responsibilities for providing services directly, the private sector must be enlisted as an alternative source of financing and competition for what are now publicly provided services.

Relieving the government of some of its production responsibilities creates opportunities for using privatization to increase efficiency and better manage state assets and liabilities. In the crisis countries the financial bailout has made the state the owner of many assets. Disposing of these assets quickly, efficiently, and competitively can preserve asset values and raise recovery rates on government investments in nonperforming bank assets. Moreover, governments can use the proceeds to reduce debt, lower interest payments, and cover other urgent spending.

Privatization is no panacea, however. Privatizing a well-performing asset may yield no social gain. Selling assets in ways that create a private monopoly can have deleterious effects, as in Chile in the 1970s (Hachette and Lüders 1993). Nonetheless, identifying activities in the public sector that could be undertaken more efficiently in the private sector, putting in place sound regulation and

rules for competition, and organizing the competitive divestiture of these assets can produce resources that improve the balance sheets of governments.

In all East Asian countries there appears to be considerable scope for mobilizing capital revenue from privatization. In Thailand the book value of net assets in state-owned enterprises (financial and nonfinancial) was 743 billion baht ($20 billion) in 1998, equivalent to about one-quarter of foreign debt. Similarly, in China the state reportedly controls about two-thirds of the 900 or so listed firms that together have a market capitalization of 3 trillion yuan ($360 billion). The government also holds unlisted shares worth 2.1 trillion yuan ($250 billion). If the state were to sell half its holdings of listed companies, it could raise 1 trillion yuan ($120 billion)—an amount roughly equal to 75 percent of the pre-1996 nonperforming loans in the financial system.

Decentralization. Decentralizing government spending and taxing powers to local levels can enhance citizen voice, public accountability, and service delivery. To do so, however, decentralization must be well designed and implemented. Effective systems of local accountability must be established, or local governments will misuse or waste funds. Similarly, spending and revenue must be appropriately balanced, or decentralization can undermine service quality. Finally, local governments must pursue responsible fiscal policies, or macroeconomic instability will occur through higher overall fiscal deficits or central government bailouts of weak local governments.

Decentralization is occurring in much of East Asia. But except in China and the Philippines, genuine local autonomy is still restricted. In Indonesia and the Philippines political representation is the key feature of decentralization—political power has shifted to address local demands for autonomy, potentially enhancing political stability. In Thailand decentralization is being pursued to improve public services and increase fiscal efficiency. In China a growing number of employees are working at local levels, and more than 70 percent of budget resources are spent by subnational governments (World Bank 1999a).

To succeed, decentralization must match authority and responsibility with financial and human resources. For example, when a central government devolves responsibility, it must ensure that local resources—

including intergovernmental transfers—are adequate to discharge these functions. Local institutions are weak in most countries. Since the Philippines passed the Local Government Code in 1991, local governments have assumed more responsibility for improving service delivery. Yet they generally lack the managerial and financial capacity to meet the increasing demand for better services. Because most local Thai governments lack the human resources and financial management capacity to deliver services, meeting the decentralization objectives of the new constitution will require long-term capacity strengthening and institution building.

Better monitoring of local governments will be essential for successful decentralization. This will entail developing appropriate accounting and reporting standards and enhancing the performance monitoring systems of both local and central authorities.

Managing financial and human resources

Making the public sector more productive means improving the use of public resources. This, in turn, requires improving the institutions that manage financial and human resources at the central and local levels.

Better public spending. While some East Asian countries are embracing a modified version of the new public management model that is sweeping the developed world, others are on a slower, less deliberate path toward global public expenditure management standards (table 5.3). Korea's capacity to manage spending, for example, is highly rated, though its system is not as close to the principles of performance management as Malaysia's. But Malaysia's follow-through is incomplete, often based more on compliance than on internalization of performance principles.

In China and Vietnam planning and implementation are reasonably effective, though not without problems. But accountability and auditing are weak, and performance management is a more distant goal. The Philippines falls in the middle of the countries examined. Indonesia's system is considered weak, with deficiencies on all good practice criteria.

A major structural problem with expenditure management in China, Malaysia, Thailand, and Vietnam is the weak link between policymaking and the budget process. These countries have national development plans as well as dual (recurrent and capital), often fragmented budgets. Korea, by contrast, has promoted interagency coordination of policymaking by transferring responsibility for overall planning and budgeting to a new, high-level Budget Planning Office.

Predictability, transparency, and accountability—hallmarks of an effective expenditure management system—are severely compromised in most countries due to the chronic use of off-budget funds (extrabudgetary funds, revolving funds, special funds). In China extrabudgetary funds absorb 40 percent of government resources, undermining ministry and agency incentives to stay within their spending allocations, exacerbating waste, enhancing opportunities for rent seeking, and increasing the likelihood that the government's strategic priorities will not be funded. In Malaysia supplementary budgets average 10–30 percent of the original budget. Many countries, notably China, also permit off-budget fiscal spending. In addition to undermining fiscal discipline, the use of off-budget funds suggests that government has less control over resource allocation among its agencies. Agencies have weak incentives to adhere to overall budget discipline.

Nearly all East Asian countries need better procedures for medium-term planning, stronger links between strategic policy decisions and spending program implementation, and more effective mechanisms for coordinating, monitoring, and evaluating spending—on and off the budget and at different levels and sectors of government. The use of performance as a guide and criterion for expenditure management will likely increase—a welcome sign as countries confront pressures to increase efficiency, accountability, and transparency.

A medium-term spending framework, or at least more strategic medium-term planning and resource allocation in the budget process, can enhance strategic prioritization and focus budget programming and approval on longer-term issues, making spending more predictable. Better performance monitoring—and performance management—is also needed at all levels of government. Taking a cue from countries like Australia and the United Kingdom, Malaysia has developed some formal instruments for better performance management by public entities. But performance management is far weaker in most other countries. In Thailand public performance management is only just beginning,

TABLE 5.3
Ratings of expenditure management institutions

Good practice criteria	Indonesia	Korea, Rep. of	Malaysia	Philippines	Thailand	China	Vietnam
Budget formulation through interministerial and legislative deliberations	○	●	●	◐	◐	◐	◐
Budget covers all or most fiscal operations	○	●	○	◐	◐	○	○
Actual spending deviates only slightly from planned levels	◐	●	◐	◐	◐	◐	◐
Timely, audited public accounts	○	●	●	◐	○	○	○
Results specified, performance reported	○	●	◐	○	○	○	○
Adequate compensation for public service	○	●	●	◐	◐	●	○
Competence-based hiring and promotion of public service	◐	◐	●	○	◐	◐	◐
Line agency flexibility and accountability	○	●	●	◐	○	○	◐
Contingent liabilities identified and managed	○	◐	○	○	○	○	○
Effective monitoring and evaluation of spending	○	◐	◐	○	○	○	○
Transparent budget process, with timely and accurate reporting	◐	●	●	◐	◐	◐	◐
Overall	○	●	●	◐	◐	◐	○

Note: Ratings are high ●, medium ◐, or low ○.
Source: World Bank staff.

through the introduction of a performance budgeting system.

New tools for mitigating fiscal risks. The realization of contingent liabilities—including explicit guarantees on privately owned infrastructure and implicit guarantees on deposits and other financial sector liabilities—has been responsible for most of the recent increase in public debt. Even the region's most advanced public financial management systems—such as Malaysia's—cannot systematically manage fiscal risks.

This shortcoming is important because East Asian countries have emerged from the crisis with a much lower ability to absorb fiscal risks. High public debt and reduced access to debt markets severely constrain the scope for government maneuver should additional fiscal risks mate-

rialize. External shocks—through terms of trade or recession—could cut into domestic growth and cause revenues to shrink, plunging public accounts into further deficit. Internal shocks, such as the Daewoo default in mid-1999 in Korea, could cause investors to flee local markets with equally severe consequences. Sustaining growth requires that government actively manage fiscal risks while accommodating restructuring and investment needs.

Containing fiscal risks means adjusting analytical and institutional frameworks for fiscal and debt management. This can be accomplished through:
- Better monitoring and reporting of contingent liabilities.
- Budget laws that incorporate guarantees and other promises of contingent government spending into medium-term fiscal planning.

- Requirements that audit institutions evaluate government analyses and risks.
- Risk sharing with private parties benefiting from contingent claims on governments.
- Strategies to neutralize or hedge risks with an integrated approach to asset liability management.

Such practices have been adopted by Australia, Canada, Colombia, the Netherlands, New Zealand, and the United States. The budget documents of many of these countries test the fiscal baseline with respect to major macroeconomic, policy, and demographic risks, clearly analyze fiscal risks, and assess the likelihood of risks occurring.

Changes in the civil service. Although detailed data on the real size, cost, and incentive structure of East Asian civil services are generally unavailable, aggregate data suggest that these countries have managed their employment establishments reasonably well (table 5.4). By and large, they have not succumbed to the pressures to inflate bureaucracies found in other regions. On conventional measures of wage bill management, most East Asian countries have performed well over the past 20 years. Korea's wage bill has stayed at less than 3 percent of GDP—in the low range of OECD levels—since the early 1970s.

Malaysia's wage bill has been more rocky, with levels reaching more than 11 percent of GDP in the mid- to late 1980s. The Philippines and Thailand have seen wage bills rise over the past 10 years. Indonesia's wage bill has been relatively low relative to GDP growth. Data on China and Vietnam are more sparse. Relative to GDP, China's wage bill is smaller and more stable than Vietnam's.

TABLE 5.4
Ratings of civil service management institutions

Good practice criteria	Indonesia	Korea, Rep. of	Malaysia	Philippines	Thailand	China
Specific legislation governing the civil service	medium	medium	high	high	high	medium
Politically neutral civil service	medium	high	high	low	low	medium
Legislated, merit-based procedures for personnel management	medium	medium	high	medium	high	medium
Open, transparent, and merit-based recruitment	medium	high	high	medium	high	medium
Open, transparent, and merit-based promotion	low	medium	high	low	medium	medium
Legal provisions ensure probity		high	high		medium	medium
Fair and transparent means of redressing grievances with civil service		high	high		medium	medium
Clearly defined institutions to develop and coordinate civil service policy	low	high	high	low	low	medium
Simple, monetized, transparent, and fair compensation	low	medium	high		medium	medium
Competitive pay	low	high	high	medium	medium	medium
Effective personnel information systems	high		high	medium	low	
Objective performance evaluation system	low		high	low	low	low
Disciplinary procedures based on transparent and fair principles	low		high			medium
Appropriate training system	low		high		low	medium
Public consultation on priorities and service standards	low		high	medium	low	low
Overall	low	high	high	high	medium	medium

Note: Ratings are classified as high ●, medium ●, or low ○.
Source: Nunberg, Reid, and Orac 1999.

Employment levels have also been relatively well managed in the region. Between 1980 and 1998 general government employment in all countries except Malaysia was contained at less than 3 percent of the population—less than that for middle-income and OECD comparators. Given the early stage of decentralization in most East Asian countries, most employees are at the central government level.

The five crisis countries have been replacing patronage with merit in professionalizing their civil services. Korea and Malaysia have taken merit reform the furthest, introducing competitive exams, performance evaluations, disciplinary oversight, career training, and professional ethics standards into recruitment and promotion practices. Most countries have also drawn clear distinctions between career and political appointees. Pay levels have generally been maintained at reasonable levels relative to the private sector.

Civil service capacity is correlated with per capita income. Korea and Malaysia are rated highly on most dimensions—reflecting their advanced stages of reform (box 5.2). China, Thailand, and the Philippines are generally assessed as having medium capacity. Indonesia is assessed at lower capacity levels for most criteria. The two high performers—Korea and Malaysia—are shifting from a rule-based merit practice to a more performance-oriented practice.

Thailand has also begun reforms toward a performance orientation, but from a lower base. Reforms are replacing formal, compliance-based mechanisms with performance evaluations, seniority-based pay, and the introduction of more managerial autonomy in selected agencies. Efforts to improve the performance of higher-level civil servants are focusing on the creation of a Senior Executive Service that will be rigorously competitive and insulated from political interference. Ancillary mechanisms to ensure probity, transparency, and accountability include asset declaration and public information legislation as well as the creation of an ombudsman and an anticorruption commission.

BOX 5.2

Korea and Malaysia: moving from merit toward performance

In light of new demands for better service and global standards of efficiency, reformers in Korea and Malaysia are overhauling civil service management.

In Malaysia the reforms were integrated with those in public expenditure management. Building on British-style civil service institutions—including a Public Services Commission that exercised independent oversight over the civil service—Malaysia's reformers first sought to strengthen fiscal controls and basic administrative functions. Since 1984 there has been a 0.53 percent ceiling on annual increases in civil service employment.

More recent reform initiatives have included total quality management and a client charter. Civil servants have been nominally incorporated into performance agreements introduced as part of the new public expenditure management system. Compliance with, rather than internalization of, performance management norms is reportedly the rule rather than the exception.

Korea's reforms have focused on reducing bureaucratic fragmentation and increasing transparency, accountability, and probity. An anticorruption commission created in 1995 has uncovered irregularities in taxation and license issuance. It has also supported the declaration of assets among high-ranking officials and candidates for public office. Two acts enacted in 1996 established due process in administrative decisionmaking and ensure citizen access to full information about government operations. Citizen recourse has also been facilitated by the creation of the Public Grievances Commission.

Bureaucratic streamlining and rationalization have been an important aim of reform in Korea. Systematic mechanisms for deregulation were introduced in 1993. In 1994 an Office of Government Policy Coordination was established to stem fragmented policymaking through isolated agencies and to evaluate performance on a government-wide basis. In 1998 the number of cabinet ministries was cut from 21 to 17 and minister-level officials were reduced from 33 to 24. An initiative to cut central government employees (excluding teachers) by 11 percent over three years began in 1998.

Ministries have been given more independence in determining their working expenses (subject to ceilings set by the Ministry of Finance and Economy). Agency heads can use budgets at their discretion. And each government department and agency that achieves budget savings by reducing staff is allowed to spend a portion of the money for performance bonuses. The bonuses can amount to as much as 100 percent of a staff member's monthly salary, and are linked to a new performance appraisal system introduced in 1995. Such bonuses cover 10 percent of staff, but proposals are being considered to raise that to 20 or 30 percent

In China the challenge is to professionalize a party-dominated bureaucracy and to streamline and reorient government institutions that were not designed for an increasingly market context. Provisional civil service regulations were introduced in 1993 to guide human resource management, and entry exams for civil servants are now in place. Competitive recruitment raises new issues for compensation, however. Low wages make it difficult for the civil service to attract talent. Although massive training is needed for the civil service, recruitment will be essential to fill the gap—especially given the projected retirement of 40 percent of the civil service over the next 10 years. Low monetary rewards, and the prospect that nonwage benefits will decline as the economy liberalizes, further undermine the attractiveness of government employment.

Constraints on Philippine civil service quality largely stem from politicization and clientelism. Although systems are in place for merit-based recruitment, promotion, and discipline, they are ineffective in the face of pressures to appoint and reward on a personal rather than professional basis. The Career Executive Service, for example, has set merit-based criteria for appointment and advancement, but only 38 percent of appointees meet the requirements (World Bank 1997b). Qualified professionals are hard to attract and retain. Fragmented management responsibilities have also hindered coordinated reforms. Civil service reform opportunities include streamlining and rationalizing basic procedures, introducing an appropriately structured remuneration system, and reducing cronyism and corruption.

While Indonesia has the formal trappings of a merit system, little in the institutional environment promotes performance or accountability in civil service management. Civil service oversight is fragmented. Budget arrangements for civil service remuneration are divided between the recurrent and development budgets. Opaque allowances and decentralized personnel management structures reduce system accountability, creating opportunities for graft. Rules of the civil service game that stimulate performance and probity are needed to build public trust in government and provide quality service to newly enfranchised citizens who are geographically and ethnically dispersed.

Enhancing accountability

Effective public policy and management can only emerge if citizens can hold public officials accountable for policy and performance. In this regard East Asia has lagged behind other regions at comparable levels of development. But as noted, many countries in the region have established the foundations for institutional accountability—an increasingly active press, an explosive expansion of the Internet, and important political liberalization.

Political opening is taking different forms in different countries. Indonesia has seen a dramatic change in political leadership. In Thailand constitutional reforms have ushered in changes in political and administrative institutions. Whatever the form, three elements are particularly important: political competition for offices of public decisionmaking, an independent press and judiciary, and fiscal institutions that grant the public maximum voice and participation.

Increasing accountability may take several years, and involves many related aspects of governance. The agenda is closely tied to decentralization—establishing institutions at subnational levels of government that can harness the energies of peoples living outside capitals. Attempts to improve accountability must also be built into public management systems. For example, public expenditure monitoring and audit, along with a transparent budget process that includes timely reporting, are key mechanisms of oversight. And performance evaluation and citizens' grievance processes are critical to ensuring the accountability of the civil service.

Fighting corruption

Anticorruption initiatives are a subset of efforts to enhance accountability. The East Asian crisis set a spotlight on corruption, creating political momentum to fight it. A growing number of countries in the region have started to combat corruption (box 5.3). Indonesia has requested international assistance to coordinate a national anticorruption strategy, and the government has realized that improving public sector pay is crucial in this effort. The Chinese government has developed a bidding law and associated procurement regulations.

Corruption is a complex phenomenon involving many public and private players, and is often the tip of

BOX 5.3

Cambodia's corruption challenge

Cambodia, like other very poor countries, has historically been rife with corruption and plagued by poor governance and political conflict. Corruption has constrained the government's ability to mobilize resources, manage public spending, implement laws and regulations, distribute social services, alleviate poverty, and foster competitive markets. Corruption appears to be a daily fact of citizen and business interaction with government.

To change this situation, the government—working with the World Bank and other donors—is developing an anticorruption program. The program has surveyed 310 private enterprises to identify hotspots of corruption. Preliminary results reveal areas of weak service delivery and public agencies prone to demanding extra payments (see box figure). Enterprises see a need for reform in several public agencies, including courts, the customs authority, the tax authority, and the police. More than 40 percent of responding businesses and individuals reported having to make extra payments frequently, mostly, or always to facilitate the provision of government services. Thus Cambodia faces a daunting task as it formulates its anticorruption program.

Many government interactions require extra payments to officials

Percentage of respondents reporting that extra payments are always, mostly, or frequently required

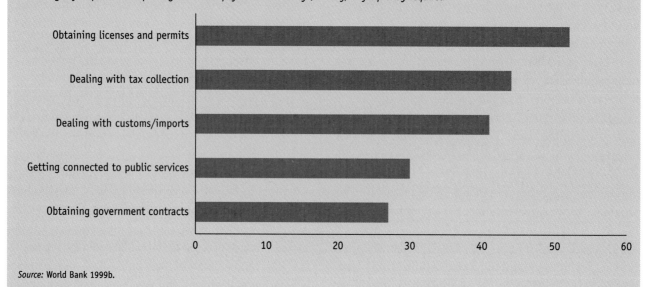

Source: World Bank 1999b.

the iceberg for institutional and governance issues. Laying the foundation in the fight against corruption includes such public sector reforms as:

- Strengthening law enforcement, including the judiciary.
- Improving transparency and accountability in budget preparation, execution, and oversight.
- Developing strongly enforced ethical codes in public administration.
- Improving procedures for merit-based recruitment, compensation, and promotion in the civil service.
- Strengthening parliamentary oversight and independent audit and investigative bodies.

Future directions for governance

Given the diverse range of East Asian governance environments and public management capabilities, any attempt at a one-size-fits-all policy agenda is ill-advised. States vary significantly in their degree of economic planning and control. Polities diverge in their extent of openness. And public administrations differ in their civil service competence and integrity and in their public expenditure management capacity.

Standards for good governance are increasingly international. Some East Asian countries have a long way to go to achieve international best practice. But the crisis has revealed governance problems even in the region's most advanced countries. All East Asian governments, however, can turn challenge into opportunity—combining the best public sector reforms from around the world with existing strengths to invent a new public management model that takes countries beyond recovery toward sustained, long-term development.

Notes

1. East Asia's urban population is expected to grow by 750 million people by 2025. In 2025 almost 55 percent (1.4 billion) of East Asians will live in cities (Douglass 1998).

2. These include such well-known sources as the International Country Risk Guide's corruption ratings, surveys carried out by Gallup International, the World Economic Forum, and the World Bank, and ratings prepared by think-tanks such as the Heritage Foundation and Freedom House.

Table note

Table 5.2. A cyclically adjusted primary budget balance estimates a government's primary balance after correcting for changes attributable to the business cycle. The general procedure entails estimating elasticities of various components of revenue and spending relative to output. The estimated elasticities are then used to make cyclical adjustments to these components of the government budget. Because components falling into the automatic category are caused by the cycle, while components in the discretionary category are assumed to cause the cycle, only the components falling into the automatic category are adjusted. Because only aggregate spending data are available, for simplicity we treat all components of total spending (G) as discretionary. Using a standard approach, we first estimate Hodrick-Prescott (1997) trend lines of output (Y), total revenue (R), and total expenditure (G) for a given period (p). By adjusting R and G in such a way, we allowed for the fact that there could be permanent changes in R and G relative to the rest of the economy. We then estimated the sensitivity of revenue to output cycles for the period. The sensitivity is measured from a regression of log (R) – log (Rp) on log(Y) – log(Yp). The estimated elasticity is denoted b and the residual is e. Thus the movement in R not attributable to the business cycle would be given as log(Rp) + e or, equivalently, log(R) – b * [log(Y) – log(Yp)]. G could be subject to same adjustment. With cyclically adjusted revenue at hand, the cyclically adjusted primary balance is thus followed naturally by taking the difference between the ratio of Rp to Yp and the ratio of G to Yp.

References

Amsden, Alice H. 1991. "Diffusion of Development: The Late-Industrializing Model and Greater East Asia." *American Economic Association Papers and Proceedings* 81 (2): 282–86.

Asher, Mukul G. 1999. "Fiscal Reform in Southeast Asia: Rationale, Issues and Prospects." Paper prepared for ASEM (Asia Europe Meeting) Regional Economist's Workshop: From Recovery to Sustainable Development, 15–17 September, Denpasar, Bali, Indonesia.

Asher, Mukul G., and Gitte Heij. 1999. "South East Asia's Economic Crisis: Implications for Tax Systems and Reform Strategies." *Bulletin for International Fiscal Documentation* 53: 25–34.

Bos, Eduard, and others. 1994. *World Population Projections 1994–95: Estimates and Projections with Related Demographic Statistics.* Washington, D.C.: World Bank.

Burnside, Craig. 1999. "Methods for Computing the Cyclically Adjusted Budget Surplus." World Bank, Development Economic Research Group, Washington, D.C.

Campos, Ed, and Hilton L. Root. 1996. *The Key to the Asian Miracle: Making Shared Growth Credible.* Washington, D.C.: Brookings Institution.

Chibber, Vivek. 1999. "Building a Developmental State: The Korean Case Reconsidered." *Politics and Society* 27 (3): 309–46.

Cho, Yoon Je. 1996. "Government Intervention, Rent Distribution, and Economic Development in Korea." In Masahiko Aoki, Hyung-Ki Kim, and Masahiro Okuno-Fujiwara, eds., *The Role of Government in East Asian Economic Development: Comparative Institutional Analysis.* New York: Oxford University Press.

Claessens, Stijn, Simeon Djankov, and Daniela Klingebiel. 1999. "Financial Restructuring in East Asia: Halfway There?" Financial Sector Discussion Paper 3. World Bank, Washington, D.C.

Diamond, Larry, and Marc Plattner, eds. 1998. *Democracy in East Asia.* Baltimore, Md.: The Johns Hopkins University Press.

Douglass, Mike. 1998. "East Asian Urbanization: Patterns, Problems, and Prospects." Stanford University, Asia/Pacific Research Center, Palo Alto, Calif.

Hachette, Dominique, and Rolf Lüders. 1993. *Privatization in Chile: An Economic Appraisal.* San Francisco, Calif.: ICS Press.

Heller, Peter. 1997. "Aging in the Asian 'Tigers': Challenges for Fiscal Policy." IMF Working Paper 97/143. International Monetary Fund, Washington, D.C.

Hodrick, R.J., and E.C. Prescott. 1997. "Postwar U.S. Business Cycles: An Empirical Investigation." *Journal of Money, Credit, and Banking* 29: 1–16.

Kaufmann, Daniel, Aart Kraay, and Pablo Zoido-Lobatón. 1999a. "Aggregating Governance Indicators." Policy Research Working Paper 2195. World Bank, Washington, D.C.

———. 1999b. "Governance Matters." Policy Research Working Paper 2196. World Bank, Washington, D.C.

Nunberg, Barbara, Gary Reid, and Jana Orac. 1999. "Public Administration Development in the EU Accession Context." World Bank, Europe and Central Asia Region, Poverty Reduction and Economic Management Sector Unit, Washington, D.C.

Scott, Graham, and Simon Smelt. 1999. "Public Sector Management in East Asia and the Pacific." Paper prepared for the Asia-Europe Meeting (ASEM) Regional Economists Workshop "From Recovery to Sustainable Development," 15–17 September, Denspar, Bali, Indonesia.

Shim Jae Hoon. 2000. "Citizens' Choice." *Far Eastern Economic Review,* 17 February, pp. 20–21.

Wade, Robert. 1990. *Governing the Market: Economic Theory and the Role of Government in East Asian Industrialization.* Princeton, N.J.: Princeton University Press.

World Bank. 1993. *The East Asian Miracle: Economic Growth and Public Policy.* A Policy Research Report. New York: Oxford University Press.

———. 1996. *Can the Environment Wait? Priorities for East Asia.* Washington, D.C.

———. 1997a. *Old Age Security: Pension Reform in China.* China 2020 series. Washington, D.C.

———. 1997b. *World Development Report 1997: The State in a Changing World.* New York: Oxford University Press.

———. 1999a. "China: Managing Public Expenditures for Better Results." East Asia and Pacific Region, Poverty Reduction and Economic Management Sector Unit, Washington, D.C.

———. 1999b. "World Bank Survey of Business Environment." Washington, D.C.

CHAPTER 6

ADJUSTING SOCIAL POLICY AND PROTECTING THE POOR

In his Bangkok office Kul Gautam, regional director for East Asia and the Pacific of the United Nations Children's Fund (UNICEF), has watched the social consequences of the economic meltdown with growing concern. He says: "Most people think of the crisis as affecting the big financial institutions—companies going bankrupt, banks suffering, some rich people becoming poorer and traders losing and gaining. All that is true, but what is often hidden from view is the impact on women and children.... Financial statistics are quickly available and are updated promptly. Social statistics—what happens to malnutrition, mortality rates, immunization rates, school completion—are not available month by month. You usually find that out two years later." That moment is coming up.

—Asiaweek, 18 June 1999, p. 40

Since the crisis hit in July 1997, households in East Asia have had to adjust to the first serious economic contraction in a generation—and to wild swings in prices of food, manufactured goods, and services. What were the magnitude and character of these changes at the household level? And how did households and governments respond?

The crisis had a large, negative effect on household welfare. Poverty increased throughout the region. Other social indicators—such as school attendance—also took a turn for the worse in some countries. But the crisis had less of an effect on household welfare than was originally feared. Moreover, households and governments reacted to the crisis in sensible ways. Households protected their consumption of critical items such as staple foods, and the labor market reflected the impact of falling wages and fewer formal sector jobs. Governments beefed up social safety nets and worked hard to gather data to inform policies.

Still, the crisis exposed limitations in the ability of private and public safety nets to cope with a shock of this magnitude—and revealed the need for policies and institutions to help households manage risks. In addition, attention must be paid to the medium-term challenge of ensuring that the poor reap the benefits of future growth.

The effect of the crisis on poverty, inequality, and households

The effects of the crisis differed between the five hardest-hit countries—Indonesia, Republic of Korea, Malaysia, the Philippines, and Thailand—and China.

The crisis countries

The financial crisis interrupted 30 years of steady growth that had made remarkable progress in reducing poverty and improving social indicators, accompanied by only modest increases in inequality in most countries. The social impact of the crisis was swift and unexpectedly complex, reflecting initial conditions, the severity of the financial shock, government policies, community and household resources, and the political context. A severe drought added to economic hardship in some countries.

Poverty. Poverty increased substantially in all the countries hit by the crisis (box 6.1).[1] Korea experienced the sharpest rise in poverty—just before the crisis, in the first quarter of 1997, 7.5 percent of urban residents were poor. By the third quarter of 1998 that share had jumped to 23 percent. It fell to 16 percent in the fourth quarter of 1998, however, and has continued to decline, at a more moderate pace, falling to 14 percent in the third quarter of 1999 (figure 6.1).

Indonesia was hit hard by financial, political, and El Niño shocks, causing the percentage of poor households to go from 11 percent in 1996 to 20 percent in 1999 (table 6.1)—meaning that an additional 19–20 million people fell into poverty. In Thailand the poverty headcount increased from 11 percent in 1996 to 13 percent in 1998 as an additional 1.1 million people dropped below the poverty line. And in the Philippines more than 90 percent of families reported being adversely affected by higher prices for food and other commodities, while 17 percent reported a job loss within the country and another 5 percent reported a job loss due to retrenchment of migrant workers. Throughout the region, investment fell much more sharply than consumption—a typical pattern in systemic shocks.

Inequality. Before the crisis there was growing concern about rising inequality in many of the region's economies. Inequality was up sharply in China, Hong Kong (China), the Philippines, and Thailand. Together with Malaysia, these economies had the highest rates of inequality in East Asia—with Gini coefficients in the mid- to high 40s. Such levels are close to the averages in Sub-Saharan Africa and Latin America, the world's most notoriously unequal regions. How did the crisis affect the income distribution in East Asia?

Aggregate indexes of inequality did not change much in Indonesia and Thailand. But the effects were quite different. In Thailand there was hardly any change in

---

BOX 6.1

Did the poor suffer less in Thailand?

The crisis caused large drops in GDP per capita and private consumption and increased poverty and unemployment (see table 6.1). Yet there is an apparent puzzle. In some countries, especially Thailand, a large contraction in GDP per capita between 1996 and 1998 (–12.7 percent), as measured in the national accounts, was associated with a modest (14 percent) increase in poverty, as measured in household surveys.

The recall periods used in household surveys may help explain this apparent disparity. Poverty estimates for Thailand are based on per capita income. The 1998 Thai household survey occurred between February 1998 and January 1999. Because households are asked about their income in the past year, however, income data from the survey refer in part to incomes in 1997 and may not capture the full impact of the crisis. As measured from the household surveys, real per capita income fell just 2.5 percent between 1996 and 1998. This analysis highlights the difficulty of comparing estimates derived from household surveys with those derived from national accounts.

Figure 6.1

Poverty increased but inequality was largely unchanged—reflecting the broad impact of the crisis

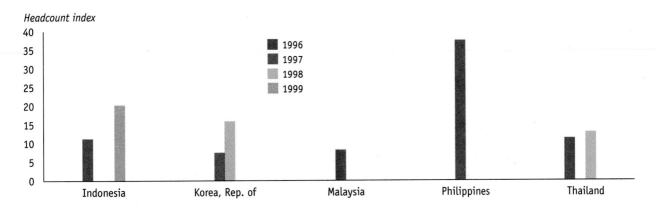

Headcount index

Legend: 1996, 1997, 1998, 1999

Indonesia · Korea, Rep. of · Malaysia · Philippines · Thailand

Note: Derived using national poverty lines. Based on consumption for Indonesia and Korea and on income for Malaysia, the Philippines, and Thailand. Data for Indonesia are for February 1996 and February 1999. Data for Korea are for urban areas only and are for the first quarter of 1997 and the fourth quarter of 1998.

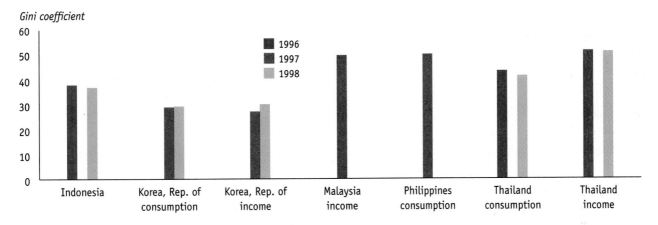

Gini coefficient

Legend: 1996, 1997, 1998

Indonesia · Korea, Rep. of consumption · Korea, Rep. of income · Malaysia income · Philippines consumption · Thailand consumption · Thailand income

Note: Data for Indonesia are for January 1996 and January 1998. Data for Korea are for urban areas only.
Source: World Bank staff estimates based on household survey data.

the percentage of people living in poverty in urban areas (1.6 percent in 1996 and 1.5 percent in 1998). But rural poverty rose from 15 to 17 percent despite the urban nature of the initial shock. The largest increases were in the South and Central regions, followed closely by the Northeast. The drop in real incomes was most severe for those with less than a primary education.

In Indonesia, urban areas and Java were hit much harder than other parts of the country. The percentage of poor people increased more sharply in urban than in rural areas. But because most Indonesians live in rural areas, more rural people became poor as a result of the crisis. While the nominal Gini coefficient changed little during the crisis, there were important differences between urban and rural areas. The nominal Gini does not take into account relative price changes—an impor-

tant issue in Indonesia because the poor face higher inflation than the rich (due to higher prices for food, which accounts for a larger share of the poor's consumption). Calculating the Gini coefficient based on appropriately deflated household incomes yields a slight drop in urban inequality (from 29.9 to 28.9) but an increase in rural inequality (from 26.5 to 28.9).

There was almost no change in the Gini coefficient for urban Korea calculated on the basis of household consumption, but the income Gini jumped from 27.1 in 1997 to 30.1 in 1998. This was partly due to the different savings behavior of households during the crisis. Korea also saw an enormous increase in the number of ultra poor (table 6.2), an outcome consistent with the large increases in poverty indicators that are more sensitive to the distribution of income. Between the first

TABLE 6.1

Indicators of economic activity and household impacts before and after the crisis

Percent

Indicator	Indonesia	Korea, Rep. of	Malaysia	Philippines	Thailand	China
Annual per capita GDP growth						
1990–96	5.7	6.3	7.0	0.4	7.0	9.2
1998	–14.4	–6.6	–9.3	–2.6	–10.8	7.8
Annual per capita private consumption growth						
1990–96	6.8	6.5	5.4	1.0	6.4	8.3
1998	–4.7	–10.2	–12.6	1.3	–15.1	5.5
Annual inflation (consumer price index)						
1990–96	8.8	6.0	4.2	9.8	5.0	11.0
1998	57.6	7.5	5.3	9.7	8.1	–0.8
Poverty incidence [a]						
1996	11.3	9.6	8.2	37.5	11.4	4.7
1998	20.3[b]	19.2			13.0	3.4
Change	79.6	100.0			14.0	–27.7
Unemployment						
1996	4.9	2.0	2.5	8.6	1.8	5.6[c]
1998	5.5	6.8	3.2	10.1	4.5	9.1[c]
Government spending (ratio of 1998 to 1997) [d]						
Education	72.3	94.2	86.3	102.6	98.7	
Health	87.8	96.8	90.3	97.6	89.3	107.5

a. Derived using national poverty lines. Based on consumption for Indonesia and Korea and on income for China, Malaysia, the Philippines, and Thailand. Data for Korea are for urban areas only. Data for Malaysia and the Philippines are for 1997.
b. Data are for February 1999.
c. Official data adjusted to include laid-off workers.
d. Deflated using GDP deflator from the IMF's *International Financial Statistics* for Korea, the Philippines, and Thailand. GDP deflator for Malaysia from the Malaysia Department of Statistics. For Indonesia, education spending is the ratio of 1998 to 1996 and health spending is from World Bank (1999b). Health spending for China is for local governments only.
Source: World Bank staff estimates based on household surveys, national accounts, labor force surveys, and budget data.

quarter of 1997 and the third quarter of 1998 the headcount index tripled—while the poverty gap quadrupled (from 1.3 percent to 5.6 percent) and the poverty severity index quintupled (from 0.4 percent to 2.0 percent). Poverty increased more for households headed by individuals with lower levels of education. But households headed by high school graduates and above accounted for two-thirds of the poor, reflecting the high education attainment in Korea.

Though the crisis worsened the welfare of poor households throughout the region, increases in poverty and inequality were generally smaller than had originally been anticipated. Why? First, the contraction in output was smaller and less protracted than expected. Second, labor mobility between the formal and informal sectors and urban and rural areas may have cushioned the impact of the crisis by distributing the burden more broadly. Third, the relative change in prices induced by currency devaluations was probably favorable to the rural poor engaged in the production of marketable surpluses, especially for export. Fourth, poor households reduced savings and reallocated items within their budgets to protect their consumption of critical items such as staple foods. Finally, public transfers—in the form of unemployment insurance and other safety nets—may also have played a role.

Labor markets. Reduced demand for labor was the most important channel through which the crisis affected most households. In addition, many high-income households suffered substantial losses in property incomes (dividends, capital gains, rents). In Korea

TABLE 6.2

Changes in number and share of Korea's poor, 1996–98

Indicator	1996	1997	1998
Ultra poor			
Number (millions)	1.2	1.1	3.0
Change (percent)	–27.7	–11.1	178.7
Marginal poor			
Number (millions)	1.9	1.7	3.3
Change (percent)	–20.6	–8.4	90.0
Poor			
Number (millions)	3.1	2.8	6.2
Change (percent)	–23.5	–9.5	123.8
Near poor			
Number (millions)	2.9	2.7	4.1
Change (percent	–13.4	–6.5	50.6

Note: The ultra poor are households with per capita consumption of less than 80 percent of the poverty line; the poverty line is equivalent to $8 a person per day in purchasing power parity (PPP) dollars. The marginal poor have per capita consumption of 80–100 percent of the poverty line. The near poor have per capita consumption of 100–120 percent of the poverty line.
Source: Kakwani and Prescott 1999.

the share of wages and salaries in national disposable income fell from 55 percent in 1997 to 51 percent in 1998, the share of profits hovered around 9 percent, and the share of self-employed income rose from 33 to 37 percent (Fallon 1999). A similar pattern is likely in the other crisis countries and is consistent with previous macroeconomic shocks in other countries, particularly in Latin America, where capital is highly mobile.[2]

In general, lower demand for labor hurts households through lower real wages, increased unemployment or underemployment, and reduced self-employment earnings. Whether the main impact comes through a quantity or price adjustment depends on the structure of the labor market. Labor market regulations may make it difficult or costly for employers to lay off workers, and collective bargaining arrangements influence the extent of downward wage flexibility. The prevalence of migrants in urban areas, domestic or foreign, also affects outcomes.

Households respond to labor market shocks in a variety of ways. Labor force participation (including child labor) may increase or decrease to make up for lower wages. Similarly, hours worked may decline or increase. Employment patterns can also change in response to the impact of a devaluation on profitability—for example,

away from construction and manufacturing, toward agriculture. And labor may move from the formal sector, which sustains the initial impact, toward self-employment or informal activities. These initial effects and responses can result in different distributional outcomes in terms of gender, age, income, and wage differences between skilled and unskilled workers.

So what does the evidence show for East Asia? The largest shocks to the domestic labor force occurred in Indonesia, Korea, and Thailand. The Philippines had participated less in the growth boom (and so suffered less from the crisis), and in Malaysia foreign labor bore the brunt of the adjustment burden. Younger, less skilled, and informal or casual workers were particularly vulnerable in all countries. Much of the adjustment to the drop in labor demand came through lower real wages. But there is substantial variation across countries depending on the importance of the formal sector and the extent of labor market rigidities. Unemployment and underemployment increased significantly in Korea and Thailand. Participation rates fell in Korea and Malaysia, stayed constant in Thailand, and increased in Indonesia—where women, particularly those 25 and older, scrambled to supplement household resources in the wake of huge income drops (Horton and Mazumdar 1999). Informal work increased considerably as labor shifted out of the formal sector and into self-employment, unpaid family work, and agriculture.

Korea experienced the sharpest increase in open unemployment, which shot from 2.5 percent just before the crisis to 8.7 percent in February 1999, before falling to 4.6 percent in October 1999. In addition, many people stopped searching for a new job upon becoming unemployed and so became part of the inactive population. Indeed, between the second quarter of 1997 and the fourth quarter of 1998 Korea's economically inactive population increased by 9 percent, or 1.2 million people. Most of the newly unemployed were low-paid workers—temporary and daily workers, the self-employed, unpaid family workers—and so would not have benefited from unemployment insurance.

The increase in Korea's Gini coefficient for real per capita income reflects the especially adverse impact of the employment shock on these more vulnerable workers.[3] Women suffered a lot—accounting for nearly three-quarters of those who became economically inactive. Women were usually laid off before men. And many, anticipating layoffs, opted for voluntary retirement. Some were subsequently rehired on short-term contracts with reduced benefits. Between October 1997 and October 1998 the number of regular female employees dropped nearly 20 percent, compared with a 7 percent fall for males. Moreover, the number of workers with short-term contracts rose for women and fell for men.

Real wages in Korea dropped 12.5 percent between mid-1997 and the end of 1998, before recovering in the first six months of 1999 (figure 6.2). Much of the decline may have reflected changes in the composition of employment: if workers shift from higher-wage formal jobs to lower-wage informal jobs, the average wage falls.

Indonesia presents a marked contrast to Korea. This outcome is not unexpected: Korea is the wealthiest, most urbanized, and most industrialized country in the region, while Indonesia is the poorest, most rural, and most agricultural. In Indonesia open unemployment rose very little—from 4.7 percent in August 1997 to 5.5 percent in August 1998—despite the massive contraction in output. Underemployment also rose, with 3.7

million more people working fewer than 35 hours a week in 1998 than in 1997 (Horton and Mazumdar 1999). Labor force participation rates, meanwhile, increased, remaining constant for men but increasing for women. Only 55 percent of women 25 and older were in the labor force in 1996, but 72 percent were in 1998. Indonesia is the only one of the five crisis countries where participation rates increased, reflecting the low initial incomes and heightened vulnerability of poor households, the severity of the economic crisis, and the inability of formal (and informal) safety nets to cope with the shock.

The main impact on family welfare, however, came through the decline in real wages. Formal wages fell 34 percent in real terms between 1997 and 1998—while agriculture wages fell 40 percent. In addition, there was a major shift from formal to informal employment and from the modern to the agricultural sector (table 6.3).

Thailand saw a larger increase in open employment than Indonesia but a smaller increase than Korea. Thai unemployment rose from 2.3 percent in February 1997 to 4.8 percent in February 1998 and 5.4 percent in February 1999. Unlike in Korea, the recovery in eco-

Figure 6.2

Wage and employment growth have recovered in Korea

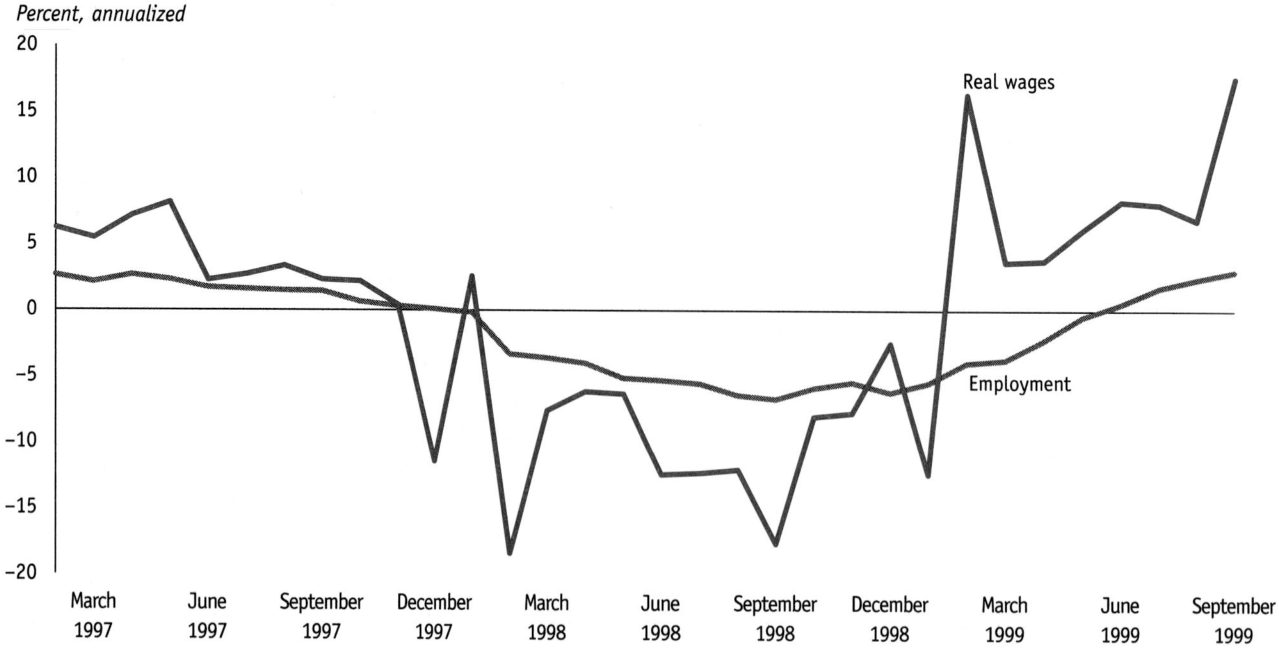

Source: Labor force surveys.

TABLE 6.3

Changes in employment in Indonesia, 1997–98

(percentage of workers)

Sector	1997	1998
Informal	62.8	65.4
Agriculture	40.8	45.0

Source: Abrahart, Betcherman, and Ogawa 1999.

nomic activity does not appear to be increasing demand for Thai workers, and unemployment remains stubbornly high. Underemployment (defined as those working fewer than 20 hours a week) also increased sharply during the crisis. Some of the cuts in working hours between 1997 and 1998 may have translated into higher open unemployment in 1999 (figure 6.3).

But as elsewhere, falling wages had the largest impact on Thai household incomes. Between February 1997 and February 1998 wages fell 6 percent in real terms. The decline was higher in urban (–8.3 percent) than in rural areas (–4.7 percent). Lower wages (hourly earnings) explain two-thirds of the decline in real per capita incomes; lower employment accounts for the rest (Kakwani and Pothong 1999). Well-integrated rural and urban labor markets in Thailand explain the widely distributed drop in wages and the increase in poverty in rural areas, where many unemployed migrants sought work. The crisis inspired significant changes in patterns of internal migration.[4]

The crisis caused fewer problems for domestic workers in Malaysia and the Philippines. Malaysia's unusually large number of foreign workers—accounting for 20 percent of the labor force—provided a cushion for Malaysian workers because migrants bore the brunt of the adjustment burden. With a drop in participation rates, particularly for women, open unemployment increased modestly, from 2.7 percent in 1997 to 3.2 percent in 1998. Unemployment in the Philippines is high (8–9 percent) relative to Korea, Malaysia, and Thailand, and—together with Indonesia—the Philippines is a net exporter of labor to the region and beyond. Unemployment increased in 1998 but has since fallen. By and large, real wages remained constant throughout this period.

Price changes. The massive depreciation of the region's currencies has caused large changes in relative prices. Such changes make the production of tradables

Figure 6.3

Thailand has seen more open unemployment

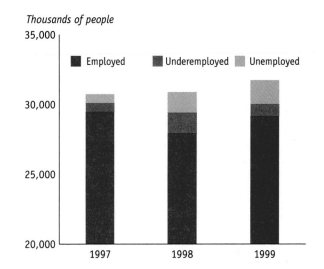

Thousands of people

Source: Labor force surveys.

more lucrative and should have benefited agriculture in particular. The rural poor are helped by such changes in prices if they are net producers of food and if consumer price increases (or world prices in domestic currency terms) are passed on to producers.

Although survey data provide detailed information on household spending, there is less disaggregation on the production side to enable a thorough investigation. Food prices rose relative to other commodities in all five crisis countries. But these changes were minor—except in Indonesia, where food prices jumped 40 percent between mid-1997 and mid-1998 (figure 6.4). The sharp increase in relative food prices was hard on the urban poor and on rural workers who are net consumers. But most rural households benefited from the shift in the terms of trade.

China

Unlike other countries in the region, China avoided the worst of the financial crisis, reflecting lower integration with global financial markets and greater avoidance of short-term debt. But a slowdown in domestic demand—evident even before the crisis—was aggravated by the decline in external demand that resulted from the crisis, and by a general loss of investor confidence in the region. Domestic factors were dominant in the economic slowdown and reflected the difficulties of deepening reforms, especially in enterprises and financial institutions.

Poverty, which had fallen impressively in the mid-1990s, stagnated in 1997–98 (table 6.4). Between 1993 and 1996, 136 million people were lifted out of poverty (based on the international poverty line of $1 a day). But since 1996 poverty has stayed at 17 percent of the population—and the number of poor people has actu-

ally increased. Poverty continued to fall between 1996 and 1998 when measured using the national poverty line (which is less than $1 a day). Poverty is overwhelmingly rural in China, though there is evidence of emerging urban poverty. Between 1996 and 1998 urban poverty doubled and accounted for three-quarters of the increase in the number of poor people. Even so, less than 1 percent of the urban population falls below the international poverty line of $1 a day.

Official data show that real rural household income growth slowed to about 4.5 percent in 1997 and 1998, compared with average increases of 6.5 percent in 1994–96. The main reasons include weak domestic demand and the slowdown in economic growth, large declines in farm procurement prices, and significant reductions in off-farm employment opportunities—reflecting poor performance in rural industry and rising urban unemployment.

Weak domestic demand and structural changes in enterprises and financial institutions depressed profitability among state enterprises and collective firms in urban and rural areas alike. In the past, off-farm employment in rural areas—representing about 30 percent of GDP—accounted for substantial reductions in rural poverty. But in 1997 nearly 15 percent of township and village enterprises were incurring losses and shedding workers. Official data indicate that employment in township and village enterprises fell 3.4 percent in 1997, and these adverse trends continued in 1998.

Figure 6.4

Relative food prices did not change much except in Indonesia

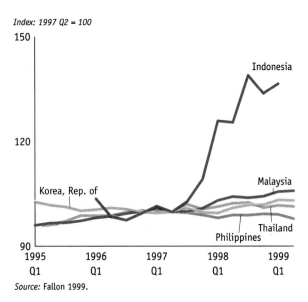

Index: 1997 Q2 = 100

Source: Fallon 1999.

TABLE 6.4
Poverty indicators for China, 1993–98

Area/poverty line	Share (percent)			Number (millions)		
	1993	1996	1998	1993	1996	1998
National						
International poverty line	29.4	17.2	17.1	347	211	214
National poverty line	6.3	4.7	3.4	75	58	42
Rural						
International poverty line	40.6	24.1	24.1	346	208	210
National poverty line	8.2	6.3	4.6	75	58	42
Urban						
International poverty line	0.71	0.46	0.98	2	2	4

Note: The international poverty line is the equivalent of $1 a day in 1993 purchasing power parity (PPP) dollars. These estimates are based on the income distribution, which is adjusted to yield the consumption distribution using average per capita consumption rates from household surveys. The 1998 consumption distribution recently became available, and alternative calculations suggest that the estimation procedure used in this table slightly underestimates poverty. The national poverty line is the equivalent of $0.71 a day and is based on income.
Source: World Bank staff estimates based on household survey data.

Declining off-farm employment opportunities in rural areas hurt the urban economy. Rising structural unemployment, associated with reforms in the midst of an economic slowdown, reduced tolerance of rural migration. Subsequent attempts to protect jobs for established urban residents (through quotas, taxes on migrant labor, and higher fees) meant that urban areas absorbed fewer rural migrants in 1997 and 1998. In 1997 the rural labor supply increased by 3.6 million—1.6 million more than in the mid-1990s.

Lower farm prices also contributed to slower growth in rural incomes. Procurement prices for agricultural products dropped by 4.5 percent in 1997 and by 8.0 percent in 1998. Since crops account for nearly half of rural income, on average, and an even higher share among poorer households, this had a significant impact on the rural poor. In fact, income from farming fell by about 1 percent in real terms between 1996 and 1998 even while overall rural income increased. The drop in crop prices reflects the glut in the grain market, partly induced by high prices in earlier years (in 1995 grain prices in China were above their world market equivalents) and by production quotas aiming at self-sufficiency.

Eradicating rural poverty remains the central focus of China's long-term development strategy. But the emerging urban poverty has become a new challenge for policymakers. Information suggests that urban poverty is closely linked to higher unemployment in China's cities. Mounting pension arrears may also play a part. While the official unemployment rate is still only 3 percent, overall unemployment (that is, including laid-off workers) is estimated at about 8 percent of the urban labor force in 1998—with rates of 12–13 percent in some urban areas.

Household responses to the crisis

Households in the crisis countries responded to the shock in many ways. For example, they reallocated spending to protect critical items in their budget. Between 1997 and 1998 per capita food spending declined in Indonesia, but the share of spending allocated to food increased—especially among the poorest households. And despite the overall drop in food spending, households increased per capita spending on staples by 5 percent in urban areas and 12 percent in rural areas. Spending on meat, by contrast, fell sharply.

Data for Indonesia and Korea suggest that households also cut back on nonessential spending that could be delayed (clothing, recreation, household goods), causing a drop in the share of such items in household budgets. Changes in household spending on education and health varied considerably by country. In Indonesia such spending fell in both absolute terms and as a share of total spending. Regression analysis suggests that the share of education spending declined the most among the poorest households. In Korea, by contrast, reductions in spending on education and health were smaller than overall reductions in household spending. It is not clear why households in some countries protected spending on items such as education and health more effectively than households in other countries. This issue requires further analysis, as it has critical implications for the design of future programs.

Another puzzle from the crisis is that households do not appear to have reduced savings by much in order to protect consumption. Indeed, data for Korea suggest that household savings were higher in 1998 than in previous years, though savings behavior varied significantly depending on household income (box 6.2). In Thailand aggregate transfers—private and public—do not appear to have increased during the crisis (*Thailand Social Monitor*, January 2000, p. 18).

Households that are unable to smooth consumption (through dissaving, borrowing, selling assets, or receiving public or private transfers) may adopt shorter-term coping measures, some of which have severe long-run implications. Reduced nutritional intake, delays in seeking preventive health care, or shortened schooling may cause irreversible losses in human capital and related income-earning potential. A family's survival may depend on a child's income, but children who work are denied an opportunity to escape poverty by improving their human capital. Working children also risk physical and mental harm, perpetuating poverty. Public policy must ensure that families do not have to resort to destructive coping mechanisms while taking care not to displace effective family or community responses to temporary income shocks.

In Thailand the use of public education and health services expanded during the crisis, including for basic services. By contrast, Indonesia saw a large drop in health care use—53 percent of those reporting an illness sought modern medical care in 1997, but just 41 percent did so in

BOX 6.2

Did households smooth consumption during the crisis?

Research on Thailand suggests that households use savings to buffer consumption from individual or community income shocks (Paxson 1992). But can households respond to economywide shocks in the same way? Preliminary data for Korea suggest that households did not smooth consumption as effectively in the face of an aggregate income shock. In 1994–97 per capita income rose steadily for all income quintiles, but in 1998 it collapsed (see box table). If households perceived the 1998 income shock to be transitory, they should have smoothed consumption to levels comparable to those in previous years. But that did not happen. For example, households in the poorest quintile would have been expected to dissave an average of 45,000 won a month in 1998. Instead they saved an average of 24,000 won a month.

There are several possible explanations for the apparent inability of households to fully protect their consumption during the crisis. First, the economywide nature of the shock may have imposed credit constraints that kept households from borrowing against future income. The systemic shock may also have depressed the market value of household assets and so the ability to prop up consumption through asset sales. Second, house-holds may not have viewed the shock as transitory. If households expected the change in income to be permanent, they would have revised their expectations and consumption patterns accordingly. Third, the estimated large positive savings may partly be an artifact of the data. The reference period in household surveys for consumption is the last month, while the corresponding reference period for income is the last year. Since estimated income figures refer to an earlier period than estimated consumption figures, these calculations may be overestimating income relative to consumption for 1998.

How households handled the income shock is important for public policy. If the data for Korea reflect actual behavior during the crisis, mechanisms that help individual households maintain consumption when a few households experience adversity may have limitations during a systemic crisis when entire communities are adversely affected—suggesting a need for direct public action. But more analysis is required to determine whether household behavior was elective or reflected constraints to dissaving, and whether the spending cuts are likely to have implications for future well-being.

Per capita real income and consumption in Korea, 1994–98

Year	1 (poorest)	2	3	4	5 (richest)	Average
			Quintile			
Per capita real income (thousands of won a month)						
1994	213.1	332.2	420.9	536.1	863.0	473.1
1995	228.1	352.9	453.1	583.3	934.5	510.4
1996	239.0	380.2	494.1	637.7	1,024.7	555.1
1997	263.8	398.3	511.2	653.0	1,049.8	575.2
1998 (actual)	206.9	330.6	428.4	558.6	958.6	496.6
1998 (predicted)*	283.4	423.2	545.6	697.7	1121.1	614.1
Per capita real consumption (thousands of won a month)						
1994	190.3	243.5	290.0	350.6	489.3	312.7
1995	206.2	255.5	307.2	373.3	517.7	332.0
1996	220.6	278.3	334.5	397.3	589.2	364.0
1997	220.8	282.0	328.2	414.0	581.6	365.3
1998 (actual)	182.9	236.7	274.6	334.6	484.1	302.6
1998 (predicted)	251.9	306.5	366.3	444.9	630.6	399.5
Average income growth, 1994–97 (percent)	7.4	6.2	6.7	6.8	6.8	6.8
Average consumption ratio, 1994–97 (percent)	88.9	72.4	67.2	63.8	56.2	65.1

Note: Predicted income in 1998 is income in 1997 times average income growth in 1994–97. Predicted consumption in 1998 is predicted income in 1998 times the average consumption ratio.
Source: Korea Family Income and Expenditure Survey; Kakwani and Prescott 1999.

1998. Among those who sought care, fewer people went to public facilities (27 percent in 1997 and 20 percent in 1998), perhaps reflecting a perceived drop in quality after budget cuts. But there is no evidence of an increase in the number of children with a low weight for their height (wasting) or a low height for their age (stunting).

In Indonesia enrollments suffered a modest decline during the crisis. The largest drops occurred in junior secondary schools, at ages 13–15, where enrollments fell 2 percent, to 3.6 percent. Small aggregate changes, however, mask a bigger effect on poor households, which may have seen a 7 percent drop in enrollments. The crisis had little or no effect on school dropouts in Thailand, but in the Philippines 7 percent of the families in a 1998 survey reported taking children out of school.

Lower enrollments among poor children during the crisis are particularly worrisome because of large pre-crisis differences in education attainment between rich and poor households in some countries (see below) and because many of these children may not return to school. Employment patterns of other family members may also change in response to the crisis. Working longer hours at lower-paid work is a common way to maintain income: Indonesian women 25 and older are exhibiting this pattern. Women may also become the victims of physical violence stemming from heightened family tension or resort to prostitution to supplement family incomes.

Information from Indonesia suggests that the poor rely primarily on their relatives, neighbors, and other community members as a safety net to cope with unexpected misfortune (Mukherjee 1999, pp. 80–83). For example, several communities in Java reported a form of rice aid known as *Perelek* or *Jimpitan*. Participating households contribute one cup of rice a month, and this pot is then used to give rice loans to needy families. When rice is given to old or disabled people, no repayment is required. Institutions like Perelek and Jimpitan are evidence of community solidarity, and they show the resourcefulness of the poor. But it is unclear how well these and other community-based safety nets can cope with widespread systemic shocks that affect all or most community members.

Government responses to the crisis

Governments responded to the crisis by implementing largely sensible policies—expanding some safety net programs and attempting to protect spending in key sectors such as education and health. But governments were hampered by their lack of preparedness, by a lack of social programs that could be expanded, by poor information, and by poor coordination.

The crisis countries

The crisis hit quickly, and its social consequences caught policymakers off guard. It proved difficult to design policies and interventions in a context of severe information gaps, rapid change, declining revenues, weak institutional capacity, and limited pro-poor programs. At the same time, citizens did not always place demands on government for social programs, possibly because of an ethos of self-reliance or because of the absence of channels for citizens' voice.

Even so, governments generally pursued sensible policies under the circumstances. Many countries tried to augment information during the crisis. Rapid qualitative assessments were used to diagnose specific areas of vulnerability. Quantitative surveys were used to systematically monitor the impact of the crisis on households and the benefits from government programs (box 6.3).

Korea went the furthest in expanding safety nets. This may reflect greater demands for public action (possibly encouraged by democratic institutions), greater government capacity to respond, and more extensive pro-poor programs before the crisis.

All countries tried to restore health and education spending once fiscal targets were loosened, with varying success. Efforts were least successful in Indonesia, where public health spending fell 8 percent in fiscal 1998 and 12 percent in fiscal 1999 (see box 6.3). Public education spending fared even worse, plummeting 41 percent between fiscal 1997 and 1998, though in fiscal 1999 it rebounded to 72 percent of precrisis levels. The dramatic reductions in real spending in Indonesia reflect the significant inflation it experienced during the crisis. The impact on service delivery is hard to determine because most of the real spending cuts would have translated into real wage declines for teachers and health workers. In Korea and Thailand social spending also declined in real terms between 1997 and 1998, but stayed constant as a share of GDP. There is also evidence that spending on primary health care was protected.

Countries also differed in their choice of instruments to mitigate the crisis (table 6.5). Given the considerable corruption associated with public service delivery, Indonesia avoided cash transfers. Specific interventions to keep children in school were adopted in Indonesia (the poorest country) and Thailand (with the highest

BOX 6.3

Monitoring the impact of the crisis

One of the challenges during periods of crisis is to identify where the impact is greatest given rapidly shifting patterns of vulnerability. It is important to obtain timely information on which segments of the population are being hurt so that resources can be reallocated and programs modified to attain maximum impact. While the crisis countries conducted regular household surveys that enabled them to track changes in poverty, the infrequency of the surveys (annual or biannual) and the long lag between data collection and analysis diminished their usefulness during the crisis. To mitigate that shortcoming, countries developed a range of instruments—rapid qualitative assessments of crisis impact, accelerated processing of ongoing surveys, addition of special modules, and new surveys. Given the urgent need for information, the first response in many countries (Indonesia, Philippines, Thailand) was to perform rapid qualitative assessments. Indonesia had the most comprehensive response to the urgent need for monitoring information.

Crisis periods pose particular challenges for evaluating changes in welfare and poverty. Recall periods in household income surveys tend to be longer than recall periods in consumption surveys, so information on income and consumption from a single survey may not be strictly comparable. Box 6.2 describes how this disparity may paint an incomplete picture of household savings behavior during a crisis. When crises are accompanied by sudden, massive bursts in inflation—as in Indonesia—accurate estimates of changes in the relative prices of key goods are important. This is because households, including poor households, respond to these changes by shifting their consumption away from goods that are relatively more expensive and toward goods that are relatively cheaper. Moreover, the consumption basket of poor households tends to differ systematically from that of better-off households—poor households tend to devote a larger share of their budgets to food, especially staples.

Finally, high inflation compounds the difficulties of gauging the significance of large changes in the level and composition of public spending during crises. In Indonesia overall real spending on health dropped 8 percent in fiscal 1998 and 12 percent in fiscal 1999. But these data mask large differences. Salary expenditures appear to have declined dramatically. Spending on some programs, including communicable disease control, also fell dramatically (from 158 billion rupiah in fiscal 1998 to 88 billion in fiscal 1999). But spending on nutrition more than doubled during the same period. Spending on donor-supported programs also went up substantially.

---

ratio of youth in the labor force). Food security was a primary concern in Indonesia and the Philippines, where the impact of the drought was most severe. Social funds were introduced in countries with active nongovernmental organizations or where government institutions were found to be failing, as in Indonesia. Finally, training programs are not particularly effective as a crisis response but were perhaps most suitable for Thailand, where a skills gap had emerged prior to the crisis.

Before the crisis, publicly provided safety nets tended to be limited in scale and coverage—reflecting reliance on rapid growth and full employment, strong family and community support, and social stigmas associated with public transfers. In Thailand the main safety net programs represented only 2 percent of the government budget in 1996. In Malaysia spending on social assistance amounted to 1.7 percent of the current budget in 1997.

With the crisis, safety nets expanded in all countries.[5] This was most evident in Korea, where spending on social protection rose from 0.6 percent of GDP in 1997 to 1.3 percent in 1998, and to almost 2.0 percent in 1999. In Indonesia outlays for the redefined "core" social safety net programs increased from about 1.0 percent of GDP in fiscal 1999 to 1.25 percent in fiscal 2000.

Nearly all the crisis countries have used public works programs to generate employment (see table 6.5). Indonesia substantially expanded the *padat karya* program in response to the crisis, creating 58 million days of labor a year for more than 400,000 people. In Korea a new public works program was introduced in May 1998; by January 1999 the program was providing 437,000 jobs and was making a dent in unemployment. Still, the program had received 650,000 applicants (figure 6.5). Community-based investment funds, such as new programs in Indonesia and Thailand, are intended to generate employment and demand-driven infrastructure.

Korea is the only crisis country that offers unemployment insurance. This young program was expanded in 1998 from firms with more than 30 employees to firms with fewer than 5 employees as well as to temporary and daily workers. That meant a substantial increase in the scheme's coverage, from 5.7 million workers in January 1998 to 8.7 million by the end of the year. The government also shortened the contribution period required to activate eligibility and extended the duration of benefit payments. As a result the number of unemployment insurance beneficiaries increased but still stood at a low 10 percent of the unemployed labor force in March 1999 (up from 1.9 percent initially).

Korea also introduced extensive wage subsidies, paying as much as two-thirds of a worker's wage if the firm could demonstrate adjustment need.[6] In 1998 the program covered 800,000 workers—and in 1999 it was expanded and the duration of the subsidy increased from six to eight months (Horton and Mazumdar 1999). A survey of enterprises suggests that just 22 percent of jobs would have been lost without the subsidy, confirming international experience that wage subsidies mostly end up subsidizing jobs that would have existed in any event.

Korea, Malaysia, and Thailand modified their severance pay schemes. Thailand extended the maximum amount of severance pay to 10 months and set up a fund to pay the legislated severance payments to workers whose firms went bankrupt. Malaysia also extended its severance pay scheme, allowing workers who quit voluntarily to receive severance pay. Indonesia, Korea, and Thailand also implemented schemes to encourage self-employment.

Other strategies for income maintenance included cash and in-kind transfers. In Korea the means-tested livelihood protection program, providing cash and in-kind aid to those unable to work, was expanded in May 1998 in terms of the number of people covered and the budget (with a nearly 40 percent increase in 1998). In drought-stricken Indonesia, public rice imports were increased while a targeted rice subsidy program was introduced in July 1998 to replace a general rice subsidy (box 6.4). Scholarships and block transfers in Indonesia's stay in school campaign provided incentives to families to keep children in school. In Thailand the low-income health insurance card program was expanded.

How effective was the public response to the crisis? The answer would ideally come from an evaluation of the impact of these programs on the poor. But this information is not available for most programs in most countries. There is information on some important indicators—enrollment rates, health care use, child labor—that are susceptible to changes in the short term. But it is not clear how much of the changes are due to private or public responses to the crisis. Understanding the effect of public programs on household welfare during the crisis should be an important part of future research.

China

China faces formidable challenges in putting in place social policies that support its transition to a market economy while maintaining social stability and enhancing equity. The most important agenda items are to:

- Maintain rapid growth, because it enables government to manage the massive structural and social transformation implied by the transition.
- Provide assistance to workers laid off from enterprises undergoing restructuring.
- Reform insurance-based schemes (pensions, health care, unemployment).
- Establish a social safety net in urban areas to help the indigent.
- Continue to fight absolute poverty in rural areas.

This long-term agenda remains important. While the crisis complicated China's ability to maintain rapid growth, important strides were made in many of these

Figure 6.5

Korea saw a sharp jump in unemployment and public works program participation

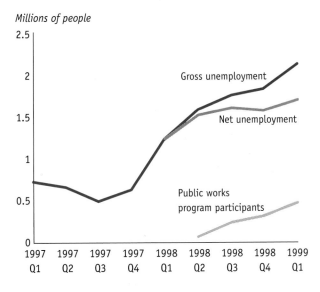

Millions of people

Source: World Bank 1999b.

TABLE 6.5
Social safety net programs in East Asia during the crisis

Country	Food security	Cash transfers	Social funds
Indonesia	New program of targeted cheap rice distribution (OPK)		Community-based programs
Korea, Rep. of		Temporary noncontributory means-tested livelihood protection program (new)	
		Social pension for the elderly (new)	
Malaysia			
Philippines			
Thailand		Social pension for the elderly and cash transfers to needy families expanded	Community-based programs (new)

Source: World Bank documents.

BOX 6.4

Indonesia's cheap rice program

Indonesia's OPK (cheap rice) program provides 10 kilograms of medium-grade rice a month at subsidized prices to households selected using indicators maintained by family planning agencies—including food intake, housing, clothing, and medical and religious practices. Households that fail to meet any of the minimum standards for these categories are eligible. On average this subsidy represents less than 30 percent of the poverty line for one person and less than 6 percent for a household of five.

Although quantitative measures of targeting efficiency are not yet available, indications are that the program is reaching the poorest, even if coverage of the poor is partial. In general, the administrative operations of the program are sound. But there are some areas requiring improvement—for example, poor families are required to pay for rice up-front. Since poor families normally make small daily purchases of rice, many are able to collect OPK rice only after borrowing from family or neighbors or selling small assets. There was no evidence of leakage along the distribution chain, although there were problems with delayed payments to rice distribution centers and the diversion of allocated funds to other uses at the local level.

Source: Klugman 1999a.

Health and education	Workfare programs	Unemployment assistance	Active labor market policies
Back to school program launched (provides scholarships for the poorest students and school grants for schools in the poorest communities) Subsidies to maintain prices of essential drugs	Existing programs expanded and redesigned		
	Public workfare scheme (new)	Unemployment insurance expanded	Active labor market programs (vocational training, wage subsidies, job placement) expanded
			Training for the unemployed expanded
			Computerized job assistance network launched and training expanded
Health card program for the poor and voluntary health insurance card program for the near poor expanded Scholarships and education loan programs expanded School fees allowed to be paid in installments, fee waivers offered, and free uniforms provided to students School lunch program expanded	Public workfare scheme (new)	Severance payments increased Employee welfare fund created to partly finance unpaid severance claims for workers from bankrupt firms	Training for the unemployed expanded Self-employment loans

reform areas, and the elements of an urban social safety net are emerging.

Fiscal stimulus. In response to the slowdown in domestic demand and in anticipation of declining external demand stemming from the global crisis, the Chinese government adopted macroeconomic policies aimed at stimulating domestic demand while maintaining currency stability. The initial fiscal stimulus package adopted in 1998 was rural based, targeted at areas experiencing the largest temporary shock (the central and western regions), and was primarily made up of labor-intensive public investments in infrastructure (water conservation, grain storage, road and rail transport, power grids). The investment program focused on employing unskilled workers and stimulating employment in the building materials sectors, which have excess capacity. Although the package's direct and indirect employment was estimated at about 5 million jobs over the program's two-year span, policies still failed to adequately spur demand.

To remedy the weak impact of the 1998 fiscal stimulus, the government announced a 30 percent increase in civil service wages in July 1999. Living stipends for laid-off workers, unemployment benefits, and minimum living allowances were also increased by 30 percent, and pension payments by 15 percent. Payments for laid-off workers' stipends alone are expected to total 24.5 billion yuan ($2.95 billion) for 1999. The composition of the second stimulus package reflected a desire to stimulate urban consumption, which has been lackluster due to increased urban unemployment and job uncertainty following layoffs from state enterprises, financial institutions, and the government administration. Less amenable to quick fixes were large declines in farm procurement prices and declining labor absorption by nonagricultural rural sectors—the two factors responsible for weaker rural incomes and rural demand.

Urban unemployment and safety nets. Government support for the unemployed has focused on laid-off workers who retain links to their enterprises. In June 1998 the State Council stipulated that all state enterprises with laid-off workers establish re-employment service centers that provide income support, contribute to life, medical, and unemployment insurance, and provide training and re-employment services. Eligibility for income support is to be limited to three years, after which workers will be transferred to the unemployment scheme and delinked completely from their parent enterprises.

While re-employment support systems have been established in most cities, support is constrained by funding shortages, regional disparities, and lagging job creation in the service and informal sectors. China places the burden of social protection at the local—mostly municipal—level. Because unemployment is far worse in localities that have neither a robust economy nor fiscal resources, default on social obligations is far more common where problems are more severe. In 1998, as part of its fiscal stimulus package, the central government augmented local government funding of social protection programs aimed at workers laid off from state enterprises in poorer regions.

But funding has not been on the scale required. As a result not all laid-off workers eligible for re-employment services and subsistence allowances are receiving them. Nor are eligible lower-income urban households receiving minimum living stipends. About 30,000 laid-off workers reportedly never received their stipends in 1999 because many local governments were unable to cover the payments. Arrears have also accumulated in pension payments, affecting at least 3.6 million pensioners in 1998.

The government has made significant strides in reforming social security systems. Responsibility for social insurance was consolidated in March 1998 under the Ministry of Labor and Social Security, bringing together departments that had been managing urban pension schemes and voluntary rural schemes. The ministry also brings together pensions and health and unemployment insurance. This consolidation should help resolve issues of unification and expanded coverage, and strengthen fund management and system oversight.

In May 1998 the government set a target that within five years a fully functional social security system would be established in urban areas to cover both state and nonstate sectors. But weak administration and oversight, as well as a lack of incentives for private participation, pose formidable challenges. Funding is also an issue. While unemployment insurance contributions were raised from 1 percent of wages to 3 percent in 1999, a large portion is used to support laid-off workers and finance re-employment services. As a result uncertainties remain on how to raise sufficient funds to meet future needs when laid-off workers become openly unemployed in the next year or so. Similarly, several fiscally weak cities are having trouble implementing the State Council's unfunded mandate to provide social assistance to the indigent.

Rural poverty alleviation. Government poverty alleviation programs have focused on designated poor areas. The programs aim to improve infrastructure and provide farmers with basic support and assistance to enhance their income-generating capacity. In 1999 fiscal funding for poverty alleviation was increased by 6.5 billion yuan to 24.6 billion yuan (2.8 percent of 1997 government revenue). While funding levels may be adequate, there appears to be considerable scope for improving program effectiveness through better targeting, greater transparency, and closer monitoring of the use of funds.

Human capital investment. In June 1999 the State Council issued a decision aiming to increase the quality and capacity of the education system. Targets set include:
- Increasing government spending on education by 1 percent a year from 1999 to 2002.
- Emphasizing quality education at all stages of the education system and reforming teaching methods.
- Granting more autonomy to provincial governments in delivering education, expanding enrollments at

the senior secondary and tertiary levels, and implementing polices promoting the development of private schools.

- Sustaining the national compulsory education program in poor areas (designed to universalize nine years of compulsory education) after 2000.

The State Council's initiatives on education reforms were partly driven by the potential expansionary impact of increased education spending, estimated at 0.3–1.3 percent of GDP.

Lessons for social policies

All the countries in the region, including those not directly hit by the crisis—such as China—are learning lessons for the design of social policies and institutions.

First, the crisis was a wake-up call that macroeconomic shocks can have disastrous social consequences and that uninterrupted growth cannot be taken for granted. Though efforts will be made to prevent similar shocks in the future, greater variability in performance may be the price that countries have to pay for the higher growth that can come through deeper integration with the global economy. This point has significant implications for economies that relied largely on growth and full employment to provide safety nets.

Second, countries were unprepared to deal with the enormous human suffering inflicted by a large-scale systemic crisis. As a result responses were delayed, partial, and fragmented. This was largely due to the information systems, safety nets, and institutional arrangements in place before the crisis—which constrained government's ability to respond adequately and quickly.

Information systems in the crisis countries were geared toward monitoring longer-term household welfare and so could not capture the sudden and heterogeneous nature of the crisis impacts. Household surveys in Malaysia (income) and surveys in Thailand (income and consumption) are conducted every two years, with results available a year after the survey. In Thailand it takes six months to analyze the data collected in labor force surveys. In Indonesia the quarterly labor force survey was abandoned because the extent of variation did not seem to merit the extra effort. Furthermore, survey instruments are often not multipurpose, making it difficult to link income and consumption data to social outcomes and government policies.

Social safety nets before the crisis were patchy and small-scale. As a result governments had little by way of a menu of programs to work with. But even where a foundation of good programs existed—such as the livelihood protection programs in Korea and Thailand—it took time to increase program budgets. The incremental budget of Korea's livelihood protection program reached only 7 percent of the new poor, while total coverage (that is, for both the former and new poor) dropped from 32 percent before the crisis to just over 17 percent in 1998. In Thailand only one-third of the elderly poor received a social pension, which on average was only one-third of subsistence requirements.

Both countries adopted supplementary budgets to expand these programs in April 1999—long after the effects of the crisis were apparent. This suggests that technical issues of targeting, and of the feasibility of scaling up existing programs, were not the only constraints. Political and cultural factors may also have been at work. Many of the crisis countries have a strong ethos of self-reliance, and governments have been keen to avoid creating a culture of dependency on public "handouts." Politically, it was not the elderly poor or indigent families (the targets of the livelihood programs) who were clamoring for public support. As a result government policies focused on vocal urban groups.

Coordination across a wide range of implementing agencies and responsible authorities was inadequate and led to fragmented responses and reduced effectiveness. In Thailand the fragmented structure of programs resulted in overlapping benefits (for example, of tax subsidies and child benefits) and inconsistent guidelines (the Labor Protection Act of 1998 requires corporate provident fund savings while the Social Security Act of December 1998 introduced a pay-as-you-go pension system). In Indonesia the employment creation program was implemented through a multitude of ministries, resulting in duplication at the local level and confusion about the various programs, their decision-making structures, and their eligibility requirements. In general, the absence of an integrated view of safety nets has led to suboptimal policies as tradeoffs and spillovers across a range of intervention domains—labor markets, pensions, poverty programs—are not considered.

Third, institutions matter for both macroeconomic management and social services; policies are only as good as their implementation. The crisis revealed weaknesses in budget management in many countries. Even after the governments of Indonesia and Thailand adopted a more expansionary fiscal stance, they had trouble increasing actual spending. Moreover, core budget institutions lacked the capacity to identify the most effective pro-poor programs.

In Indonesia disbursements of social safety net spending during the first nine months of fiscal 1999 were only 37 percent of the annual budget. Part of the explanation lies in difficulties in expanding programs and establishing new ones. Rapid increases in budgets strain implementation capacity and may compromise targeting effectiveness and increase the risk of corruption and misuse. Concern about the transparency with which funds were spent likely contributed to the delay in program implementation in both Indonesia and Thailand.

Contrasting experiences with public works programs in Indonesia and Korea show how institutions matter. Korea's workfare program has good design and implementation and is making a difference in the lives of the poor. Indonesia's public works program is plagued by weak targeting of projects (box 6.5). In the six Indonesian regions where rapid appraisals were carried out, almost two-thirds of poor households did not participate in the projects—while many nonpoor households gained access. There may also be significant leakage because of weak governance and accountability.

Social policies to protect the vulnerable

Social policies in East Asia must reckon with the unfinished agenda of the precrisis years and respond to the new demands of an aging and increasingly urban population. Moreover, households are likely to be more vulnerable than before in a globalizing world with weaker traditional family support systems. These demands will likely find greater expression in the political arena than before, creating opportunities for constructive discussion of social issues—as well as risks that the agenda will be hijacked by special interest groups, to the detriment of the generally voiceless poor. Sound policies and effective institutions will be crucial to restore growth with equity, handle systemic crises, and put in place a safety net for people bypassed by growth. The international community may also have a role to play.

Regional trends: challenges and opportunities

The faces and structures of East Asian societies are changing rapidly. East Asia is becoming older, more urban, more formal, and more open economically and politically. These trends have important implications for social policies. Demographic changes will bring issues of old age security to the fore and require changes in public spending. Economic changes—driven by shifts in employment, greater urbanization, and continued globalization—will bring greater labor mobility and increased household insecurity. Increased political participation will put social

---

BOX 6.5

Implementing public works programs: lessons from Indonesia

Evaluations of public works programs in Indonesia suggest that just over one-third of poor households have participated. There has been significant leakage of benefits to the nonpoor. In Jakarta 9 percent of poor households worked on the scheme once, compared with 30 percent of middle-income households. In Medan only 5 of more than 400 poor households participated in the public works program, because the contractor used his own workers. The high level of leakage can be traced to several factors:

- Collusion with the project coordinator enabled some workers to work less than the prescribed hours at effectively higher wage rates.

- Projects implemented by the Manpower Department gave higher priority to displaced workers (who may not be poor).
- Sites and projects were not always selected to benefit the poor. Participation by the poor was also limited by weekly payment of wages, inconveniently located projects, rigid working hours (with no possibility of working part-time), and lack of consideration of local skills, abilities, and experience. Many of these criteria, in addition to types of work that were socially unacceptable for women and timing inconsistent with domestic responsibilities, led to lower participation by women. The government is looking into ways to reduce leakage and improve the participation of women.

Source: Klugman 1999b.

issues on the political agenda. All three trends will put pressure on informal, family-based mechanisms for household protection and increase demands for more formal, government-mandated schemes.

Demographic trends: rapid aging populations. Most countries in the region have rapidly aging populations, thanks to falling fertility and rising life expectancy. The old age dependency ratio—the population 65 and above to the population 15–64—is still relatively low, mostly from 5 to 8 percent, with the big exception of China (9.5 percent). But the ratio is projected to double in 30 years and triple in 40 years, reaching 27 percent by 2040—near the projected level in Eastern Europe and Central Asia and well above other developing regions. This aging is extremely rapid by historical standards: it took France 140 years and Sweden 86 years for their elderly populations to double.

Changing demographics have important consequences for public spending and social protection schemes. Life expectancy at age 65 currently ranges from 11.2 to 16.2 additional years for men and 12.2 to 19.7 additional years for women. Over the next 40 years the expected increase in life expectancy at age 65 is an additional 2 to 4 years. This suggests potentially greater vulnerability among the elderly and the need to focus on old age security, including pensions and health care. At the same time, the youth dependency ratio—the population 0–14 to the population 15–64—is projected to fall from about 41 percent now to 31 percent by 2040. This too has important consequences for government spending, particularly for education.

Changes in fertility and life expectancy in the region are closely related to income levels. Korea is furthest along in the demographic transition, with an old age dependency ratio projected to reach 40 percent by 2040. The corresponding figure for Lao PDR is 8 percent and for Cambodia, 11 percent. There are exceptions: China's population is aging more rapidly than its income level would suggest, and the reverse seems true for Malaysia. But in many countries there will be fewer working-age people supporting a growing share of elderly, with important implications for the coverage and design of pension schemes.

Economic trends: urbanization and services. In 1960 all East Asian countries had largely agrarian populations, with less than one-third of the total living in urban areas. Major societal changes in the past 40 years have increased the percentage of the urban population—most dramatically in Korea, where the urban population rose from less than 30 percent in 1960 to more than 80 percent in 1995. Urbanization will continue to increase over the next 30 years. By 2030 there will be few East Asian countries where the share of the urban population is less than 50 percent. In many others, such as Malaysia and the Philippines, at least 70 percent of the population is expected to be urban.

Projected trends in urbanization go hand in hand with economic transformation. In 1996 agriculture still accounted for a significant share of GDP and an even higher share of employment in many countries, reaching 70 percent or more in China and other transition economies. With continued industrialization and market liberalization, agriculture's share of employment is expected to drop quickly. Despite the recent setback induced by the crisis, more workers will be part of the formal labor market in market and transition economies alike.

These trends will probably weaken traditional support and coping mechanisms. In predominantly agrarian societies with large families, informal arrangements—such as intergenerational income support for the elderly—have worked well. Cultural traditions in Asia, which emphasize family values, have helped preserve these arrangements to some extent, but Japan and Korea suggest that the forces of "modernity" are strong. More than two-thirds of parents 60 and older still reside with an adult child in Malaysia, the Philippines, Thailand, and Vietnam. But in Korea only 49 percent did so in 1994, down from 78 percent in 1984. In Japan the proportion of people 60 and above whose family is their main source of income was 6 percent in 1990, down from 16 percent in 1981. (Though that is still much higher than in Western countries, with 0.1 percent in the United Kingdom and 0.7 percent in the United States.) Though Asian societies may exhibit greater familial solidarity than Western ones, the extent and coverage of private transfers are unlikely to be sufficient. Rapid urbanization combined with falling fertility and higher old age dependency ratios will place increased pressure on informal, family-based, and community-based income support systems.

At the same time, an increase in formal sector jobs generates a greater need for formal social protection mechanisms. Korea's recent experience illustrates the point: agriculture and the informal sector were unable to absorb the unemployed (unlike in Indonesia), resulting in the region's largest increase in open unemployment. But rising incomes, greater institutional capacity, and a more easily accessible tax base are all associated with increasing formalization, making it easier to meet these demands.

Finally, recent trends in trade, technology, capital flows, and political systems have led to an increasingly integrated world order. Sustained and expanding engagement with the global economy was an essential ingredient in the East Asian miracle and will continue to provide a strong impetus for productivity improvements in the region. But globalization can also increase volatility. Moreover, there is no guarantee that the benefits of global and regional integration will be shared across individuals, households, ethnic groups, communities, and countries. Globalization is likely to increase opportunities, but it may also make some groups more vulnerable. The answer is not to return to autarkic policies. Rather, countries should emphasize sound macroeconomic management, ensure that broad segments of society share in the fruits of global integration, and implement mechanisms to mitigate shocks when they occur.

Political trends: increased democracy and participation. The transition toward greater democracy and political participation in parts of the region is influencing the social agenda. Nongovernmental organizations (NGOs) and civil society more broadly are demanding greater accountability for the use of public resources, most strikingly in Indonesia but also in Thailand. This is healthy. But experience from the Philippines suggests that a vibrant NGO community does not always get results in the political arena. As political systems mature, concerns articulated by civil society groups will need to be integrated with mainstream political institutions.

These new demands on government will tend to push up government spending on social safety nets. Market economies will scale up their support in response to increased demands from a more vocal middle class. Transition economies (especially China) will cut their support for state employees in favor of more affordable and equitable systems.

Many countries will have to reach compromises on labor relations. Labor unions are already demanding that industrial relations be redefined to protect workers during hard times and to share benefits during good times. Navigating this relationship will be important—a balance should be struck between the legitimate concerns of workers and the need to maintain flexible labor markets. A possible compromise is retaining enterprise-level wage flexibility while putting in place mechanisms (such as unemployment insurance) that mitigate downside risks.

Another concern is that the political debate on social issues may revolve around the needs and aspirations of the new middle class—to the detriment of poor households and regions. Giving greater voice to the poor, and to champions of the poor, will be important. The international community should help keep this issue squarely on the table in discussions with the region's countries.

Principles for sound social policy

Every East Asian country will strike its own social bargain, reflecting an agenda, constituency, and process unique to that country. But some principles can be articulated drawing on the region's history, international experience, and lessons from the crisis.

Growth remains the greatest weapon against poverty. While the crisis interrupted steady gains in reducing poverty and improving overall welfare, it should not lead to a questioning of the importance of sound fundamentals, whether for macroeconomic or social policies. Indeed, the crisis highlighted how important growth is for poverty reduction—and how devastating contractions in output can be for the poor.

Growth has made the biggest contribution to reducing poverty in the region. Between 1978 and 1984 poverty dropped by 27 percentage points in Indonesia, and growth accounted for 70 percent of that impressive performance (figure 6.6). But distributional shifts have been significant in the region, and with rare exceptions (Malaysia in 1973–89, Indonesia in 1978–84) these have been adverse—resulting in higher inequality (including in Malaysia in the 1990s; World Bank 1997, 1998). In some countries distributional shifts have been large enough to swamp the positive contribution of growth and lead to a rise in poverty. Thailand in 1975–86 is the most striking example, but rural China in 1985–90 and the Philippines in 1988–91 had similar outcomes. Growth is essential. But the quality of that growth is also important. Given the overwhelmingly rural nature of poverty in East Asia, policies that contribute to rural growth are essential.

Policies should promote equitable access to services. Labor remains the poor's most important asset, and policies that increase the demand for labor and the quality of that labor are essential for broadly based growth. Improvements in human capital have made important contributions to the region's past growth, and widespread provision of basic health and education services is widely credited for the impressive gains in poverty reduction in the "miracle" countries.

But in many of the region's more advanced countries, poverty has become concentrated among those with little or no education. Continued investments in human capital are arguably even more important today than in the past, because the premium for skills is expected to increase in a world increasingly reliant on knowledge and technology. The risks of being left behind may also have increased.

It will become increasingly important for governments to ensure equitable access to health and education. Most East Asian countries have attained high enrollments at the primary level (with the notable exceptions of smaller, poor countries). The challenge now is to broaden access to secondary education and to improve the quality and relevance of that education. Given their incomes, some countries in the region, particularly Malaysia and Thailand, lag behind in expected secondary enrollments—more so in 1995 than in 1980 (figure 6.7). Broadening access to secondary education should become a priority for these countries.

The cost of education is a concern for the poor in some countries. In Vietnam the direct private costs of

Figure 6.6

Growth has done the most to reduce poverty

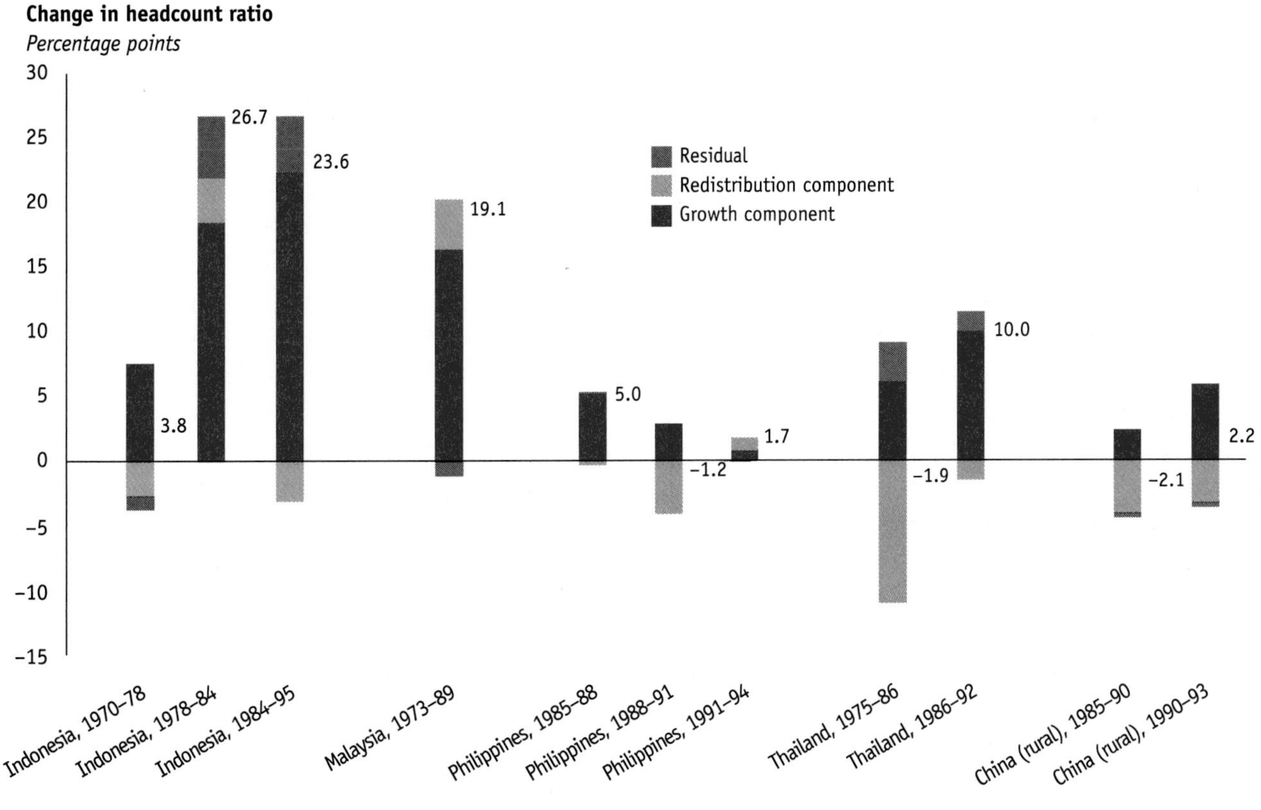

Change in headcount ratio
Percentage points

Note: Negative numbers signify an increase in poverty, and negative bars suggest that the component contributed to an increase in poverty.
Source: World Bank 1997.

Figure 6.7

Some countries have lower gross secondary enrollments than their incomes would suggest

Secondary enrollment rate, 1980

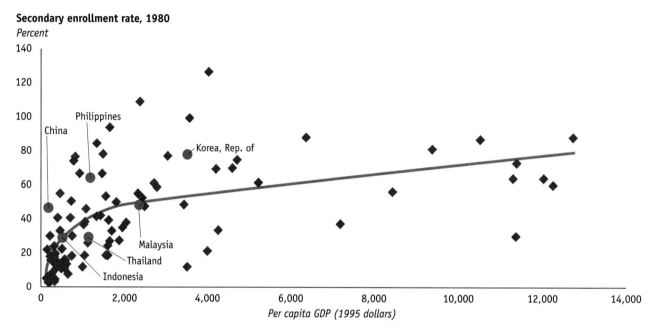

Percent

Secondary enrollment rate, 1995

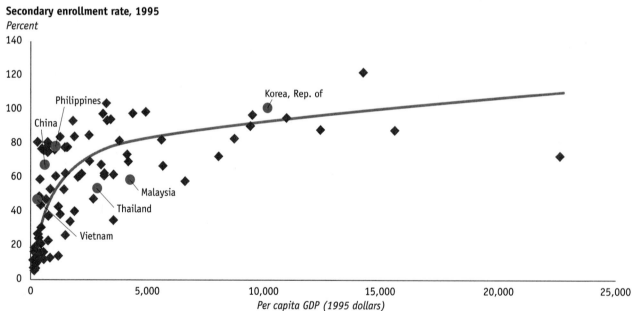

Percent

Source: World Bank data.

sending a child to upper secondary school for a household in the lowest income quintile is 58 percent of mean household income (World Bank 1996, p. 55). Because students and their parents are generally unable to borrow against future income, such high costs may be an insurmountable barrier for access to secondary education for poor children.

Many countries continue to see large disparities in education attainment between the rich and the poor. In the Philippines there are big differences in education attainment between the poorest households and the middle and richest households (figure 6.8). In Indonesia there are big differences between all three groups. This pattern is partly driven by differences in urban-rural education outcomes. In both countries rural children have much lower education attainment than their urban counterparts. Thus governments in the region must continue to make efforts to provide affordable, high-quality, relevant education to poor children—especially in rural areas.

Equitable access to public health care is also critical. In several East Asian countries out-of-pocket payments for health care account for a large share of total health care costs. This is highly inequitable—and along with poor quality, contributes to underuse of health services by the poor. Demographic changes will be favorable for some social expenditures but not for others. Given declining fertility, a constant overall level of resources should help increase per pupil spending on education and per patient spending on maternal and child health care. But aging populations may increase strains on the budget if fiscally sustainable solutions are not found to provide pensions and health care to the elderly.

Governments should be sensitive to the distributional implications of policies. Ideally, the incidence of government—as measured by the distributional impact of tax and spending policies—should be pro-poor. Governments need better information about the incidence of spending and taxes, and this information should be built into the budget process so that policy-

makers and political leaders are aware of tradeoffs when policy decisions are made. This is particularly important because the large increases in public debt resulting from government assumption of bank recapitalization costs will put tremendous pressure on noninterest spending in the crisis countries. Government policies need to ensure that the poor are not left holding the bill at the end of this process.

Countercyclical fiscal policies and programs can cushion adverse shocks. Sound macroeconomic policies help reduce the occurrence of systemic shocks. But policies that help households mitigate sudden downturns in income, some of which may be idiosyncratic, are also important—especially because much of the poverty observed at a given point may be transitory (Jalan and Ravallion 1998; Pritchett, Suryahadi, and Sumarto 2000). Because the region's economies are known for fiscal prudence, an expansionary stance during downturns would help smooth the adjustment without undermining fiscal sustainability and investor confidence. Programs with a built-in stabilization function, expanding automatically during crises, are especially useful because they help sustain economic activity and help vulnerable groups directly. Moreover, programs focused on the poor may have large multiplier effects

---

Figure 6.8

Education attainment tends to be lower for poor 15–19 year olds

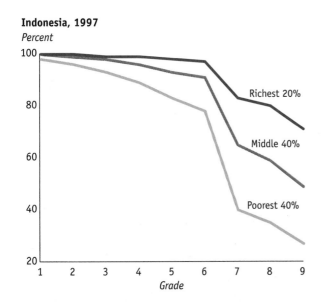

Indonesia, 1997
Percent

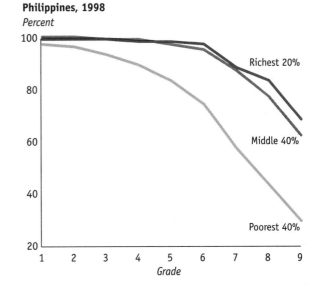

Philippines, 1998
Percent

Source: Filmer 1999.

since the poor typically consume a larger portion of their income than the nonpoor.

Such programs already exist in the region or were introduced in response to the crisis. They could become part of the permanent social safety net, operating at low levels of activity in good times but capable of responding to increasing demand in bad times. One concern, however, is that programs created or expanded during a crisis may generate constituencies that resist any attempt to scale them back thereafter.

Programs with automatic stabilization properties include insurance-based schemes (such as unemployment insurance), public works programs, and means-tested (or proxy tested) transfers. The choice of instrument will depend on the country and will normally be related to income, institutional capacity, and cultural norms and values. Social insurance programs typically require contributions and have specific rules on eligibility. Welfare or social assistance programs are typically financed out of general revenues and have eligibility requirements based on an assessment of need. Most governments in the region have opted for programs that do not reduce the incentive to work, and so have been reluctant to introduce unemployment insurance or expand income transfers. Although program design can help reduce adverse work incentives, effective insurance and transfer programs require a lot of information and institutional capacity to design, target, and manage well.

In principle, all means-tested programs can be responsive to a shift in vulnerability. But leaving aside resource constraints on program expansion, the effectiveness and frequency of testing are key to a timely response. In some cases it may be possible to identify proxy indicators that are reliable correlates of poverty and that are easier to measure than income. But targeting is complex, and few low-income countries do it well. Some countries rely on community information to identify the needy. This approach may be appropriate if local elites are not apt to capture the programs. But it makes the program response less automatic—an undesirable feature in a crisis.

Higher-income countries in the region have the capacity to implement targeted safety net programs, but there have been concerns about the possible disincentives associated with these programs. Ideally, safety nets should provide a consumption floor and encourage

investment in the assets of the poor—especially human capital accumulation—or social and physical infrastructure for the poor (Lustig 1999). Targeted human development programs have been used successfully in Latin America, including Mexico (box.6.6). These programs transfer income in cash or in kind to poor households with children, with the transfers conditioned on school attendance and health care visits. The income support reduces poverty and augments the household's future earning capacity by directing resources toward improving the nutrition, health, and education of children. Targeted human development programs should appeal to the East Asian ethos of self-help by linking transfers to productivity-enhancing interventions.

Programs that rely on self-selection provide an alternative to means testing, but they can be administratively cumbersome. Public workfare designed to reach the able-bodied poor is the best example. These programs provide an important countercyclical force and an effective poverty alleviation mechanism. Their benefits to the poor are maximized if they create assets that the poor value (schools, rural roads) and transfer income to maintain current consumption. Because unemployed workers have to show up for work to receive the benefits, workfare programs solve the incentive problem that unemployment insurance schemes have with informal or self-employed workers. In addition, demand for workfare can be an effective barometer of the distress in a community, which can be used to signal the need to scale up other pro-poor programs.

If leakages can be minimized, the costs of safety nets need not be large even if they reach many beneficiaries. For example, Progresa costs about 0.2 percent of Mexico's GDP and 1 percent of the federal budget—and the program reaches almost 2 million households (see box 6.6). The workfare program Trabajar in Argentina costs about 0.25 percent of GDP and reaches 350,000 unskilled, unemployed workers. Moreover, it transfers an average of 26 percent of family income, and as much as 74 percent of family income in households in the bottom 5 percent of the income distribution (Lustig 1999).

Better information, institutions, and coordination are needed. Effective social policies in general and crisis management in particular require better information systems, more responsive institutions, and better coordination across agencies and programs. The crisis

Targeted human development programs: Mexico's Progresa

Progresa is a targeted human development program in Mexico that provides a range of education, health, and nutrition interventions. In 1998 the program reached 1.9 million poor rural households—three-quarters of which were in the bottom quintile of the income distribution.

A thorough evaluation of Progresa is under way. But the preliminary results in terms of targeting effectiveness and school enrollments are encouraging. Poor people in beneficiary communities are more likely to enroll their children in school than are poor people in control communities, especially for children at the secondary level (grades seven to nine). Enrollments in grades three to six are 2.2 percentage points higher than they would be without the program, and secondary school enroll-

ments rose 4.9 percentage points. The continuation rate from primary to secondary education also increased significantly under the program. Secondary enrollments averaged 55 percent for children who had completed the program, compared with 43 percent in communities not reached by the program. Even after adjusting for past variations in enrollment rates, the increase remains significant.

Progresa has also eased education inequality in beneficiary communities. Before the program began, children of poor families attended grades one to eight less often than children of better-off families. This pattern was reversed after just one year of program grants, with the enrollment rates of the poor now higher in all but one grade.

Source: Lustig 1999.

---

revealed the need for a strategic and coordinated view of social policy and underscored the importance of transparent and accountable institutions. International evidence makes apparent the need for cohesion in crisis management. A number of countries (Korea, Thailand) created interministerial councils to ensure complementary approaches across the ministries engaged in social policies. The effectiveness of these bodies should be assessed to see whether they can continue to serve a useful function in normal times.

It will also be important to lock in some of the moves toward increased accountability. Decentralization and increased community involvement are likely to continue to provide a push for more responsive government institutions. While decentralization has potentially enormous rewards, there are also dangers. Decentralization of social services may weaken the quality of services, especially during a transition, and may increase regional disparities and inequity.

Future social policies and tradeoffs need to be made based on more solid information and analysis. The region has many micro surveys, but survey instruments could be made more relevant to policymaking. Adding modules or supplemental questionnaires that help assess the effectiveness (availability, quality, price) of social services and targeted programs is a priority in all countries. Questionnaires should also distinguish between public and private transfers and services. Surveys could be more frequent in some countries—for

example, a quarterly labor force survey should be standard in most countries. In addition, there are significant benefits from surveys that integrate quantitative and qualitative assessments, because the two types of data can be highly complementary. Finally, making survey data more widely available, building local capacity for analysis, and bolstering dissemination efforts would enhance the impact of information on policies.

In addition, there is a need to evaluate programs that purport to reach the poor. Such evaluations would arm governments with the information needed to make critical decisions on public spending in times of severe budget constraints. Some countries use program evaluations to make important policy choices. It may be possible to use program evaluations to reach not only a technical consensus on program rankings but also a political one. This would make countries better prepared for crisis and improve fiscal spending for the poor.

Notes

1. Comparable precrisis and postcrisis data are available for Indonesia, Korea, and Thailand. Malaysia's 1999 Household Income Survey is not yet publicly available. The Philippines conducted a new survey (Annual Poverty Indicators Survey, or APIS) in 1998 that included a panel element, with the intention of garnering information about the impact of the crisis. But consumption data between the regular survey (Family Income and Expenditure Survey, or FIES) conducted in 1997 and APIS are not comparable because the APIS consumption questionnaire was truncated. Nor are income data in the

two surveys comparable because of the shorter reference period used in APIS (six months, as opposed to one year in FIES).

2. A recent study (Diwan 1999) of 53 episodes of financial crisis in 135 countries from 1975 to the mid-1990s finds that the share of labor in GDP falls sharply following a financial crisis and recovers only partially in subsequent years. On average the share of labor in GDP was found to drop by 5.5 percentage points per crisis, although net losses (after partial recovery) were a smaller but still sizable 3 percentage points of GDP. The long-term trend decline in the share of labor observed over the past three decades in crisis countries, amounting to 4.1 percentage points of GDP, may reflect the manner in which financial crisis tend to be resolved—at the expense of labor.

3. Income data are available only for households where the head earns a wage or salary.

4. First, the flow of workers to Bangkok, particularly from the poorest region (Northeast), dropped dramatically from precrisis levels. Second, the type of workers who moved to Bangkok changed, with the proportion of unskilled workers decreasing from 25 to 14 percent of all migrants, and those with secondary or higher education increasing from 28 to 41 percent. These two changes reflect the collapse of unskilled and semiskilled opportunities in the capital. Third, the crisis changed the seasonality of migration, with similar emigration from Bangkok in both wet and dry seasons. Finally, the type of migrant leaving Bangkok changed, with more families (rather than individuals) moving as a result of the crisis (Thailand Social and Structural Review 1999).

5. Reliable spending estimates for social safety nets are difficult to obtain because programs are small and span a large number of ministries. Moreover, it is difficult to establish definitions that are consistent across countries and over time in a given country. For example, in Indonesia safety nets used to cover a wide range of programs, including basic health and education services. But in fiscal 2000 the government moved to a narrower "core" safety net.

6. Need could be demonstrated by shutting down two or more days a month, cutting hours by more than 10 percent, granting employees a month or more of leave, transferring workers to affiliates, or switching to a new line of business while retaining at least 60 percent of existing employees (Horton and Mazumdar 1999).

References

Abrahart, Alan, Gordon Betcherman, and Makoto Ogawa. 1999. "Indonesia: The Necessity for Reform: Labor Legislation and Social Protection." World Bank, Washington, D.C.

Abubakar, Syarisa Yanti. 1999. "Migrant Labour in Malaysia: Impacts and Implications of the Asian Economic Crisis." Malaysia Institute of Economic Research, Kuala Lumpur.

Asher, Mukul G. 1999a. "Social Safety Nets in East Asia: How Desirable? How Feasible?" National University of Singapore.

———. 1999b. "Social Security Reforms in Southeast Asia." National University of Singapore.

Betcherman, Gordon, Amit Dar, Amy Luinstra, and Makoto Ogawa. 1999. "Active Labor Market Policies: Policy Issues for East Asia." World Bank, Social Protection Unit, Washington, D.C.

Birdsall, Nancy, and Stephan Haggard. 1999. " Beyond the Crisis: A New Social Contract Renewing Growth with Equity in East Asia." Carngie Endowment for International Peace, Washington, D.C., and University of California, San Diego.

Booth, Anne. 1999a. "Education and Economic Development in Southeast Asia: Myths and Realities." Paper prepared for a conference on the social, institutional, and political causes of the Asian crisis, November, Lund, Sweden.

———. 1999b. "Education, Employment and Social Insurance in South East Asia: A Review of the Evidence and Policy Options in the Post Crises Era." Paper prepared for ASEM (Asia Europe Meeting) Regional Economist's Workshop: From Recovery to Sustainable Development, 15–17 September , Denpasar, Bali, Indonesia.

———. 1999c. "The Social Impact of the Asian Crisis: What Do We Know Two Years On?" *Asian-Pacific Economic Literature* 13 (2): 16–29.

Campbell, Duncan. 1999. "Globalization and Change: Social Dialogue and Labor Market Adjustment in the Crisis-Affected Countries in East Asia." International Labour Organization/EAS-MAT (East Asia Multidisciplinary Advisory Team), Bangkok, Thailand.

Diwan, Ishac. 1999. "Labor Shares and Financial Crises." World Bank, Washington, D.C.

Edwards, Alejandra Cox, and Chris Manning. 1999. "The Economics of Employment Protection and Unemployment Insurance Schemes: Reflections on Policy Options for Thailand, Malaysia, the Philippines and Indonesia." Paper presented at the World Bank–International Labour Organization–Japan Ministry of Labor/Japan Institute of Labor seminar on Economic Crisis, Employment, and Labour Markets in East and South-East Asia, 13–15 October, Tokyo.

Fallon, Peter. 1999. "The Impacts of Crises on Poverty and Income Distribution: Some Lessons from East Asia and Elsewhere." World Bank, Washington, D.C.

Fallon, Peter, and Robert E.B. Lucas. 1998. "Losers and Winners during Economic Crises." World Bank, Washington, D.C.

Filmer, Deon. 1999. "Educational Attainment and Enrollment Profiles: A Resource Book Based on an Analysis of Demographic and Health Surveys Data." World Bank, Washington, D.C.

Filmer, Deon, and Lant Pritchett. 1998. "Estimating Wealth Effects without Expenditure Data—or Tears: With an Application to Educational Enrollments in States of India." Policy Research Working Paper 1994. World Bank, Washington, D.C.

Goto, Junichi. 1999. "Labor Market Integration in East Asia—Present and Future." Inter-American Development Bank, Washington, D.C.

Horton, Susan, and Dipak Mazumdar. 1999. "Vulnerable Groups and the Labour Market: The Aftermath of the Asian Financial Crisis." Paper presented at the World Bank–International Labour Organization–Japan Ministry of Labor/Japan Institute of Labor seminar on Economic Crisis, Employment, and Labour Markets in East and South-East Asia, 13–15 October, Tokyo.

Jalan, Jyotsna, and Martin Ravallion. 1998. "Determinants of Transient and Chronic Poverty: Evidence from Rural China." Policy Research Working Paper 1936. World Bank, Washington, D.C.

Kakwani, Nanak, and Nicholas Prescott. 1999. "Impact of Economic Crisis on Poverty and Inequality in Korea." World Bank, Washington, D.C.

Kakwani, Nanak, and J. Pothong. 1999. "Impact of Economic Crisis on the Standard of Living in Thailand." National Economic and Social Development Board, Development Evaluation Division, Bangkok, Thailand.

Klugman, Jeni. 1999a. "The Poverty Impact of Government Safety Nets during Recent Periods of Economic Crisis." World Bank, Poverty Reduction and Economic Management Network, Poverty Unit, Washington, D.C.

———. 1999b. "Social Safety Nets and Crises." World Bank, Poverty Reduction and Economic Management Network, Poverty Unit, Washington, D.C.

Lustig, Nora. 1999. "Crises and the Poor: Socially Responsible Macroeconomics." Presidential Address, Latin America and Caribbean Economists Association Meeting, Santiago, Chile.

Marquez, Gustavo. 1999. "Labor Markets and Income Support: What Did We Learn from the Crises?" Inter-American Development Bank, Washington, D.C.

Mukherjee, Nilanjana. 1999. "Indonesia: Consultations with the Poor." Paper prepared for a World Bank Global Synthesis Workshop, 22–23 September, Washington, D.C.

Paxson, Christina H. 1992. "Using Weather Variability to Estimate the Response of Savings to Transitory Income in Thailand." *American Economic Review* 82: 15–33.

Pritchett, Lant, Asep Suryahadi, and Sudarno Sumarto. 2000. "Quantifying Vulnerability to Poverty: A Proposed Measure with an Application to Indonesia." World Bank, Washington, D.C.

Pyne, Hnin Hnin. 1999. "Gender Dimensions of the East Asian Crisis: A Review of Social Impact Studies in Korea, Indonesia, the Philippines and Thailand." World Bank, Environment and Social Development Unit, Washington, D.C.

World Bank. 1996. "Vietnam: Education Financing Sector Study." Washington, D.C.

———. 1997. *Everyone's Miracle? Revisiting Poverty and Inequality in East Asia.* A Directions in Development book. Washington, D.C.

———. 1998. *East Asia: The Road to Recovery.* Washington, D.C.

———. 1999a. "Beyond the Crisis: Structural Reform for Stable Growth." Thailand Social and Structural Review. Poverty Reduction and Economic Management Unit, Washington, D.C.

———. 1999b. "Towards an East Asian Social Protection Strategy." Washington, D.C.

Yusuf, Shahid. 1999. "Rethinking the East Asia Miracle." World Bank, World Development Report office, Washington, D.C.

CHAPTER 7

DEVELOPING STRATEGIES FOR A NEW MIRACLE

Asia is waking up from its two-year nightmare. But what a world to wake up to. Just ask Wong Ngit Liong, managing director of Venture Manufacturing Ltd. Two years ago, a custom order might take his company as much as eight weeks to fill. Today, the same order might have to be turned around in a couple of days. Could Asia's recovery lull the region back to business as usual? It had better not. As Mr. Wong's shrinking turn-around time shows, keeping up with the demands of a fast-changing world means there can be no business as usual. The landscape has changed for policymakers too. The world, Asian leaders are finding, has become a much more competitive place.

—Asian Wall Street Journal, 25 October 1999, p. S2

East Asia is once again the world's fastest-growing region (figure 7.1). The economic turnaround launched in 1999 has brought the region back from the abyss of rising poverty, falling living standards, and systemic convulsion of its productive and financial sectors. The sacrifices that farmers, workers, and middle classes made in tightening their belts and deferring consumption have been rewarded with rising incomes, falling unemployment, and a new competitiveness in international markets.

Still, the incomes of low- and middle-class citizens have not been fully restored, and the 13 million or so people that the crisis pushed into poverty can take little solace in these improvements. But rather than detract from the impressiveness of the recovery, these qualifications underscore the imperative of maintaining its pace, broadening its reach, and projecting it well into the future.

The challenge ahead is to convert today's recovery into a new era of rapid and sustained growth—an era with achievements rivaling those of the East Asian miracle years. Doing so is at once possible and difficult. It will be possible because East Asians save a lot, work hard, and have a demonstrated capacity for flexibility and institutional change. It will be difficult because future growth hinges less on increasing physical capital and more on raising the pro-

Figure 7.1

East Asia will grow faster than other regions

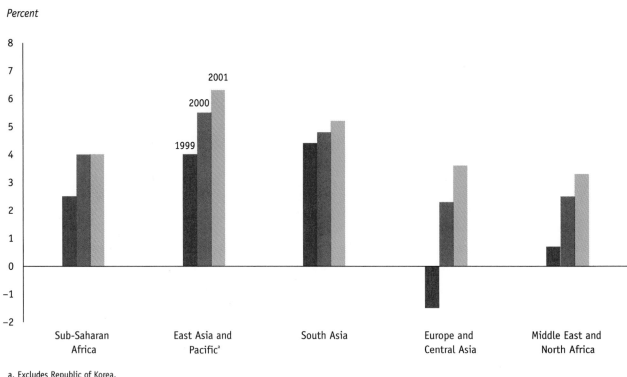

Percent

a. Excludes Republic of Korea.
Source: World Bank 2000a.

ductivity growth of all factors—by working smarter, adopting new technology, and combining people, knowledge, and capital in new ways. Raising productivity requires modern business, government, and social institutions that allow resources to be used more efficiently and flexibly, that enable technologies to be created and adopted more rapidly, and that harness the energies of all East Asians—including the poor.

The stakes for the region's poor are high. Today, 890 million East Asians live on less than $2 a day (see table 1.2). If regional growth averages 7 percent a year over the next decade and is equally shared, rising incomes would lift about half these people above the poverty line, reducing the number to below 452 million in 2008 (figure 7.2). Slow growth of 3 percent would leave more than 700 million people in poverty.

Policies that shape the pattern of growth—captured in changes in the distribution of income—also make a big difference. If incomes become more equally shared in processes of rapid growth (and Gini coefficients drop by 10 percentage points), the number of poor people could be cut to 383 million—much lower than the 509 million if this same growth is unequally shared. Similar dramatic outcomes can occur even if the more stringent $1 a day poverty line is used: rapid growth of 7 percent and improving income equality would reduce poverty from 278 million to 22 million.[1]

Whether a new era of growth is possible—given shifting demographics, expected savings, and productivity growth—is the subject of the next section. The subsequent section summarizes this report's main suggestions for institutions and offers a strategy for East Asia to realize its potential. The final section outlines ways regional cooperation and the international community can contribute to East Asia's success.

A new era of high growth?

East Asia's growth over the next decade will probably have to rely on fundamentals different from those that drove its superlative economic performance in the past.

Figure 7.2

Today's 892 million poor could be far fewer in 2008 if growth is rapid and broadly shared

Millions of people living on less than $2 a day in 2008

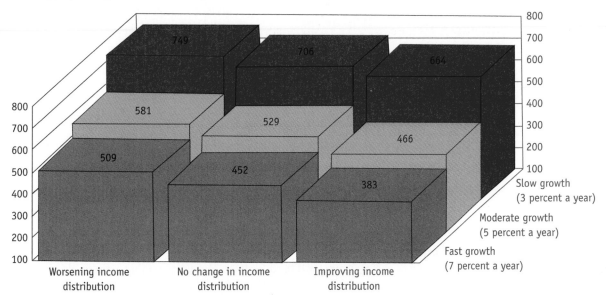

Note: Worsening income distribution assumes a 10 percentage point increase in the Gini coefficient. Improving income distribution assumes a 10 percentage point drop in the Gini coefficient.
Source: World Bank data.

The past as a predictor of the future: productivity

The East Asian miracle resulted from the region's high savings and capital accumulation, sustained investments in education, and market-friendly institutions (World Bank 1993). These factors enabled a rapid accumulation of physical capital and an ever more knowledgeable labor force, and allowed the main countries in the region to achieve average annual per capita growth of 5.1 percent in 1980–95 (table 7.1).

This growth can be decomposed into 6.1 percent growth in physical capital, 2.4 percent growth in human capital,[2] and 1.3 percent growth in total factor productivity. Growth in productivity is a residual meant to capture the application of new technology and information, improvements in how workers and capital are combined, and the efficiency with which inputs are used. Productivity gains at the industry level may have been larger (Nelson and Pack 1998). While different methodologies and choice of country samples can produce different numbers, these findings are broadly consistent with those of other studies.[3]

Performance varied significantly across countries. The Republic of Korea was the best performer (other than China), growing at nearly 8 percent per capita. This reflected extraordinary savings and investment rates that led to 9.5 percent per capita growth in physical capital. Korea also had the greatest success in raising education levels and (except for China) productivity. In contrast, the Philippines experienced stagnant per capita growth due to weak macroeconomic and trade policies that hampered investment and productivity growth.

Regaining—and maintaining—high growth rates will require greater emphasis on improving productivity. In fact, without higher productivity, output growth per capita will decline slightly, from 5.1 to 4.2 percent (figure 7.3).

Why? Consider investment in physical capital per worker. Since there are no technical reasons to expect savings rates to fall significantly (box 7.1), investment rates in the next decade will likely be only marginally lower than in the 1990s. But some East Asian countries have already created a large stock of capital, so the additional new capital per worker will be less (in percentage terms) than in the past.

TABLE 7.1

Dynamics of per capita growth, 1980–95

(percent)

Component	Indonesia	Korea,Rep. of	Malaysia	Philippines	Thailand	China [a]	Average	United States
Output	5.0	7.8	3.9	−0.3	6.0	8.2	5.1	1.6
Physical capital	6.4	9.5	5.4	0.1	7.6	7.3	6.1	1.5
Human capital	2.7	3.4	2.2	1.7	2.3	2.3	2.4	1.0
Labor force share in population	1.2	1.2	0.7	0.4	1.4	0.8	0.9	0.3
Labor force quality measure	1.5	2.2	1.5	1.3	1.0	1.5	1.5	0.7
Productivity	0.9	2.1	0.5	−1.4	1.9	4.0	1.3	0.3

Note: A constant returns to scale production function is used for this exercise. The share of physical capital in output is assumed to be 40 percent and the share of human capital to be 60 percent. The regional average is computed as a simple average. See the table note at the end of this chapter for a description of the methodology used to calculate the data in the table.

a. This productivity estimate for China includes a component—growth due to sectoral reallocation and to change in ownership from state to private owner—that has been estimated to account for about 1.5 percent of growth (World Bank 1996). Subtracting this component brings the productivity estimate to 2.5 percent of growth.

Source: World Bank staff estimates.

Assuming the same rate of annual investment in the next decade as in the 1990s, capital per person will grow more slowly in East Asia—at an average of 5.3 percent, compared with 6.1 percent in the past 15 years. This conclusion is consistent with Solow models that show diminishing returns are likely to set in, but only slowly over long periods (World Bank 1999, p. 5). These trends, however, do not hold for China, Malaysia, and the Philippines over the time period of the analysis.

Moreover, demographic factors will push down the contribution of labor to growth. Human capital is comprised of the number of workers and their average education attainment. But the region's labor force participation rates are already high by global standards, and women have easy access to employment. And workers in advanced East Asian countries already enjoy relatively high average education. These factors mean that the labor component—as measured narrowly by these variables—is unlikely to increase much.[4]

As with capital, raising education levels will be both difficult and unlikely to contribute much to East Asia's long-term growth—except in low-income countries, where education attainment is lower. Increasingly, raising productivity will involve improving the quality of education and realizing marginal gains in attainment rates.

Looking to the future: the role of institutions

If institutions facilitate savings and productivity growth to the same degree as in the past, growth rates will continue to be robust. Table 7.2 shows projections for 2001

assuming that the pace of policy reform continues and the international environment performs as expected. The table also shows potential growth through 2010 assuming that modest increases in productivity offset the slightly lower savings rates associated with rising incomes.

GDP growth could easily range from 5–7 percent in China, Korea, Malaysia, and Thailand—countries where high investment and respectable productivity growth have produced high growth in the past. Potential growth for Indonesia and the Philippines is 4–6 percent and depends more on realizing productivity growth that has been absent in recent years. The region's smaller economies have considerable potential but are more dependent on external factors. Still, the policy levers they control—particularly governance—can have huge impacts on long-term growth rates.

High growth will not come automatically. Success requires that institutions provide a favorable context for savings, investment, and productivity growth. Better institutions matter for growth (Barro 1996; Levine 1998). Using the World Bank's country policy and institutional scores, a 20 percent improvement in macroeconomic, trade, financial, and public institutions can add 1.2–2.0 percentage points to a country's per capita growth (see table 7.2).[5]

These results are similar to Hanna and Lawson's (1999) findings, which were constructed using the quite different World Economic Forum measures of international competitiveness. That study found that a 20 percent improvement in the WEF measure would add 2.1

Figure 7.3

Output growth per capita will fall if productivity growth does not improve...

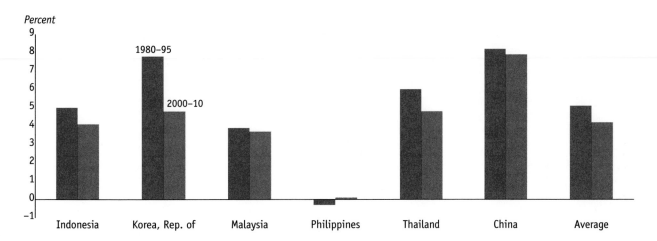

...because of declining capital accumulation...

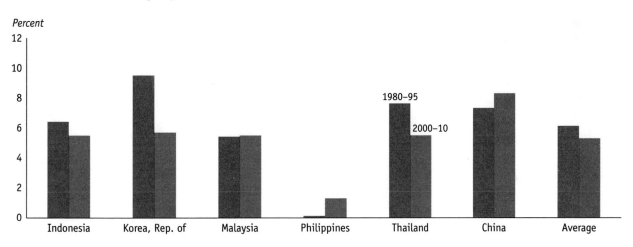

...and declining growth of effective labor

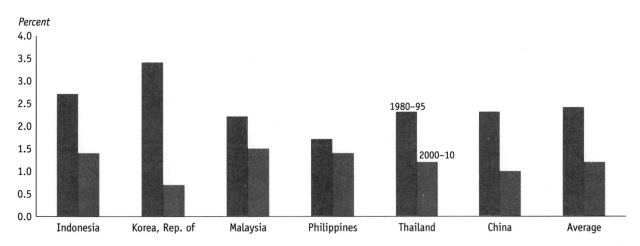

Source: World Bank staff estimates.

Is East Asia demographically doomed to slow growth? No

Fears that East Asia will experience slower growth because of falling savings and investment seem, in light of a recent study, unfounded. Bloom and Williamson (1998) argue that because East Asia's dependency ratio (the share of young and elderly people in the population) is certain to increase, savings rates will probably fall—because higher dependency ratios imply higher consumption. Moreover, since individuals are assumed to save less as they age and the average age will rise, savings could be predicted to fall. The authors' calculations indicate that the East Asian miracle was driven by high savings associated with population dynamics—a "demographic dividend"—but that this trend will reverse and work against continued high savings.

The anticipated impact of a lower savings rate is not consistent with recent evidence, however. Loayza, Schmidt-Hebbel, and Serven (1999) present cross-country evidence that the savings rate changes only slowly over long periods. In addition, recent analysis from the World Bank Savings Project indicates that the negative relationship between demography and savings is weak and is overshadowed by other factors—cultural norms, sound financial institutions, and so on. These factors tend to keep savings rates stable over long periods in most countries. Moreover, a reformulation of the life-cycle hypothesis of savings to include demographic variables reveals a weak fit between the simulated model and the data (Pritchett 1997). Savings may fall. But if they do, it probably will not be because of axiomatic links to demographic change.

TABLE 7.2
Past, projected, and potential real GDP growth in East Asia, 1999–2010
(percent)

Country	Estimate 1999	Projection 2000	Projection 2001	Growth potential 2002–10	Percentage point increase in GDP from better institutions[a]
Indonesia	0.2	4.2	5.0	4.0–6.0	1.4
Korea, Rep. of	10.7	7.0	6.0	4.5–6.5	2.0
Malaysia	5.4	6.0	6.1	6.0–8.0	2.0
Philippines	3.2	4.3	5.0	4.0–6.0	1.6
Thailand	4.2	4.8	5.0	5.0–7.0	1.8
China	7.1	7.0	7.2	5.5–7.5	1.8
Vietnam	4.7	4.6	5.0	4.5–6.5	1.4
Cambodia	4.0	5.5	6.0	5.0–7.0	1.2
Fiji	7.8	3.2	3.2	3.0–5.0	1.4
Lao PDR	4.0	4.5	5.0	5.0–7.0	1.2
Mongolia	3.3	4.3	4.5	4.0–6.0	1.4
Papua New Guinea	3.8	4.5	5.9	4.0–6.0	—
Solomon Islands	−0.5	−1.0	2.0	3.0–4.0	1.4

a. Percentage point increase in GDP associated with a 20 percent improvement in institutions and policies as scored by the World Bank and determined by cross-country regression estimates.
Source: World Bank staff estimates.

percentage points to economic growth. Thus even if savings and investment rates fall from their high perches over the next 10 years, potential productivity gains from better institutions could enable growth rates to attain their past velocity.

But take note: the institutions and policies that produced the East Asian miracle must now contend with globalization, demands for greater participation, and the legacies of the crisis. These forces will challenge the region's policies and institutions. The speed at which countries change their institutions will determine whether they can unleash their full growth potential over the next decade.

A strategy for institutions and growth

East Asia's development over the next 10 years will rest on three strategic initiatives for institutions and growth:

managing globalization, revitalizing business, and forging a new social contract. The first deals with how nations relate to the regional and global economies through finance and trade, as well as the forward-looking institutions that affect competitiveness. The second treats the way countries allocate resources through banks and corporations. The third is the way people and their governments interact through public institutions and social policy.

Managing globalization

In responding to the crisis, East Asian governments have not shrunk from globalization. To the contrary, even as private capital continued to bleed out of the crisis countries, policymakers searched for ways to intensify their links with global financial markets—but with policies and institutions that would reduce their exposure to sudden capital flight. Policymakers have worked hard to restore the confidence of international investors, lowered barriers to foreign participation in their economies, and resisted temptations to raise trade barriers (Pangestu 1999).

Many countries have opened once-protected domestic sectors to foreign direct investment. Indonesia raised foreign ownership limits in the financial and retail sectors from 49 to 100 percent, and in manufacturing from 51 to 100 percent. Korea raised foreign ownership limits in finance, manufacturing, and retail from 15–20 to 100 percent, and in utilities from 0 to 49 percent (Claessens, Djankov, and Klingebiel 1999). Korea also amended its Foreign Direct Investment Act to permit takeovers in nonstrategic sectors without government approval, raised the ceiling on foreign participation from 10.0 to 33.3 percent without approval by the company's board of directors, lifted restrictions on foreign ownership of land and real estate, and allowed foreign equity investment in nonlisted companies (IMF 1999a, pp. 39–40). Malaysia lifted limits on foreign ownership of utilities from 30 to 49 percent and maintained fully open markets in manufacturing and retail. Thailand permitted banks to be fully owned by foreigners for 10 years and is essentially open in manufacturing.

The exceptions to these trends toward closer integration have tended to prove the point. Malaysia's experiment with capital controls, undertaken largely after it had achieved financial stability and widely interpreted as a retreat from globalization, was quickly transformed from a prohibition on capital repatriation to a progressively smaller tax on short-term outflows. China's tightening of its foreign exchange regulations occurred as a minor footnote in the larger story of its World Trade Organization accession offer—an offer that would give foreign businesses market access to financial and other services. The agreement, announced in November 1999, would lower barriers to foreign entry and competition in many formerly closed areas, including insurance, banking, retail, and telecommunications.

This new openness came with important changes in regulations that allowed governments to mitigate the risks associated with globalization. Nearly all East Asian countries have tightened requirements for bank supervision, information disclosure, financial standards, and capital adequacy. Rules on loan classification, loan loss provisioning, and interest accrual have been universally tightened—according to the World Bank index of bank regulation, Indonesia, Korea, Malaysia, and Thailand improved from 1.75 to 2.45 (Claessens, Djankov, and Klingebiel 1999, p. 26).

China has also upgraded its bank regulations. Since 1997 it has ended credit quotas, improved the capital base of banks, adopted international loan classifications, issued new provisioning rules (though actual provisioning still lags), and set up mechanisms to begin asset resolution. These measures are intended to ensure better risk management consistent with international standards, so that—among other things—greater financial integration can proceed at lower risk.

All East Asian countries sought to expand trade with their neighbors and with the world. Of the five crisis countries only Thailand raised tariffs substantially—some even above its bound rates (WTO 1999). Indonesia, the Philippines, and Malaysia imposed only minor increases in tariffs; Korea did not increase any of its tariffs (Bora and Neufeld 2000). Of the East Asian countries not yet in compliance with the Agreement on Trade-Related Investment Measures, only Malaysia and the Philippines have asked for extensions of the transition period to meet their obligations under the agreement. Indonesia and Thailand have met their obligations (Bora and Neufeld 2000).

These changes mark a shift in development strategy. Still, it will take several years for their effects to be felt. It will take time to put in place a new system and make it work in ways consistent with the simultaneous and sometimes conflicting demands of local culture and globalization. Moreover, future challenges could derail growth.

Challenges for integration. East Asia did not manage financial integration well (chapter 2). Macroeconomic policy after 1992 in Indonesia, Korea, Malaysia, and Thailand facilitated too much reliance on foreign capital inflows and short-term debt. In 1996, when investors began showing concerns about debt levels, policy became expansionary to offset the effects of these expectations. In 1997 the situation became unsustainable. Meanwhile, domestic banks intermediated inflows poorly and without adequate hedges. In Indonesia corporations took on heavy exposure to offshore debt. This came on top of already high leverage ratios associated with rapid growth and overreliance on bank sources of funding.

By reducing or removing structural sources of macroeconomic vulnerability, national policies are the most important in helping to prevent crisis. Such policies include:

- Maintaining consistent macroeconomic policies, especially monetary and exchange rate policies.
- Managing external liabilities, with effective monitoring of private debt, removal of policy distortions that create incentives to borrow abroad (especially short-term), and measures that discourage excessive short-term borrowing.
- Accelerating the implementation of financial sector policies that emphasize prudent regulation, effective supervision, and full transparency—all with the objective of ensuring that banks match their assets and liabilities in accordance with sound banking practices.
- Improving disclosure on macroeconomic variables and corporate and financial data to equity investors and bond holders.

These recommendations are easy to recount, harder to translate into policies, and even harder to incorporate into the economic institutions needed to make them enduringly effective. Nonetheless, that is East Asia's challenge.

Challenges for trade, investment, and competitiveness. East Asia is re-emerging from the crisis as a world export powerhouse. A lack of trade competitiveness did not cause the East Asian crisis. Long-term trends in exports show that the region was competitive going into the crisis and has come out even more so. Exports from Southeast Asia and China have grown more rapidly than competing products in world markets.

True, more advanced economies—Hong Kong (China), Korea, Singapore, Taiwan (China)—were beginning to lose market share in the mid-1990s in North America and Europe (chapter 3). But that trend may have reflected increased foreign investment in China and elsewhere as these economies shifted toward services. Moreover, nearly all the economies in the region produce exports that are among the fastest-growing segments of world trade. Exports of their major products are growing quickly as a component of world trade. Finally, because East Asia is once again a fast-growing region, all countries benefit from internal growth.

In other respects, however, the bloom was falling off the East Asian rose before the crisis. Foreign direct investment to the region (save China) was flagging relative to other regions. As a share of GDP, foreign direct investment barely advanced in the 1990s, and the region's share of global foreign direct investment tapered off (UNCTAD 1999, p. 53). Foreign direct investment in China surged after 1992, some portion of which entailed recycling of Chinese residents' funds back into the country as foreign investment eligible for preferential tax treatment.

Other regions, notably Latin America, fared much better in the 1990s. One conclusion is that East Asia failed to keep pace with policy improvements elsewhere. While other regions were busy implementing more welcoming policies, including new access to areas once monopolized by the state, East Asia mostly maintained a restrictive stance to foreign direct investment in favored sectors.

The crisis is changing East Asia's stance toward foreign investment. Korea has learned that opening to foreign investors can increase efficiency and deliver new capital to cash-strapped businesses. Foreign entry through acquisitions surged from less than 10 percent in 1993–96 to 50 percent in 1998. Thailand, after much political debate, has allowed foreign investors to participate in its financial sector. Even China, with the region's most restrictive foreign direct investment policies, has undertaken startling new commitments as part of its World Trade Organization (WTO) accession offer (see box 3.1). All these changes mark an important development in East Asia's attitude toward globalization—countries in the region have decided to opt in rather than retreat.

But much remains to be done. Governments can help themselves through unilateral actions to improve trade and foreign investment policies, including further lowering trade protection, narrowing tariff dispersion, and reducing exemptions—these tend to create uneconomic rents and drag down productivity. Over the long run East Asia must raise its productivity through a more flexible education system (particularly at secondary and tertiary levels) and reforms that encourage innovation and adoption of new technology. A heavy-handed role for the state in education and state monopolies in information industries seem increasingly anachronistic and unlikely to generate the benefits associated with flexibility.

Trade is also amenable to collective action. Especially important is reducing trade barriers within the region in accord with the Association of Southeast Asian Nations (ASEAN) Free Trade Area (AFTA). The AFTA, established in 1992, aspired to establish free trade by 2008 for most products and countries. In 1994 it agreed to try to reach that goal by 2003. With diligent implementation, 98 percent of tariffs will be 0–5 percent by 2003 (2006 for Vietnam and 2008 for Lao PDR and Myanmar). Agricultural tariffs will be lowered a bit more slowly. ASEAN members have made substantial commitments to AFTA—54,367 of 55,525 tariff lines will be cut. To be effective, regional agreements must ensure that trade creation outweighs trade diversion by moving toward a general reduction of trade protection inherent in liberalization based on most-favored-nation arrangements.

Similarly, trade commitments made through the Asia-Pacific Economic Cooperation (APEC) group should be honored swiftly.[5] When the group met in 1994, it set a goal of realizing a free and open trade and investment area in Asia and the Pacific by 2010 for industrial economies and 2020 for developing economies. Unlike AFTA, trade liberalization through APEC is voluntary, unilateral, and nondiscriminatory. Although progress toward liberalization outside the WTO has been disappointing, APEC has complemented the WTO's work in areas like the Information Technology Agreement, which was endorsed by APEC before being accepted by the WTO. APEC trade ministers recently agreed to support the launch of a new round of WTO trade negotiations. The ministers also encouraged the acceleration of accession negotiations for APEC's non-WTO members, and agreed that these countries should be able to participate in the forthcoming WTO round. APEC also agreed to include manufacturing in the WTO negotiations. APEC's support for the abolition of agricultural export subsidies will send a powerful message to the European Union.

The international community has provided indirect support for East Asia's recovery. Despite the sudden drop in international prices, Western Europe and the United States have maintained open markets. Moreover, OECD countries have generally adopted policies that promote a stable and expanding global economy. In the immediate future the most pressing item on East Asia's trade agenda will be moving forward with China's accession to the WTO. Should China become a WTO member, expanded trade would raise incomes worldwide by $60–90 billion (Martin and Hertel 1999). A second agenda item is the launch of the recently deferred millennium round of trade discussions. These will further liberalize trade in services, agriculture, and textiles. Facilitating trade flows is probably the most important policy move—unilateral, regional, and multilateral—that governments can make to ensure high and sustained growth.

Revitalizing business

The systemic collapse of East Asia's financial sectors forced the crisis countries to rethink the relationship between banks and corporations and between businesses and governments. Moreover, lessons have rippled across the region, prompting even countries only marginally affected by the crisis—such as China—to change their objectives for business organization.

Fundamental changes have been made to laws governing banks, to the structure of the financial sector and industry, and to the governance of corporations and banks. Indonesia, Korea, and Thailand have strengthened financial sector regulation and invested substantially in prudential supervision. Malaysia, after initially backing away from world-class standards, later infused them with new vigor. China too has enacted new, internationally acceptable standards for prudential regulation.

The crisis has radically altered the structure of the financial industry. Thailand has closed 57 of 91 finance companies. Korea has shut down more than 200 institutions, including the merchant banks responsible for building up private debt before the crisis. And Indonesia has shut down 66 of 237 banks. Moreover, Korea and Thailand have for the first time allowed foreign ownership of banks.

More new ownership is likely. Indonesia has invested 18 percent of GDP in providing liquidity to banks and over 30 percent in recapitalizing banks. Korea has invested 5 percent of GDP in providing liquidity support and another 11 percent in recapitalizing banks. Malaysia has provided 13 percent of GDP in liquidity support and another 2.4 percent in recapitalization, while Thailand has invested 20 percent in liquidity support and 17 percent in public and private banks. China, with a much larger potential problem, has committed $33 billion to bank recapitalization (see table 4.3).

Liquidity support and recapitalization efforts—undertaken to preserve depositor and investor confidence in banks—have left governments with huge ownership shares in the economy. The Indonesian government now holds 78 percent of bank assets through state banks or large shares of private banks. The Korean government holds 58 percent of bank assets, Thailand holds 32 percent, and Malaysia holds 18 percent. An even larger process is under way in China, where the state is divesting state enterprises and assets acquired through the recent closure of investment and trust corporations.

Since 1997 governments have implemented new financial regulations and laws providing new governance systems for corporations and banks. In all the crisis countries except Malaysia, governments have passed new laws on corporate bankruptcy and equity and creditor rights. The first wave of bankruptcies has begun and will impose new discipline on corporate behavior for years to come. As in the financial sector, governments are allowing increasing foreign ownership in once-closed sectors, such as telecommunications. The shift in strategy has rekindled confidence among domestic and foreign investors—and been requited with strong economic recovery.

But efforts to revitalize business are incomplete and vulnerable to policy complacency or reversal. Not enough progress has been made on banking and corporate distress to resolve the uncertainties hanging over the recovery and future prospects. Attention has rightly focused on bank and corporate restructuring. Four challenges loom.

First, despite capital injections, banks' balance sheets are weak. Nonperforming loans are five times loan loss provisions in Indonesia, Korea, Malaysia, and Thailand—and much more than that in China. Banks need more capital. The capital shortfall ranges from 2 percent of bank assets in Malaysia to 18 percent in Indonesia, with Korea (4 percent) and Thailand (8 percent) in between.

Second, corporations are still overindebted, with loans accruing interest that cannot be paid. The process is lagging far behind in Indonesia—by late 1999 just 17 percent of debt restructuring was complete. Thailand, with 29 percent of its debt restructured, was not much further ahead, though it enjoys far more favorable political circumstances. Korea had restructured 48 percent of its debt and Malaysia, 32 percent; both have to press forward. In the immediate future, a large share of corporations in the crisis countries project operating profits insufficient to cover interest expenses.

The outlook may not be entirely dim, however, because the operational restructuring that often accompanies debt restructuring may be less of a problem than was originally anticipated. In the depths of the crisis it seemed that complete restructuring of real activities and business organization might be required. After all, profits were declining in the years just before the crisis, and many companies had overinvested in nontradables. But with current relative prices and exchange rates, it appears that firms' operations are on sounder foundations (chapter 4).

Third, the crisis has made government the owner and manager of many large corporations and banks at just the time when globalization demands a shift toward a smaller direct role for the state complemented by a stronger regulatory role. Thus the crisis countries face two tasks. They must sell off many of these assets in a way that maximizes their value to the state and reduces rising public debt. And they must do so in a way that imposes adequate penalties on past owners, introduces competition in the subsequent business organization, and (hopefully) broadens the ownership of capital. The enormity of this agenda is only now being realized.

Fourth, East Asia's experience points to the importance of reducing the government's role in allocating resources. Directed credit, loan guarantees, tax credits, and distorting trade restrictions have often failed to create new, internationally competitive industries. Yet they have created private expectations that government, having encouraged an industry's development, would come to its rescue in the event of financial difficulties. Such provisions may have worked during early stages of development, but many have already been phased out. Even China was eliminating directed credit before the crisis. Under agreements with the WTO and APEC, the most distorting trade incentives are being phased out. Tax subsidies are a final remnant of government intervention in resource flows.

Whether governments respond adequately to these four challenges will shape the pace of future income growth. Only with better-capitalized banks can savings be efficiently intermediated into the investments needed to realize a country's growth potential. Only with restructured balance sheets can corporations be the creditworthy, dynamic clients that banks and capital markets need to realize rapid growth. And only by realizing maximum gains from government-held financial assets and ensuring that subsequent business organization is competitive can the public sector reduce its debt and ensure effective market performance.

Forging a new social contract: the role of government

The social contract—the implicit agreement between the governed and their government—is changing in East Asia. Even before the crisis, East Asians were becoming less inclined to accept limited participation in government, limited accountability from officials, and a partial social safety net in exchange for fast-rising incomes. The cessation of growth unleashed forces of political change, leading to new governments in Indonesia, Korea, and Thailand.

The crisis has left different legacies for these new administrations. One is debt. Rising public debt service has squeezed noninterest public spending just when governments want to spend more protecting low-income groups from falling wages and employment, and to invest more in infrastructure, cities, and customs administration. The crisis revealed that many public institutions are not equipped to face the challenges of a modern, globalized economy. Most budget institutions have had trouble adjusting to new priorities and adapting to more flexible and innovative spending.

Although political administrations have changed in most crisis countries, the institutional tasks of public sector reform have barely begun. Fiscal pressures—emanating from debt burdens and larger changes in society—and globalization are making countries rethink the role of the state. Under pressure to do more with less, governments will have to focus on regulations that support market development, contain its negative spinoffs, and help incorporate those left behind; they may have to enlist private investment in activities that are now the sole domain of the state. Governments are also rethinking the organization of the state and according more responsibility and power to subnational governments. Finally, governments are being compelled to improve institutions of public management—revenue and spending agencies and ministries—as well as the civil service.

The crisis also revealed that growth is no substitute for an effective social safety net—and the deep recession has heightened insecurity. The poor, the sick, and the elderly are likely to demand new protection from rapidly changing markets. Growth is a prerequisite for reducing poverty, increasing incomes, and creating jobs. But societies integrated with the global economy are not immune from recessions or external shocks. East Asia has lagged other developing regions in helping families provide security for the elderly. Moreover, countries were unprepared to deal with the scale of human suffering inflicted by a systemic crisis. Delayed, partial, and fragmented responses imposed high costs on East Asians. The institutions, information systems, and safety nets in place before the crisis constrained governments' ability to respond adequately and quickly.

These facts point to new policy directions. Governments have to foster institutions able to respond to an aging, increasingly urban population that is likely to feel more vulnerable in a globalizing world with weaker traditional family support systems. Government information systems must respond faster in times of crisis. And social safety nets have to be stronger—and able to expand (or contract) in line with economic conditions. Policies on pensions and unemployment insurance will vary by country. Across the region, however, citizen demands for effective programs will likely find greater expression in the political arena. Making the poor part of the growth process—by raising their productivity—will become increasingly central to ensuring that rising incomes are broadly shared.

Balancing the agenda: a country affair

Each East Asian country has to strike the right balance as it rises to the challenges of managing globalization, revitalizing business, and forging a new social contract. For the crisis countries, the agenda is focused on the most advanced aspects of institutional improvements—managing open capital accounts, working out the lingering effects of the crisis, improving public administration, educating the poor. To increase productivity, Korea's government has turned to institutional priorities—particularly in education—associated with linking to the knowledge economy. Malaysia and Thailand are completing the restructuring agenda, increasing competition in business and finance, and improving education both for the poor and for the relatively well educated. In Indonesia and the Philippines, improving governance and bringing the poor into the growth process can pay especially high dividends to efforts to strengthen institutions.

For China and Vietnam the agenda revolves around institutional reforms to accelerate the transition from plan to market. Private firms must play a central role, with the government focusing on regulation to balance the social and environmental repercussions of market-led development. New institutional arrangements will support stable, rapid growth and should precede full openness in the capital account. But today's cumbersome restrictions cannot long stave off the steady march of financial integration that has already begun, so governments must use the next few years to manage the process—to avoid being overrun by it. China, with its well-developed program and WTO offer, has charted a sophisticated path toward integration. Vietnam is only beginning to formulate its bold course.

The region's small countries, though badly hurt by the crisis, emerged with their basic institutions relatively free of crisis-driven pressure to change. As a result the small countries have not kept pace with the struggle of the more advanced countries to develop institutions that harness global market forces to national advantage. The small countries risk being left behind. To profit from globalization, they must rise to their most daunting challenges. Managing globalization entails coping with sharp terms of trade shifts associated with widely fluctuating commodity prices, and doing this requires better government institutions. Public governance should convey confidence—not corruption—to investors. Policies should convey neutrality to best promote local development. And social policies should create opportunities for the countries' large, poor, and often rural populations to benefit from an expanding economy. In Mongolia the governance agenda involves consolidating a still-fragile democracy, improving public spending institutions, and investing in public infrastructure. Many of the same things could be said for Cambodia, but moving swiftly to restore public—and investor—confidence in public institutions is an unusually high priority. Lao PDR and resource-rich Papua New Guinea face similar challenges. The other Pacific Islands have inflated, aid-dependent public sectors that, along with regulations protecting certain businesses and interest groups, deprive the region of foreign and domestic investment that could elevate growth.

Regional and multilateral initiatives for a new era of growth

East Asia is a $2.1 trillion regional economy and the home of 1.7 billion people. Thus common regional policies offer a potentially powerful force in the global economy. The crisis showed that regional activities could supplement multilateral arrangements to cope with volatile capital flows, currency crises, and contagion.

In addition to the regional trading arrangements discussed above, regional economic arrangements often include modalities for mutual consultation, surveillance, and collaboration on a broad range of economic policies. Regional arrangements for policy coordination in East Asia include a network of bilateral repurchase agreements among central banks, the Executives Meeting of East Asia and Pacific Central Banks, the Six Markets Meeting, the APEC Finance Ministers Meeting for financial cooperation, and the ASEAN Ministers Meeting. One of these arrangements' objectives is to establish a cooperative framework to cope with currency crises through frequent exchanges of information and the network of repurchase arrangements involving dollar-denominated foreign exchange reserves.

In addition, a framework for regional financial cooperation emerged spontaneously following the baht crisis. Japan was by far the largest contributor (box 7.2). Although a proposal for an Asian Monetary Fund did not get off the ground, in 1997 finance ministers and

Japan's Miyazawa Initiative

Among bilateral donors offering support to East Asia's crisis-affected countries, Japan deserves special mention. In October 1998, as it became apparent that more official capital would be needed to offset huge outflows, Japan pledged $30 billion to support the crisis countries. Half of the pledged amount was to be dedicated to short-term capital needs during the process of implementing economic reforms. The rest was earmarked for medium- and long-term reforms. By February 2000, $21 billion had been committed, with $13.5 billion for medium- and long-term reforms.

Korea has been the largest recipient ($8.4 billion), followed by Malaysia ($4.4 billion), Indonesia and Thailand ($2.9 billion each), and the Philippines ($2.5 billion). The initiative has supported economic adjustment, financial and corporate restructuring, social safety nets, infrastructure, and export financing. Some programs cofinanced reform packages with the IMF, World Bank, and Asian Development Bank. In the second phase of the initiative, Japan has partially guaranteed sovereign debt issues, enabling countries to use limited public resources to mobilize private capital, thereby promoting private debt markets.

deputies in the region agreed to establish a cooperative arrangement of regional surveillance, called the Manila Framework, in a way consistent with the IMF–World Bank framework. The ASEAN Economic Monitoring Process has also been strengthened since the crisis, supported by international financial institutions. Financing from international financial institutions—the IMF, World Bank, and Asian Development Bank—has been supplemented by financing from countries in the region.

Regional consultation and economic monitoring should include exchange of macroeconomic and structural information on fiscal positions, monetary and exchange rate policies (including domestic and foreign assets and liabilities of central banks), capital flows, external debt, financial system conditions, and corporate developments. With effective consultation and monitoring, the region's economies will face peer pressure to pursue disciplined policies conducive to stable currencies and external accounts.

Other policies worth discussing in regional forums could include efforts to improve common standards, transparency and mutual surveillance, policies on short-term capital flows, and trade and investment. Several entities—including private organizations, the World Bank, and the IMF—are developing standards that could be adopted and promulgated through regional entities. Exchange of information among governments and central banks could also lead to greater macroeconomic collaboration, including concerted policies, temporary swap agreements, and the like.

New regional efforts through APEC and ASEAN could include establishing common disclosure requirements for private firms based on agreed accounting principles, perhaps by way of implementing globally agreed principles. Also feasible are:

- Disseminating data on reserves and external debt, including initiatives under way under the auspices of the IMF.
- Improving fiscal transparency and practices—a process that can elicit technical support and sponsorship from the IMF and World Bank.
- Developing common procedures and methods to quantify tax expenditures and (possibly competitive) production subsidies.
- Setting standards for good social practices, now under development by the World Bank.
- Creating a system for early warning modeling (this field is still in its infancy, so first efforts might be to monitor developments by international financial institutions and the private sector on behalf of regional ministers).

Policies on short-term capital flows could be directed toward minimizing volatility across the region and between the region and the rest of the world. Short-term capital flows were the primary source of financial contagion and volatility in the region. Developing market-friendly ways to offset the potential social costs of short-term capital volatility could help countries establish a common policy framework that would avoid disadvantage to any. Policies now under discussion could raise the cost of short-term borrowing by taxing inflows, setting higher reserve requirements, or requiring central bank fees for sovereign guarantees. These could be linked to better regulation of banks to ensure that assets are better matched to liabilities (World Bank 2000a).

The international community was a significant actor in the East Asian drama. As private capital fled the region, official capital poured in and helped stabilize capital accounts. Official flows to Indonesia, Korea, Malaysia, the Philippines, and Thailand rose from –$1 billion in 1996 to $29 billion in 1997 and $22 billion in 1998 (in gross terms). Between fiscal 1996 and 1999 the World Bank more than doubled its disbursements to the region, from $4 billion to $9 billion.

Almost always, multilateral initiatives were accompanied by substantial financial support from Japan and other OECD countries—and even in some cases from economies in the region, such as China and Singapore. Bilateral flows averaged nearly $4 billion in 1997–99, up from a mere $300 million. The region will continue to receive long-term official and multilateral support, but the amounts will taper off and the composition of lending will likely shift back toward low-income East Asia and toward conventional project lending (away from balance of payments support).

Several initiatives are being considered in discussions on international financial architecture among the G–22 and by the boards of the IMF and World Bank (World Bank 2000b; IMF 2000) (box 7.3). In addition to standards and disclosure these include debt standstills in emergency financial packages, the amount and form of external aid, and appropriate conditions for lending, particularly the balance between short-term macroeconomic targets and structural policies (Eichengreen 1999; Fischer 1999; Bhattacharya and Kawai 1999). East Asia—and other developing countries—would benefit from an expeditious and supportive resolution of these discussions.

BOX 7.3

Fostering a supportive international financial architecture

The East Asian crisis led to a proliferation of discussions on international financial architecture. The general objective within the international community is to enhance international capital flows and reduce their volatility. One area of focus is better information and transparency. More and timelier information on the exposures of international lenders, particularly to short-term lending, would point out potential weaknesses sooner. The World Bank and IMF, among others, have been working on new standards for disseminating data on reserves and external debt, and subscribing countries are slated to adopt these in 2000 (Nellor 1999). In addition, new codes of good practices on fiscal, monetary, and financial practices have been approved.

Another area is banking and supervision, where strengthening of the Basle core principles is ongoing. A third area is securities markets. The International Organization of Securities Commissions has prepared principles and standards for disclosure, and implementation is being discussed. A fourth area, accounting and auditing, is under review by the International Accounting Standards Committee, with the objective of uniform standards by 2002. The IMF and World Bank have begun a pilot program of financial sector assessments to assess countries' financial systems and their efforts to implement these principles. Bankruptcy and corporate governance have been the subjects of the United Nations Commission on International Trade Law's model law of cross-border insolvency, now under dissemination to government, as well as the OECD Task Force on principles of corporate governance. These measures can help prevent crisis by providing better information to markets.

More contentious is the balance of official and private finance in response to massive capital flight and crisis. Even before the East Asian crisis, the G–10's 1996 report, *The Resolution of Sovereign Liquidity Crises,* urged the IMF to try to minimize moral hazard for debtors and creditors and "strengthen the ability of governments to resist pressures to assume responsibility for the external liabilities of their private sectors." Though in most situations a strong policy response by the country—coupled with official resources—can provide the basis for stabilization and a return to growth, there may be situations in which the catalytic effect of the program is insufficient. In these situations it may be necessary to take steps to secure additional private involvement, whether through the accrual of arrears or other mechanisms to ensure that burdens are shared with private creditors (Fischer 1999a).

There are two reasons for this. The first is to ensure that investors do not make their decisions with the expectation that they will be bailed out should investments turn bad. Second, official lenders have limited resources that, in some situations, simply cannot finance stabilization and recovery programs. East Asia tested the limits of the possible in this regard. A companion change being considered is to modify standard bond and lending contracts to require majority (rather than unanimity) on debt restructuring programs, and to allow greater discrimination on the part of payments to individual creditors.

These issues are now being debated (see Eichengreen 1999; Fischer 1999b; World Bank 2000b; and IMF 2000). Outcomes that lead to more transparent, rules-based procedures may provide better measures of the costs and benefits of lending, reduce moral hazard, and reduce unpredictable shocks to markets.

Toward a new development strategy

The tumult that jolted the region and the world has prompted a sea change in the way East Asian countries approach globalization, in the way business is organized, and in the social contract between governments and governed. In the wake of the crisis, nearly every country has initiated the profound institutional changes—in trade and finance, in business, and in government and social policy—needed to launch a new era of high growth. A strong recovery has been the reward for the difficult first stages of implementing new policies.

It remains to be seen whether the recovery will facilitate the second stage of reform that will lead to years of continued rapid growth. Recovery could lead to policy complacency and slow reform under pressures from vested political interests—in which case today's recovery would become weighed down by tomorrow's debt service, mounting nonperforming loans in banks, and broken corporations, leaving the region exposed to the next wave of international shocks.

Two parts of the answer are clear. East Asian countries have the resources, human and financial, to achieve a new era of broadly shared rapid growth. In that sense they enter the new millennium largely in control of their destiny. And by embracing globalization and attempting to manage it to national advantage, countries have made an impressive start.

Ten years from now, standing firmly in the new millennium, East Asians will look back and see the crisis of 1997 as a major turning point in their history. And they will see the results clearly—as either an opportunity for institutional change that was missed or the beginning of a profound historical transformation.

ANNEX
Studies of total factor productivity growth in East Asia

Country, author	Publication year	Period covered	Annual change in productivity (percent)
Indonesia			
World Bank	1993	1960–89	1.3
Kawai	1994	1970–90	1.5
Nehru and Dhareswar	1994	1960–90	0.2
Bosworth and others	1995	1960–94	0.8
Drysdale and Huang	1995	1962–90	2.1
Sarel	1996	1978–96	1.2
Average			1.2
Standard deviation			0.6
Korea, Rep. of			
World Bank	1993	1960–85	2.2
Bosworth and others	1995	1960–94	1.5
Young	1995	1966–90	1.7
Average			1.8
Standard deviation			0.4
Malaysia			
World Bank	1993	1960–89	1.1
Kawai	1994	1970–90	1.6
Nehru and Dhareswar	1994	1960–90	−0.2
Bosworth and others	1995	1960–94	0.9
Drysdale and Huang	1995	1950–90	−0.5
Sarel	1996	1978–96	2.0
Average			0.8
Standard deviation			1.0
Philippines			
Kawai	1994	1970–90	−0.7
Nehru and Dhareswar	1994	1960–90	−0.8
Bosworth and others	1995	1960–94	−0.4
Drysdale and Huang	1995	1950–90	0.2
Sarel	1996	1978–96	−0.8
Average			−0.5
Standard deviation			0.4

Country, author	Publication year	Period covered	Annual change in productivity (percent)
Thailand			
World Bank	1993	1960–89	2.5
Kawai	1994	1970–90	1.9
Nehru and Dhareswar	1994	1960–90	0.1
Bosworth and others	1995	1960–94	1.8
Drysdale and Huang	1995	1950–90	1.7
Sarel	1996	1978–96	2.4
Average			1.7
Standard deviation			0.9
China			
World Bank	1996	1985–94	2.2

Source: Aswicahyono and Hill 1999; World Bank staff estimates.

Notes

1. At $1 a day, the number of poor people in East Asia was estimated at 278 million in 1998. Annual growth of 3 percent with no change in the distribution of income would leave 150 million people below this poverty line in 2008, compared with 63 million if growth averaged 7 percent. With fast growth and a better distribution of income—the best case scenario—22 million people would be living on less than $1 a day. With a worsening income distribution, even fast growth would cut the number of poor people to just 132 million.

2. *Human capital* is defined as the labor force adjusted for quality (as proxied by average educational attainment). It has three components: the share of working-age population (estimated by the United Nations), the participation rate (estimated by the International Labour Organization), and a proxy for knowledge in the labor force (the average education attainment of the population, adjusted by the rate of return to education estimated in the education literature). For further details, see note to table 7.1.

3. Many studies have derived estimates of past growth dynamics in East Asia, each with its own model formulation and choice of dependent variables. Each of these formulations, including those in this chapter, are arbitrary, and the results are subject to the choice of parameter values and to measurement error of the variables (both inputs and GDP). Estimates of total factor productivity growth, which are obtained as a residual of output growth after measured inputs have been subtracted, should be treated with caution. Frequently cited studies include Collins and Bosworth (1996), Young (1994, 1995), and World Bank (1993). The estimates here are consistent with these and other studies in finding that accumulation of physical and human capital explains growth to a larger extent than does productivity growth.

4. Future growth in education attainments will also be different, with higher secondary rather than primary attainments. Projections reflect the fact that the share of the higher-educated population in the total is generally lower than those educated at the primary level. As demonstrated in several studies (notably Mincer 1974 and Psacharopoulos 1994), the returns to incremental secondary education are lower than for incremental primary education. The lower returns and slower increase in average education attainments lower the direct measured impact of growth in human capital on overall economic growth.

5. These scores are based on evaluations by country staff of 20 policy and institutional variables for each country. The relationship between scores and growth was studied by William Easterly of the World Bank. His regression equation related per capita growth to past growth trends, indicators of technological development, and education, together with institutional quality as given in the country scores. These provide the basis for estimating the responsiveness of per capita growth of GDP to institutional improvements in the East Asian economies.

6. The members of APEC are Australia, Brunei, Canada, Chile, China, Hong Kong (China), Indonesia, Japan, Korea, Malaysia, Mexico, New Zealand, Papua New Guinea, Peru, Philippines, Russia, Singapore, Taiwan (China), Thailand, United States, and Vietnam.

Table note

Table 7.1. Total factor productivity growth is estimated using the conventional growth accounting approach. The following equations were used to calculate the data in the table. The production function equation, $Y = AK^a H^{(1-\alpha)}$, specifies output (Y) as a function of physical capital (K) and human capital (H). The human capital equation, $H = We^{\theta^*\mu}$, expresses H as a function of raw labor (W, the number of workers) adjusted by a quality component reflecting the education level in the economy. The equation for the number of workers, $W = Ndp$, expresses the number of workers (W) as the product of the population (N), economically active population (d, for demographics), and labor participation rate (p). The quality component, $e^{\theta^*\mu}$, comprises the exponential function (e), the average years of schooling (μ), and a parameter (θ) known as the Mincer coefficient, which is the income elasticity of an additional year of education (see Mincer 1974 or Psacharopoulos 1994). Finally, the physical capital stock equation is $K_t = (1-\delta)K_{(t-1)} + I_t$, where $I_t = s_t Y_t$ is the investment rate and s_t is the savings rate, at time $_t$.

On a per capita basis, the production function becomes $y_t = Ak_{(t-1)}^\alpha h_{(t-1)}^{(1-\alpha)}$, where $y = Y/N$, $k = K/N$, and $h = H/N = dpe^{\theta\mu}$. The per capita growth equation is $g_y = g_a + \alpha g_k + (1-\alpha)g_d + (1-\alpha)g_p + (1-\alpha)g_{\theta\mu}$. With this formulation we can assess growth of output in terms of capital, demographic trends (g_d), trends in participation rates (g_p), improvements in education attainment ($g_{\theta\mu}$), and changes in total factor productivity (g_a). Standard data sources were used for this exercise. Data on output and investment were from Summers and Heston (1991). Data on output and investment for China and Indonesia were adjusted to ensure consistency with the national account data: annual growth rates from the national accounts were applied to the initial Summers/Heston data values to generate a new series. Human capital data were from the World Bank, the United Nations, and the International Labour Organization. Data on the average years of schooling (μ) for all countries in the exercise except China were from Nehru and Dhareshwar (1993). Data on China were from Barro and Lee (1993). The income elasticity of an additional year of education, the Mincer coefficient (θ), was from the education literature (Psacharopoulos 1994 and Mincer 1974). We use a Mincer coefficient of 0.1 (the estimate for middle-income countries; the analysis was unchanged if coefficient values of 0.07 or 0.13 were used). In constructing the physical capital series, we obtained the initial capital stock from Nehru and Dhareshwar (1993). We use a fixed (α) value of 0.4 for all economies in the sample (use of other values of α, such as 0.3 and 0.5, did not have a qualitative effect on the analysis). We assume a delta (δ) of 0.06.

References

Aswicahyono, Haryo, and Hal Hill. 1999. "Perspiration vs. Inspiration in Asian Industrialization: Indonesia before the Crisis." Paper prepared for ASEM (Asia-Europe Meeting) Regional Economist's Workshop: From Recovery to Sustainable Development, 15–17 September, Denpasar, Bali, Indonesia.

Barro, Robert J. 1996. *Getting It Right: Markets and Choices in a Free Society.* Cambridge, Mass.: MIT Press.

Barro, Robert J., and Jong-Wha Lee. 1993. "International Comparisons of Educational Attainment." *Journal of Monetary Economics* 32 (3): 363–94.

Bhattacharya, Amarendra, and Masahiro Kawai. 1999. "International Financial Architecture: Lessons from the East Asian Crisis." World Bank, Washington, D.C.

Bloom, David E.M., and Jeffrey G. Williamson. 1998. "Demographic Transitions and Economic Miracles in Emerging Asia." *The World Bank Economic Review* 12 (September): 419–55.

Bora, B., and I. Neufeld. 2000. "Tariffs and the East Asian Financial Crisis." United Nations Conference on Trade and Development, Geneva.

Bosworth, Barry P., Susan M. Collins, and Y-C Chen. 1995. "Accounting for Differences in Economic Growth." Paper presented to a conference on Structural Adjustment Policies in the 1990s:Experience and Prospects, Institute of Developing Economies, Tokyo.

Claessens, Stijn, Simeon Djankov, and Daniela Klingebiel. 1999. "Financial Restructuring in East Asia: Halfway There?" Financial Sector Discussion Paper 3. World Bank, Washington, D.C.

Collins, Susan M., and Barry P. Bosworth. 1996. "Economic Growth in East Asia: Accumulation versus Assimilation." *Brookings Papers on Economic Activity* 2. Brookings Institution, Washington, D.C.

Drysdale, Peter, and Yiping Huang. 1995. "Technological Catchup and Economic Growth in East Asia." *Economic Record* 73 (222): 201–11.

Eichengreen, Barry. 1999. "Towards a New International Financial Architecture: A Practical Post-Asia Agenda." Institute for International Economics, Washington, D.C.

Fischer, Stanley. 1999a. "Learning the Lessons of Financial Crises." Paper prepared for Emerging Market Traders' Association Annual Meeting, 9 December, New York.

———. 1999b. "On the Need for an International Lender of Last Resort." *Journal of Economic Perspectives* 13 (4): 83–104.

G–10 (Group of 10). 1996. *The Resolution of Sovereign Liquidity Crises: A Report to the Ministers and Governors.* Basle: Bank for International Settlements.

Hanna, Don, and Sandra Lawson. 1999. "A Further Rebound in Asian Growth: Is Restructuring a Must?" Global Economics Paper 20. Goldman Sachs Economics Website (http://www.gs.com).

IMF (International Monetary Fund). 1998. "Korea: Third Quarterly Review." Staff paper. Washington, D.C.

———. 1999a. "Korea Economic and Policy Developments." Staff paper. Washington, D.C.

———. 1999b. "Thailand: Statistical Appendix." Staff paper. Washington, D.C.

———. 2000. "Report of the Acting Managing Director to the International Monetary Fund and Financial Committee on Progress in Reforming the IMF and Strengthening the Architecture of the International Financial System." Washington, D.C.

Kawai, Hiroki. 1994. "International Comparative Analysis of Economic Growth: Trade Liberalization and Productivity." *Developing Economies* 32 (4): 373–97.

Levine, Ross. 1998. "The Legal Environment, Banks, and Long Run Economic Growth." *Journal of Money, Credit, and Banking* 30 (3): 596–613.

Loayza, Norman, Klaus Schmidt-Hebbel, and Luis Serven. 1999. "What Drives Private Saving across the World?" World Bank, Washington, D.C.

Martin, William, and Thomas W. Hertel. 1999. "Would Developing Countries Gain from Inclusion of Manufactures in the WTO Negotiations?" Paper prepared for ASEM (Asia-Europe Meeting) Regional Economist's Workshop: From Recovery to Sustainable Development, 15–17 September, Denpasar, Bali, Indonesia.

Mincer, Jacob. 1974. *Schooling, Experience and Earnings.* New York: Columbia University Press.

Nehru, Vikram, and Ashok Dhareshwar. 1993. "A New Database on Physical Capital Stock: Sources, Methodology and Results." *Revista de Analisis Economico* (Chile) 8 (June): 37–59.

———. 1994. "New Estimates of Total Factor Productivity Growth for Developing and Industrial Countries." World Bank, International Economics Department, Washington, D.C.

Nellor, David. 1999. "Changes in International Financial Architecture." Paper presented at the Australian National University conference on Corporate Restructuring in Asia, 21 September, Canberra, Australia.

Nelson, Richard R., and Howard Pack. 1998. "The Asian Miracle and Modern Growth Theory." Policy Research Working Paper 1881. World Bank, Washington, D.C. Pangestu, Mari. 1999.

Pangestu, Mari. 1999. "Trade Liberalization in APEC: With Focus on East Asia." Paper prepared for ASEM (Asia-Europe Meeting) Regional Economist's Workshop: From Recovery to Sustainable Development, 15–17 September, Denpasar, Bali, Indonesia.

Pritchett, Lant 1997. "Demography and Savings: What Is to Be Done?" Paper presented at the World Bank conference on Macroeconomics and Population Momentum: A Learning Forum, 21 July, Washington, D.C.

Psacharopoulos, George. 1994. "Returns to Investment in Education: A Global Update." *World Development* 22: 1325–43.

Sarel, Michael. 1996. "Growth and Productivity in the ASEAN Economies." Paper presented to an Association of Southeast Asian Nations conference on Macroeconomic Issues facing the ASEAN Countries, Jakarta, Indonesia.

Summers, Robert, and Alan Heston. 1991. "Penn World Table (Mark 5): An Expanded Set of International Comparisons,

1950–1988." *Quarterly Journal of Economics* 106 (May): 327–68.

UNCTAD (United Nations Conference on Trade and Development). 1999. *World Investment Report.* Geneva.

World Bank. 1993. *The East Asian Miracle: Economic Growth and Public Policy.* A Policy Research Report. Washington, D.C.

———. 1996. *The Chinese Economy: Fighting Inflation, Deepening Reforms.* Washington, D.C.

———. 1999. *Global Economic Prospects and the Developing Countries 2000.* Washington, D.C.

———. 2000a. *Global Development Finance 2000.* Washington, D.C.

———. 2000b. "International Architecture: A Progress Report." Report to the Board. Document SecM2000-114. Washington, D.C.

WTO (World Trade Organization). 1999. Trade Policy Review: Thailand. Geneva.

Young, Alwyn. 1992. "A Tale of Two Cities: Factor Accumulation and Technical Change in Hong Kong and Singapore." In Olivier Blanchard and Stanley Fischer, eds., *NBER Macroeconomics Annual.* Cambridge, Mass.: MIT Press.

———. 1994. "Lessons from East Asian NICs: A Contrarian View." *European Economic Review* 38: 964–73.

———. 1995. "The Tyranny of Numbers: Confronting the Statistical Realities of the East Asian Growth Experience." *Quarterly Journal of Economics* 110 (3): 641–68.